P9-CNH-016

## More Praise for *Dog Talk* by Harrison Forbes

"Harrison Forbes talks 'dog' fluently. As one of this country's leading dog trainers and behaviorists, he truly understands canines and can solve any doggy dilemmas in his unique, no-fuss style. Whether he's importing and training German Shepherds for high-security police work or schooling Chihuahuas to cope with apartment-style living, he has some great stories to tell. If you love dogs, you'll love this book."

—Sandy Robins, pet lifestyle expert, author, and regular pet contributor to MSNBC.com and dogcentral.msn.com

"Harrison Forbes is a treasure for the pet-loving public. He has the combination of experience and intelligence that cuts to the essence of those topics that matter."

—Rolan Tripp, DVM, veterinary content consultant for Animal Planet and founder of animalbehavior.net

"Harrison Forbes is who I use for all my dog advice."

—James Gandolfini

"Entertaining and informative, Forbes's stories will inspire the average owner and help them build a bond with their own dog."

—*DogChannel.com*

"In the newest life-with-dogs memoir, veteran dog trainer and radio show cohost Forbes forgoes the maudlin for some genuine insight into dog behavior and psychology.... Forbes doesn't offer any pat answers to handling a challenging dog besides a lot of patience and hard work. Still, those interested in the hows and whys of dog attacks and aggression will find the book useful, and Forbes's tone of love and respect for his charges is itself both instructive and encouraging."

—*Publishers Weekly*

"As Forbes talks about dogs he has trained and potentially dangerous situations he has encountered, he is also teaching the reader a tremendous amount about why dogs act and react the way they do."     —*Booklist*

# DOG TALK

*Lessons Learned from a Life with Dogs*

# Harrison Forbes

WITH

# Beth Adelman

 St. Martin's Griffin ✹ New York

DOG TALK. Copyright © 2008 by Harrison Forbes. All rights reserved. Printed in the United States of America. For information, address St. Martin's Press, 175 Fifth Avenue, New York, N.Y. 10010.

www.stmartins.com

The Library of Congress has catalogued the hardcover edition as follows:

Forbes, Harrison.
    Dog talk : lessons learned from a life with dogs / by Harrison Forbes with Beth Adelman. — 1st ed.
        p. cm.
    ISBN 978-0-312-37873-8
    1. Dogs—United States—Anecdotes. 2. Dogs—Behavior—United States—Anecdotes. 3. Dogs—Training—United States—Anecdotes. 4. Human-animal relationships—United States—Anecdotes. 5. Human-animal communication—United States—Anecdotes. 6. Forbes, Harrison. 7. Dog trainer—Tennessee—Biography. I. Adelman, Beth. II. Title. III. Title: Dog talk.
    SF426.2.F65 2008
    636.7—dc22

                                                                    2008009291

ISBN 978-0-312-58246-3 (trade paperback)

First St. Martin's Griffin Edition: October 2009

10  9  8  7  6  5  4  3  2  1

# CONTENTS

# ACKNOWLEDGMENTS

Harrison Forbes

To my veterinary mentors, Dr. Ben Lifsey, for all of the wonderful guidance on raising raccoons; Dr. Danny Walker, who put up with the pesky kid who asked so many questions and let me work at the clinic at such a young age; and Dr. Cary Carter, my stellar co-host, true friend, and great human being. Thanks to Appie Kamps, master Dutch KNPV trainer and true animal whisperer; Remco Witcamp, the best Dutch decoy and great friend; Bob Frisbey, the greatest Schutzhund helper, who shares my love for a challenging harddog; Mark "Commander" Leamer, for imparting years of street K-9 knowledge; and to Dave Taylor, Terry Davis, Ken Lichlider, and all the law enforcement trainers and handlers. To my great friend and greatest narc dog trainer, Mark Robertson—thanks for all the years of wisdom and shared good times; Louis and Mark Only, who both have now passed away, who fostered my love of animals; Scott Parrish, for the learning years at Zoo World Pets; James Keach and Jane Seymour; Issac

Tigrett, for making me believe I should chase my dream; Nikki Moustaki, for great introductions in the pet world; Rachel Wientraub at *The View*, for her tireless support and guidance; Bill Way, for the introduction to the radio world; Tom and Suzanne Harrison at Diverse Talent Group; Roger Haber, attorney and adviser. A special thanks to Daniela Rapp and all the staff at St. Martin's Press (especially Matt Baldacci, Marketing Director; Lisa Senz, Associate Publisher, Reference Group; Dori Weintraub, Deputy Director of Publicity; and Jeffrey Capshew, Director of Broadway Sales)—you all "got it" from the start and stayed with me through all the changes. Thanks to Jeff Kleinman at Folio Literary Management, and to Beth Adelman, for skillfully guiding me through the inner workings of the publishing world, putting up with a hot-tempered hillbilly, and championing my cause. Thanks to Greg Alexander, the best business partner I've ever had. Thanks to my family—Grandaddy Rice, Mom, Dad, Lee, Jill, and the kids—for support through all the tough times; and thanks to all the listeners and viewers of *Pet Talk*: you kept me on track.

### Beth Adelman

Jeff, thank you for remembering me after all those years, for setting me on this path, and for having the patience of a saint.

Harrison, thanks for being as smart as you are and for telling really great stories. We make a good team.

Linda, you also have the patience of a saint. Thanks for listening and caring about what you are listening to, and for typing it all perfectly.

And Craig, thanks for everything. Absolutely everything.

# DOG TALK

# Introduction

I'm going to start this book with a confession: I'm a hypocrite. For fourteen years now I've been telling listeners to my radio show, *Pet Talk,* not to buy a puppy from a retail store, not to buy a puppy on impulse, not to buy a puppy at Christmastime, and not to buy a puppy if you have children under the age of four. But when the only girl born in your family in fifty-nine years looks up at you with her baby blue begging eyes and says, "Daddy, can I have this little puppy? Please, I want her sooooo bad," all logic and fortitude melt away as you turn to daddy putty and you hear a voice that sounds like yours saying, "Okay, baby." Then your heart seizes up and you think, "I can't believe I just did that!" But it's too late. "Do as I say, not as I do." Isn't that the mantra of hypocrites?

Oh yes . . . and the puppy was a seven-week-old shih tzu with a lazy eye. Because I also always tell my listeners not to get a puppy that young and not to take one with health problems. While I'm at it, I might as well be a *big* hypocrite.

I've built my reputation as a dog trainer by working with some of the world's toughest police and protection dogs, finding ways to deal with dogs who were very difficult to handle. Most of those dogs lived in my kennel—although some of them came in and out of the house and eventually became beloved members of our family.

While I've also worked with many of the little guys, I've never been especially fond of owning small, yappy dogs. It was a different story with my wife, Jill, though. She grew up with a small dog and always wanted another one for our kids. She astutely figured out that I'd never get one just because she asked, so she successfully passed the torch of that want and need to our four-year-old daughter, Alexandra Jane. Jill saw to it that the flame of that desire never went out, and the need for a smaller dog, a house dog, a dog who would be Ally Jane's little pet, had been a theme in our house for some time.

I finally promised them we could get a small dog when all the kids were older than four, because I am the kind of guy who practices what I preach—most of the time. This meant another two years; Chandler, my youngest, was two at the time. But you know how patient little kids are.

A few months before Christmas, Ally Jane started hitting me pretty heavy with the requests. Every time we saw a puppy on television or passed one on the street, she wanted it. She climbed up in my lap one day with those very sad puppy dog eyes and the pouty lips and said, "I just want a puppy, Daddy. If that's all I get for Christmas, that's okay. All I want is a puppy."

That's when I took my first step down that slippery slope of hypocrisy. "We're not going to get a puppy," I said, "but we'll find an adult dog."

And I meant it. I started checking newspaper ads offering dogs for adoption, and went to see several of them. Just a week earlier, I'd talked to some people with an adult Yorkshire terrier. On the phone, he sounded like the ideal dog. But they didn't live nearby, so we agreed to meet at a spot halfway between where they were and where I was. And I'm really glad we did, because the dog had never been away from home before and he was completely wound up and freaked out. If we'd met him in his home, he would have seemed just fine and I'd never have known there was a problem. With all the traveling we do, that dog would have been a disaster. Sure, I could have worked with him and helped him develop his confidence, but why start out with a nervous, unsocialized dog when you've got three little kids in the house? (I also have a son named Parker who is eight.)

When I saw that dog, I was reminded of one of those things I know all too well and always apply when I test dogs for police work: Dogs can react very differently when they're outside their comfort zone. Things aren't always as they appear, and a smart trainer knows that. The fact that I forgot about this and only ended up meeting the dog away from home by chance just tells you how far away from my good sense I'd already stepped.

The day I officially became a hypocrite was the Sunday before Christmas. We were in Memphis visiting my mother. By then I had seen so many different dogs that they were starting to run together. There was a place called The Puppy Corral that was twenty minutes from Mom's house, and we ended up passing it on the way home. I wasn't stuck on one particular breed, and I thought it would be useful to see several breeds at once so I could compare them. Not to get a puppy, mind you, but just to give me an idea of the kind of adult dog I wanted to look for. Everyone was in the car, and there just wasn't any way for me not to take the kids into the store with me.

But it was only to look. Because this store is the epitome of the things I preach against. They're supplied by commercial breeders, they're overpriced, and the genetics of these dogs is questionable. Still, this particular place had been in business twenty-five years and had a pretty good reputation and a good health guarantee. They have little sitting areas where you can take the puppies out and play with them, so I decided while I did some breed research I could also teach the kids about temperament testing. It would be a learning experience for me and for them. That was all. I swear.

The showroom was huge—maybe 3,000 square feet. They had about 200 dogs in the place, but they just kept about two or three of each breed in display cages and kind of rotated them around. There were stand-alone stations with three or four puppies in playpens, and there were walls of cages with a pup in each, and attendants everywhere helping you look for what you wanted. There was also a bunch of people mopping up the concrete floor with disinfectant whenever a puppy peed, so the place was very clean. In concept I don't like what they do, but I had to admit they did it well.

My kids went crazy because there were adorable puppies everywhere. And within five minutes I realized this was not going the way I had hoped. I started pointing out to the kids some behaviors I saw in the dogs that I didn't like. They just wanted every puppy they picked up. Jill didn't let Chandler sit on the floor, but she held him while he enthusiastically petted every dog we saw. At this point, I should have realized what was happening and herded them all to the exit.

But I didn't. Somehow, I was still convinced this was a great opportunity to teach the kids, that we could walk out of there without a puppy. We were in a unique situation of being able to look at so many breeds at the same time. I always tell my radio listeners not to get stuck on a particular breed, but to look for a type of dog. Sometimes it's really important to compare apples and oranges, and where else were we going to do it? At least, that's what I told myself.

There was a brown and white Lhasa apso I liked, and he did really well on all the little things I use to gauge temperament. For example, when we put him down in a pen, he went toward the kids rather than away from them. When they rolled a tennis ball, I watched how long he was interested in the ball, and when his interest broke off I noted whether he went off by himself or back to the kids. "These are the same tests I do for police dogs," I told my kids. I guess I didn't notice that nobody was listening.

Now, if I roll a ball, all I'm interested in for a police dog is his sustained interest in the ball. I don't really care if he goes back to the handler, because interest in the handler is not as important as interest in the toy. Think about this for a second: When you're training narcotics dogs, you're using a reward of playtime with a ball or a tug toy or something similar to get them to do the work. The dog isn't doing it because he likes the smell of the drugs; he's doing it because he has an insatiable drive for the reward.

But a pet dog has to be oriented to people. You want him to have some kind of interest in a toy, but he should be able to move away from it and seek out the attention of a person. So I made the kids sit down on the floor inside the play area and not run and pick the puppy up or even call him. I rolled the ball for the Lhasa apso and we just waited to see if the dog would go back to them.

He followed the ball for less than ten seconds and then ran back and played with the kids and was really cuddly. Everything was going fine. He was a cute dog, kind of fluffy, really sweet.

But then my wife picked him up and he instantly started scrambling to get down. Jill didn't think anything of it—"He just wants to get down and play"—but I saw something else. I kept picking the dog up and passing him around and pretty soon it was clear this dog was uncomfortable being held. I wanted to see if he would fight when I tried holding him close to me, and the answer was yes.

I was looking for a dog who would submit to being picked up and feel confident and okay about it. That's indicative of a dog who will follow a leader, which means he will be easier to teach. But this dog had an independent spirit and was not inclined to be compliant.

He was cute as a button and really healthy, but his attitude bothered me. Then I did a noise test with him. I dropped a metal drinking bowl on the hard concrete floor while the dog was in the middle of playing. It's absolutely normal for a loud noise like that to startle a dog, but the key is watching how they recover. If it startles them to the point where they can't get over it within ten to fifteen seconds, there's a problem. The ideal is a dog who is either mildly startled for a split second or not startled at all and then goes over to investigate the bowl.

The Lhasa did okay with the startle test, but I just wasn't feeling right about his struggling when he was picked up. Which was fine with me, because *we were not there to get a dog.*

We looked at a French bulldog, other Lhasa apsos, shih tzus, a miniature schnauzer, a toy poodle, two Yorkshire terriers, a cairn terrier—maybe eight or nine dogs who I actually got out and tested. And by "tested" I don't just mean the ball and the bowl and picking the dog up. I watched everything about them: their body language, were they proud, did they walk around confident with their tail up or did they slink around, how did they react when people walked by?

We were getting ready to leave—because, after all, we were only there to do research—when they brought out this tiny little black-and-white ball of fluff. I mean, so tiny that it worried me. She was a shih tzu, and they swore she was seven weeks old but she looked more like four weeks. She weighed less than two pounds. I actually made them go back and check her birth date.

I handed the puppy to Ally Jane and stepped back to see what would happen. That's when I noticed that one of the pup's eyes was looking forward and the other was going off to la-la land. So this is an underweight shih tzu with a googly eye. Time to go home.

At that point, though, Ally Jane was holding the pup and the puppy was nuzzling into her and obviously passed the holding test, plus she was tiny and cute. My daughter and her mom were really liking this dog.

So then I did an extended version of the ball test, because I wanted to make sure that she could see and focus properly. I held her and rolled the ball across her field of vision, looking to see if she was focusing enough to pinpoint its location. She scampered after the ball, picked it up and gave a little growl, really oblivious to all the noise and people in the store. She was showing a lot of personality and was able to focus and have fun. Within about thirty seconds she was playing and romping like she was a part of the family, and her growling and wrestling with the ball was showing a feisty temperament that I liked. She was comfortable and confident. Then she ran right over and tumbled headfirst into Ally Jane's lap. That told me a lot: "I'm confident with body contact with people I don't know," she was saying. She was diving into everybody's arms and when she got there she was very settled—not in a cowering way but proud and full of herself. She was just enjoying being held and kissed and loved.

Then I did the noise test. I dropped the bowl when she was sitting there playing with Ally Jane. And she did the best possible thing: She turned her head to look but didn't startle. She just turned around, looked at it, ran over, and sniffed it. Then she turned back to Ally Jane and just flew into her and started grabbing her pants legs and playing with her and play growling.

Ally Jane just loved her. And she had already named the dog: Abigail Elizabeth. I knew right then it was all over. The princess had won.

I did the holding test and the good old charisma and chemistry test and this dog was the one everybody loved. I can't really give you one particular reason why this puppy was the one, but that's the nature of chemistry. She just was. And that's when I got "the face." The face of the girl I love the most in the whole world. The one that said, "Daddy, please can I have this little puppy?"

But we did not take the shih tzu home. Instead, I left a deposit with the store to hold her. There was a fight about that, but this is one of those rules I never break. I know what you're thinking: I'd already broken all the rules by leaving a deposit. But you just don't take a dog home after one visit. You have to let your emotions settle down a little bit, make sure you still want the dog as much after some time has passed. Did I really think Ally Jane wasn't going to want that shih tzu a day from now, a week from now, a month from now? I may be a hypocrite, but I'm not stupid.

Ally Jane, meanwhile, cried all the way to the car. "I want her now! Why can't we have her now? Let's take her home." My wife wanted her, too. Parker, though, was playing the tough guy. He had started working with Nord, one of my protection dogs, and had heard me preach the anti-little-dog mantra so many times that he felt obliged to show some manly disdain. So it was the women against the men. (Lucky for me Chandler was too young to say much.) "Stinky old daddy" is what Ally Jane called me. My wife called me that, too.

And then came the pouting. Ally Jane stuck out her adorable little girl lip and then asked every twenty minutes, "When are we going to get her? Why can't she come today? Can we go back and get her tomorrow? Can we go back and get her tonight?"

Actually, I wanted an extra two weeks because I was going to be traveling a lot and I wanted to be home for a while when the puppy came into the house. Plus, I made the folks at the store pull all the feeding records on her, because she was so tiny that I wanted to make sure she was eating. And I made them rewrite the health guarantee she came with so I would have two weeks from the day of purchase to get the pup seen by my veterinarian to guarantee her health.

But it didn't work out the way I planned, because a dad can take only so much pouting. I went and got Abigail Elizabeth on Christmas Eve, less than a week after we'd first seen her. A few days before, the whole family went to Target to buy the puppy bowls and beds and everything we'd need. There were all these accessories and things that I was never able to get for my working dogs. It was kind of weird for me, but I was surprised at how quickly I got into it.

When you get a big dog you intend to train for protection work, you buy him a leather buckle collar and a strong leather leash and some stainless steel bowls and a couple of very sturdy chew and tug toys, and that's about it. But when you get a baby shih tzu . . . well, I started looking at the little dog carriers—purses, really—and comparing the pink leather one to the black one and then the frilly flowered one that would match the pink pet bed. There were so many more choices than I was used to and suddenly I *cared* about whether the pink carrier matched the pink bed.

My family started teasing me. They said in a couple of weeks I'd be walking around with the pink dog purse with the dog sticking out of it. And actually, a time or two, I did.

I suppose this is as good a time as any to explain that I've been a dog trainer and behaviorist for more than twenty years, and have trained more than 600 dogs for police departments all over the country. I compete in protection dog sports, too. How I got into this line of work and the dogs I have worked with are partly what this book is about.

The things I've learned over all those years of dog training and shared over all those years of broadcasting is the other part of what this book is about. That's important, because this book is not just for people who think police dog training is kind of cool—although it definitely is.

This book is for everyone who likes dogs and is interested in dog behavior and why dogs do what they do. If you want to know what makes dogs tick, well, so do I. And I have spent the past two decades trying to figure it out.

I also wrote this book to help people understand that they are a lot more in control of their dog's behavior than they think. Any good dog trainer will tell you that your energy travels down the leash just like an electric cord. And your dog's energy travels up the leash. It works both ways. That's the biggest curse or gift we can give our dogs. I've never seen a nervous dog with a real calm, mellow dog owner. You can give your dog good calm energy and a confidence that enables him to feel good about being in all kinds of situations.

When your dog was a puppy, anytime he was exposed to something new, his mom was standing there and he immediately looked to her to see what she was doing. If she shivered and cowered and got nervous, he learned to shiver and get nervous. If she was confident, he was thinking, "Okay, this must be cool.

Let's go on to the next thing." Without his mom, your dog takes those cues from you. Think about how empowering that is.

So now, as I said, it's Christmas Eve. We all piled into the car for the two-hour drive from where I live, near Jackson, to The Puppy Corral outside of Memphis. On the way, I was thinking that for all these years, whenever I've brought new dogs home they've always been my police dogs. If any dog ever chewed up anything or had an accident in the house, it was my fault. With this puppy, I was savoring the fact that the whole housetraining process was going to be on my family's shoulders and I could point fingers and make them clean stuff up. I was looking forward to saying things like, "You wanted this dog, you begged for it, and now you got it."

By now I had forgiven myself for getting this puppy. Everyone was so excited that I just got pulled along with them. Maybe a white collar would look nice with the pink carrier . . .

We picked up Abigail Elizabeth (a name that, at the time, was probably twice as big as the puppy), signed the papers, and started the long drive home. She was such a tiny little puffball, but she was great in the car and didn't get sick or stressed. The first fifteen minutes into the drive I looked in the rearview mirror and she was sound asleep in Ally Jane's lap. That picture was worth everything. Ally Jane had her hand resting on the puppy, and she was so happy and so excited. I knew then that I'd done the right thing by making her wait a week for the dog. This way, it was a big event and not like just picking up a toy at Wal-Mart. I hoped building up the puppy's homecoming like that would help her see how serious a thing it is to get a dog.

When we got home, I set up a baby gate to confine Abigail

Elizabeth to the utility room and then explained to my family about keeping a dog that young in a small area of the house so she wouldn't get into trouble. Of course, as soon as I left the house they'd get the puppy out and let her run around. And, as puppies do, she started going to the bathroom all over the house. But I never cleaned up a single drop. I let my wife and my daughter do it.

You may be wondering at this point why I've started a book about police dogs with Abigail Elizabeth's story. The reason is simple: The techniques I use with police dogs also work with a shih tzu. The basic behavioral drives of a ninety-five-pound German shepherd are not all that different from the basic drives of a four-pound Chihuahua. (In fact, I've always said that if Chihuahuas weighed ninety-five pounds, they'd be people killers.)

I want to dispel a lot of myths about police dogs, because they are so much more like regular housedogs than people think. And I want you to feel empowered to be in control of your own pet and to think about the little things you do that may be making it harder to get what you want from your dog. If you have a small dog who's a little snappy and crusty about things, it's not as dangerous as if he were a hundred-pound dog, so maybe you let it go or tell yourself he's just a grumpy little dog. Gradually, you get into a routine where the dog's behavior shapes the way you live your life, where you sit, when you have people over, who can touch the dog, and so on, rather than the other way around.

If you learn anything from my experiences with the biggest, toughest dogs around, it's that it doesn't have to be that way. With just a couple of tweaks and fixes, you can make your life with that pet a whole lot better and take that relationship up a couple of notches, so you have a dog you really enjoy.

Any trainer who says he "knows it all" has a narrow view of dog training. You might know a technique that works with one dog but it might not work with another, so you have to draw from all of your experiences to help each dog be what he is meant to be. In some ways, this book is a chronicle of that journey for me.

But dog behavior is still dog behavior. Here's another way to think about it. Suppose I'm the CEO of a Fortune 500 company and I see my vice president of finance is so disorganized that he can't get his work done. The things I would do to help him get everything organized and running smoothly are the same things I'd do if my stay-at-home spouse was disorganized and disheveled all the time. I'd take the same basic approach to running a Fortune 500 company as I would to running a small household. And I'd take the same basic approach to training a shih tzu as I would to training a rottweiler.

As it turned out, Abigail Elizabeth presented some interesting problems for us (I'll tell you about those at the end of this book), and I learned a lot from working with her. I love seeing the way Ally Jane lights up around her. In fact, there's something special about each of the dogs I've had—parts of my heart will always be with them. PJ, for example, was there for me during a difficult transition in my life. Tico was goofy and all personality—a great working dog. Bart and I had a quiet connection right from the beginning; he returned my love in a way that was so focused and individual.

With all these dogs, I had a certain understanding. "You'll

respect me and I'll respect you," they seemed to be saying. "I will do what you want, but there comes a point when I will stand up for myself." In no dog was this mutual respect more deeply felt than it was with Lex. We understood each other utterly and completely. A dog like that comes along once in a lifetime. You'll meet Lex in Chapter 1. And when you do, you'll understand why I'm still not ready to give my whole heart to another dog since Lex.

# 1

# Lex

The ringing of the phone jerked me awake. I turned over and looked at the clock. It was one in the morning. When the phone rings at that time of night, it's never good. I think of heart attacks, car accidents, trips to the emergency room. As I picked up the receiver, I realized I was holding my breath.

The person on the other end of the line identified himself as a police officer. A lot of K-9 officers called me, but never this late. He was in a panic, talking fast, and I couldn't focus on what he was saying until I heard the name *Lex*. My mind cleared in an instant. Lex was a German shepherd I had imported from Czechoslovakia a year and a half ago, and then sold to a one-dog K-9 police unit outside St. Louis. I clicked on the light and swung my feet out of bed, suddenly tense.

"It's not the dog's fault," the officer was saying. "I did exactly what I wasn't supposed to do. I just lost my head."

Lex's original and very experienced handler had been fired from the police department, and the chief had given the dog to this guy—very gung-ho, but he'd never worked with a police dog before. Before he left, the experienced handler wrote down a list of do's and don'ts. Number one on the list: Don't hold the dog close to you on a leash or by the collar and let anybody approach you, because for sure he'll go off. Number two: Don't let anybody try to hug the dog or get in his face.

The officer was so thrilled, the first thing he did was drive home and run into the house with the dog, hollering to his wife, "Honey, honey, I've got Lex! He's mine now." Everybody was excited, and all that excitement created a frenzied kind of atmosphere, which always keys up a dog. Lex was in a strange place with a guy he barely knew holding his leash. Then this woman he'd never seen before ran over, grabbed him by each cheek, looked him in the face, gushed, "Oh, such a good boy!" and leaned over to give him a big kiss on the muzzle.

Lex ripped half her face off, then bit her husband when he stepped in the middle of it. He managed to drag Lex into his patrol car, but the department certainly didn't want to keep the dog and nobody even wanted to go near him. Lex would be put down in the morning.

I sell every one of my dogs on a buy-back agreement, which means if they don't want him, I have the first right to buy him back. I didn't know enough about Lex's situation at that moment to know how he had gotten to that point, but I knew for sure I wasn't going to let any dog be put down because of someone else's mistake. "Just wait for me," I told the officer. "I'm coming to get him."

I realize this sounds like a strange way to begin the story of the dog of my heart. But I want you to know who Lex really was. He was no dog from a Disney movie and this was no "man meets dog and instantly falls in love" scenario. He came into my life abruptly—and, as you'll see at the end of the book, left it rather abruptly as well. He could be touchy and dangerous, and I can't remember a single night he sat next to me on the sofa and watched TV. If he felt someone was challenging him, there was no middle ground. He ripped holes in my clothes—and occasionally in me—when I couldn't get out of the way quick enough.

Lex was also a German shepherd out of the ugly duckling bloodline—kind of small and rangy looking, and just seventy pounds (most working German shepherds are ninety pounds or more). He looked almost like a coyote. He moved like one, too. A lot of big, proud, showy dogs walk head up and chest out. Lex didn't do that. His body movement was very predatory; he'd hold his head down and just keep moving and scanning in front of him. He wasn't real masculine looking, either. Lex was one ugly little underdog.

But in the months and years that followed, I came to love Lex more than any dog I'd ever owned. I loved him because he had the heart of a samurai warrior. Because he was sensitive and fierce. Because he didn't take any crap from anyone, including me. Because he was the most brilliant dog I've ever known—not in the sense of following commands, but in the more profound sense of thinking for himself. Because all his life he never stopped learning. Because I knew I could rely on him 100 percent in any situation.

We had our good times and our bad times, and we had plenty of arguments that occasionally left me with some rips in my shirt and him with a headache. We ended up sort of like an old married couple—loving the best and the worst in each other, and knowing each other inside and out. There came a time when we knew each other so well that it seemed we could read each other's minds. I may have known other dogs almost as well, but no dog has ever known me like that.

The night of that phone call, I went back to sleep for a few hours, then got up at 5 a.m. and drove from Tennessee to St. Louis. It takes five hours, and that gave me lots of time to think about what I was getting into. I'd only spent a short time with Lex before I sold him, but I knew he was a great working dog.

I got Lex back in 1995. At the time, I had a business called the National Canine Law Enforcement Training Center where I imported working dogs from all over Europe to be trained and sold here in the United States to police departments. All these dogs already had some sort of basic training, and many had done protection work because their breeders belonged to clubs that competed in various protection dog sports.

Lex was with me just a few weeks before I sold him, but I knew he was exceptional. When I got a dog, I always put him through a large battery of tests to make sure he was what the European broker promised—good nerves, abilities, talent, and so forth. I knew immediately Lex was a special dog because he was easy to handle from the get-go. No matter how charged up he got from a training exercise, I could always make him stop in his tracks with just a single command. He wasn't really friendly or affectionate, but he was keen to do the work.

He had a very strong personality, too. He had really high fight drive (I'll explain what I mean by that in a bit), and I knew you had to be careful not to put him in situations where he could blow up, because he would. He also had nerves of steel and wasn't afraid of anyone. It was like he was ready to run the show. I don't mean that he tried to dominate you, but he certainly wanted to keep things even between you and him.

With that high drive, he had to go to someone who knew how to handle dogs. The officer I sold him to was a good, experienced handler who liked a big, high-powered, tough dog and knew how to channel the energy of a canine like Lex. Unfortunately, he also liked an aggressive, mouthy dog who put on a big show.

Police officers do what we call maintenance training for as long as they work with a dog, to keep his skills sharp and teach him new ones. I kept in touch with this handler, and I knew he did a lot of maintenance training that brought out the worst in Lex. He constantly set up scenarios where he was being attacked and the dog had to step in. Sometimes, they'd walk down a street and a whole bunch of decoys (people wearing protective clothing who pretend to be the bad guys) would jump out from behind buildings and out of doorways. In one scenario, the handler had people going up to pet Lex and then attacking the officer, so the dog was wired to think, "This guy's acting like he's nice, but any second he may turn bad." The handler had decoys break into his house and attack him, and bust into Lex's pen in the middle of the night when he was sleeping and go after the dog.

Lex was already a dog with a lot of natural aggression who

was always ready for a fight. Now, this kind of training taught him that the boogeyman might be around every corner. Nobody could be trusted except his handler. And he never had a moment when he felt he could relax and let his guard down. He was always keyed up. In fact, he had developed irritable bowel syndrome from the constant stress, and he suffered from it the rest of his life.

During my long drive in the early morning, I had enough time to admit to myself that I might have made a mistake when I placed Lex. But if that was a questionable placement, there was no question that when the department gave Lex to a totally inexperienced officer, it was a huge mistake. And it sure played out that way.

Eighteen months later, when Lex came back to me, it was getting harder and harder to import dogs with his drive and skills, and I appreciated those qualities in him even more. I wasn't sure what I wanted to do with him or whether I would sell him to another police department. I just wanted to work with him first and see what was up.

When I picked Lex up, I loaded his crate into my car and kept my distance. I wasn't afraid of him, because I knew at his core he was a stable dog with a good temperament. But he definitely seemed keyed up and even a bit paranoid.

On the long drive home, I thought about my next move. There is a part of every dog that you can continue to mold all their lives. Every dog has a range, some narrower than others, of how much you can change them by changing their living arrangements, their handler, their stress level, and so on. Even though Lex was almost five years old, I knew what kind of dog he was and I respected him. Something had gone terribly wrong with the way he was being trained and handled. I knew he had been molded to be aggressive to the point of almost turning him into a monster. My job was to mold him back as far as I could.

The first thing I wanted to do was just mellow him out by letting him decompress on my farm. I wasn't going to require him to really do anything except be a dog. No training, no confrontations. He'd been in a high-stress situation for too long. The idea was just to let him settle in and calm down. When he did, I hoped the dog he was at his core would reemerge.

That doesn't mean I left him sitting in the kennel. I did stuff with him all the time, but the things we did had a few very specific goals. One was to establish myself as the leader without instigating a confrontation. I did that by opening the gate to his pen and just walking somewhere with purpose and ignoring him. Dogs who have been trained for police work usually spend their lives clipped to a leash, so simply being let out is really freeing for them. And then there's the natural curiosity any pack animal has to see where you are going and what you are doing. After a while, they can't help but start to follow you. And that's a subtle initial starting point for the dog of, "I'm following you, so I guess you're the leader."

By not requiring him to do anything at all, I accomplished my second goal, which was to wipe the slate clean and just let Lex relax. In those days, too many trainers would take a dog like Lex and say, "By God, I'm going to show him who is boss." They might yank him out of his pen and make him do a bunch of obedience exercises and beat him up when he showed any kind of resistance, or just dominate the heck out of him. Well, that kind of works, but you've also started off a relationship on the wrong foot, with a big helping of mistrust. And although the dog may be compliant, it's come through the wrong vessel.

That kind of training brought out all the bad characteristics in such dangerous, volatile animals. What really set me apart and enabled me to work with so many aggressive dogs is that I got inside those dogs' heads from the beginning with a calmness that could never come about through manhandling. I didn't require them to do anything at all except be their own doggy selves. And that enabled us to build some trust, which is the key to everything else.

Lex had a lot of issues. He was very confident, but he was also very, very suspicious. So part of his training regimen for the rest of his life was calm, confidence-building exercises, things that kept him from feeling like the boogeyman was going to get him. Some of his suspicion was genetic hardwiring—it's not all that uncommon in German shepherds—but that first handler had pushed it way over the top with all the surprise attack exercises they'd done.

A lot of people with suspicious or fearful dogs make a similar mistake, unintentionally reinforcing the behavior. It starts with them isolating the dog. And by that I don't mean sticking him alone in the backyard—although that's part of it. Isolation, for a dog who has some natural fearful or suspicious tendencies, is when you are walking down the street with your dog on a leash and somebody comes toward you with their own dog. You may be worried about what your dog will do, so you start getting nervous. Or maybe you are worried about what *his* dog will do. Either way, the dog picks up on your nervous energy. Then you move your dog over to the side until they pass, and when they do, you go, "Whew!" You just taught your dog that people coming down the street are bad and he should be nervous when they approach and ought to be watching out for them. Whatever you just confronted, the whole package, was something to be afraid of or suspicious about. Now, imagine what it would feel like to experience every walk around the block as a potential threat. That's what had happened to Lex.

I knew it was fixable with him, because his nerves were rock solid. By that I mean his core temperament was almost incorruptible. He was not plagued by genetic weaknesses in temperament such as fear of noises or flashes of light or unfamiliar people or situations. Those kinds of inborn fears are very difficult to work around. If a dog has great nerves, you can deal with everything else. But if a dog has weak nerves, that's definitely going to limit what you can do with him. Good nerves are like a solid foundation to a house. Even if the wind blows the roof off, you can repair the house. But with a shaky foundation—what I call a nervy dog—no matter how well you build the house, it will never be stable. I'm not saying you can't train a nervy dog and make him better, but you've got to have realistic expectations about what you will be able to accomplish.

Right from the start, Lex and I had a special nonverbal link. I knew what he needed and he was drawn to my strength. I have a presence that can be a little much for soft dogs, or medium-tempered dogs, but the strong dogs respond to it. That presence has nothing to do with me being physical or raising my voice. It's something else—something dogs recognize and understand.

One of the things I liked about Lex was that he was very

attentive to his handler. Even in the beginning, when we were just running around the farm, he'd always look up and check in with me, just to say, "I'm over here doing this, but every couple of minutes I'm going to look and see what you're doing." Some dogs go off in their own world, with their own smells, going their own way, and they ignore their handler. That doesn't mean they're bad dogs, but you have to work harder to get their attention. Lex wasn't that way. He always seemed to know when I needed to tell him something. Just when I'd start thinking, "I want him to run over here," it's almost as if he would feel my thought and turn around and look, as if to say, "You calling me?"

The way Lex was tuned in to me gave me phenomenal control over him. Often when you have a dog who has a tendency to be aggressive, for the rest of his life you have to keep him away from situations that could set him off. But I could always stop Lex before he got out of hand. I could read him well enough that I saw when he was getting too keyed up, and then I used my voice to take control. In the beginning I used specific commands, but later I could just change my tone of voice and he'd stop whatever he was doing. When he was close by, sometimes all it took was a small hand signal or a look.

It soon became clear to me that Lex was too good not to do real police work. He was full of explosive energy, he was smart, hardworking, and temperamentally sound. He was also unable to relax. He always needed to be doing *something,* and if he wasn't working, he was pacing or barking. So I wanted him to have the chance to work.

And I wanted him to work with me, because I respected his

abilities and I wasn't going to risk him being mishandled again. Besides, I *really* liked this dog.

When I sold a dog to a police department, I often did a ride-along with them for a few weeks to help them integrate the dog into the department. It got me interested in doing some police work myself. So I became certified and ended up working part-time for the Gibson, Tennessee, police department. They wanted a patrol dog, but not all the time. Lex and I did a few shifts a week for them. It was the perfect situation for both of us.

It only took about six weeks before I could work Lex on the street as a police dog. That's how responsive he was to good handling. But it took a little over a year before his suspicion level came down a few notches. If someone came up to me and I had Lex at my side, he would go off like a bomb, barking and snarling and straining at the end of the leash. To work on that, I took him to a Schutzhund club. Schutzhund is a dog sport developed in Germany in the 1930s. It's a working dog trial that has three components: obedience, tracking, and protection, meaning attacking a decoy bad guy in very specific scenarios. It was originally designed to be a prequalification for dogs going into police or military service—a kind of standardized test, like the LSAT for law school. It's practiced today in the United States as a competitive sport. I started doing Schutzhund training with Lex to give him some work that didn't involve high-intensity protection scenarios.

Lex quickly gained quite a reputation at my Schutzhund club, and everyone was inclined to keep their distance. But I finally recruited a few guys to help us out. Lex loved hot dogs, so I cut up a dozen or so and put them in little plastic bags.

Then I had some of the other handlers hold the hot dogs and feed Lex as he mingled among them. No one made eye contact or said his name—they'd just hand him a piece of hot dog when he came up to sniff, then continue their casual conversations. I wanted everyone moving around very calmly to show Lex that no one was out to get him.

We repeated that exercise a lot, more often with pieces of cheese, and it came to be known as the easy-cheesy. Over time, Lex got the message. He gained control of himself and wasn't always looking over his shoulder the way he was when I first got him. He also turned out to be great in Schutzhund, and I competed with him at the top levels.

But Lex was really at his best when he was thinking for himself in situations that were less contrived than those in Schutzhund. And that super-high fight drive never subsided. It's what made him a great working dog.

I want to explain what I mean by "high fight drive." For training, you basically deal with two drives. You've got prey drive, which is the chase-the-rabbit thing. That's the reason a dog chases a car or a ball. It's the drive that kicks in when a dog sees a squirrel running across the yard. That drive to chase and catch is genetic.

The flip side of prey drive is defensive drive. It's normal for a dog to defend himself if he feels threatened. But a dog with too much defensive drive will get defensive in situations that are actually low stress—he reads too many things as a threat that aren't. Sometimes, dogs like that are afraid of everything.

Now, for police work, ideally you want a nice balance. The dog should have a lot of prey drive, but also have a strong defensive drive. That translates into a dog who has a lot of confidence and will defend himself if somebody hurts him or puts him in a position where he feels threatened. What you do in training is teach the dog to understand what really is a threat and what isn't, and then lay out some basic rules of engagement. You coach those drives into some sort of parameters, so the dog doesn't get out of control.

Lex had very high fight drive. Some people lump fight drive in with defensive drive, but I really think it's something different. It's a dog's willingness to engage, even if he doesn't fear for his life and isn't backed into a corner. And Lex's fight drive was off the charts. It forced me to become a very different kind of handler. I had to be on guard, anticipating all of his moves. And I think that's a big part of what brought us so close together. I was hyperalert to his body language to avoid trouble, and as I showed him how well I understood him, he became hyperalert to me. In time, I knew when he was likely to get a little out of control and I could head off any problems. Because Lex was 100 percent reliable on commands, I could always find a way to call him off before things got crazy.

One of the most important lessons I learned working with Lex is that you can't really contain that kind of drive. It's going to come out somehow. Lex had this amazing ability to maintain a kind of super-extended adrenaline rush. He would be wound up in the back of a patrol car for eight hours on a shift, pacing and barking and spinning at every car that went by. He was cranked up to level ten all the time. I had to wear the earphones I'd use when I practiced on the shooting range, so that his barking wouldn't wear me out. There were times when he'd really get on my nerves, so I'd make him lie down and shut up. That was almost punishment for him. He needed to be able to get revved up and go.

The challenge with Lex was finding the things he loved to do more than anything, and letting him do those things regularly. Lex was like a pressure cooker, and being able to hit the release valve was an important part of managing him. I let him run around a lot and just be a dog, especially at first, but that's not the thing he loved most. What Lex loved most was work.

If I let him loose in a big field, even if it was hot, he was not going to find some shade, plop down, and hang out. He was constantly moving from one place to the next, smelling, stirring, looking for something. It was like, "If I keep moving around enough, somebody's going to say, 'Hey, I want you to do something. Here's something over here to do.'" I felt sorry for him a lot of the time, because it seemed he had a tortured soul that just couldn't be satisfied. He wasn't even interested in other dogs. It wasn't that he was aggressive with them—he just didn't care. He was so interested in work, he was hardly even interested in female dogs.

When I started doing maintenance training with Lex, he trusted me not to put him in those creepy scenarios he had been exposed to before. I was never unfair to him in what I asked him to do. I try to build a dog up over time by always putting him in situations he can deal with. As he solves each puzzle, the next one gets a little harder. Lex had a lot of natural confidence, and I used his maintenance training to reinforce that. As a result, the training brought out the best in him.

The more intense and unpredictable the scenario, the better

he liked it. Whenever you took a battle to another level of intensity, he would always match it with his own. The good dogs will stay with you as you escalate the intensity in an exercise, but eventually they all reach their limit in an exercise and back down. Lex always had another level. If you went crazy on him in the middle of an engagement, he could go crazier. There was no backing him down, ever.

Sometimes I would hide a couple of decoys in the woods in bite suits and then we'd pull up in a patrol car, lights blaring, and I'd send him out to find and engage the "bad guys." The correct response from the dog in this kind of situation is to physically battle the decoy, and you have to let him do it or else when he's on the street he'll bark a lot but not do much else.

Just so you know what's happening in these scenarios, the decoys are wearing full Kevlar bite suits. Only their face, hands, and feet are exposed. Kevlar is the same material that's used in bulletproof vests. You can shoot a .22 caliber bullet into a Kevlar bite suit and it will not penetrate. Neither will a dog's teeth. It still hurts when the decoy gets knocked down, and they sure feel the pressure of a bite, but they don't get bit.

I'd tell the decoys to really resist, and they'd be battling and throwing buckets at Lex. But the more intense it was, the more they amped it up, the harder that dog fought. We set up situations where we dumped water on him, threw things in the air, pulled him on slick floors, screamed and hollered and banged sticks together, and it didn't matter. He loved it. The only time his tail really wagged was during those training scenarios. It would be straight up in the air like an antenna and he'd just be twitching with excitement, he was so happy.

Most dogs are not that way. They prefer the familiar. When you take them out of that comfort zone, you start to see cracks in the mortar. But Lex worked better when the problem was more interesting. And that's the mark of a spectacular police dog, because when you get called out to a situation, almost every time it's someplace the dog has never been or a situation with elements he has not encountered before. We used to call Lex "The Sponger" because he was able to absorb and deal with new information all the time. And that comes from a combination of intelligence, courage, and confidence.

Lex became explosive in protection work, and his warrior spirit was legendary. As I mentioned before, we'd do training exercises where the pressure would start low and keep escalating, taking it to the next level and the next, trying to find the dog's barrier. But Lex didn't have one. He could match you fight for fight on everything and it was almost like the farther up the ladder you went, the stronger and more intense and more focused he got. You never want to push a dog past his limit, but Lex had no limit. He was always moving forward, ready to take whatever you could throw at him.

There were times in training where we would have what I call training "accidents." In other words, we'd have the decoy add some pressure to the situation by knocking something over or making a very loud noise or covering the dog's face. You have to be careful with these things in the training phase, because you don't want to push a dog too far and damage him, mentally. But often, because Lex was clearly having such a ball, the decoys would do way more than you should—falling on top of him, tripping over him, holding him down. I remember one time a decoy stepped on Lex's foot, then tripped and fell right on top of him. This was a big guy and he was smack on top of Lex, almost smothering him. With 99.9 percent of dogs, you'd have to stop right there and go back and do some training to build up their confidence again. Lex was like, "You want to bring that game? Well, here's *my* A game." He battled and subdued those guys every time.

I remember one time we were training in a building. We had some very good dogs there, so we were doing some really high-pressure, heavy distractions. We set it up so the dog came into a building and ended up being challenged by a decoy who was backed into a corner, so there was no way the dog could get around behind him (a favorite attack route for many dogs). The decoy had buckets and bells and all kinds of stuff, and when the dog bit him, he'd pick up a bucket and yell and drop it over the dog's head. Covering their face would make 80 percent of dogs let go and back up. But Lex knew how to maneuver his body to get out of it but not let go. And if he did let go, he immediately rebit in a better spot.

Now, there are some things you need to understand about bite work. First of all, most dogs go for an extremity—an arm or a leg. Lex would come in and bite somebody right in the stomach, which is a very confident bite for a dog. A rebite is when the dog momentarily lets go, and then clamps down again in a different bite. Typically, when a dog rebites it's because he's afraid. But that wasn't the case with Lex. He would only rebite to gain an advantage.

Lex understood about leverage and the physics of balance with a bite, and that's something you can never teach. For example, if he bit your arm, he'd also try to hook one of your legs and drive his body into you. Then he'd either push you down or use his weight like a wrestler to bring you down. As light as he was, he really knew how to drive himself into you.

As intense as Lex was in the bite work, though, he never lost his head. Good decoys will tell you that when a dog gets on a bite and you start putting pressure on him, his eyes kind of glaze over and some dogs even shut their eyes. It's not uncommon, especially with dogs who have a little bit of fear in them. It's as if they're thinking, "Okay, I'm just going to have an out-of-body experience here. I've got to hang on, but I'm going to think about running along the beach chasing butterflies." Those dogs clamp down on a bite, but when you tell them to let go and you're in a dark building in the middle of what they think is a pretty realistic fight, they are holding on for dear life and are hardly listening. They've shut the world out and you can't get them to stop. We call that a "hard out."

Lex never did that, either. He always had a wonderful clear-headedness, even in the heaviest situations. He was super dependable, which is why I had so much confidence in him. I knew it didn't matter whether we were out on the sports field or really biting a human being in a ditch somewhere in the middle of the night, his brain was always wide open and he heard everything I said.

I remember one traffic stop I made on a roadblock we were working with the Tennessee Highway Patrol. They run regular sobriety checkpoints, and we were stopping traffic one night on the main highway through Gibson. As the officers were checking licenses and registrations, I would walk Lex around in between the cars. He was a certified narcotics dog, and if he indicated that he smelled narcotics in a particular car, under Tennessee law that is considered probable cause, which means we could detain the car and search it without a warrant.

Inevitably on these kinds of roadblocks, you pull over some people who are drunk or have drugs in the car or have warrants out on them, or have some other reason for wanting to avoid the police. A lot of times, they'll see the lights and stop real short, pull into a driveway or a field and turn around and head the other way. So if you are going to run a roadblock well, you set it up in a place where the drivers don't see it until they get pretty close, and where there are not many places to turn around. Normally what you do is station a patrol car right at the spot where people first get sight of the roadblock. You use two cars, so you have the approach covered in both directions. That way, if someone bolts, you have a car in place to run them down.

We were taking turns sitting in the patrol cars. I needed to rest Lex, because he had been searching cars for an hour and it was a really hot night. So the two of us were sitting in a patrol car on the edge of town, at the crest of a hill where people would see the roadblock just as they passed me. It was dark, and the car was partly hidden behind a little stand of trees.

A car drove past, then suddenly did a 180-degree turn in the road and started taking off the other way. I hit the lights and chased it down. I was very careful as I approached the car, because a traffic stop is probably the most dangerous thing a cop does. There are too many unknowns. When you're chasing roadblock runners, you already know that somebody's hiding something or they wouldn't have turned around and run. So it's scarier, but you're also already on the alert. I was alone, so I took Lex out of the car with me and put him in a down-stay in the grass near my car as my backup.

As I approached the car, the driver, a woman, started cussing me out in a way that would make your hair curl. She had probably half a case of empty beer cans lying on the floor of the car and one open next to her. She was drunk and was yelling and hollering the way only drunks can. Then she got out of her car, without me asking her to get out. I was keeping my distance from her and telling her to calm down and stand up against her car.

Lex saw her come out of her car and was fit to be tied. He was probably twenty feet away from us. I looked over and snapped my fingers for him to stay down. He did, but he looked like a frog. He was jumping up and down in place, bouncing from a down position straight up in the air and then back to a down. He had his tail up and was gnashing his teeth, barking, and snarling, because he knew there was something big-time wrong with this woman. The way she was yelling at me was not to his liking and he was ready to engage.

When I looked over at him, I saw that every time he went up in the air and came down, he was about a foot closer. I would yell at him to lie down and he'd do it, but he kept cheating, getting closer and closer. He gave me this look that said, "I'm not going anywhere, I'm staying here," but all the while he kept creeping up. All his training and instincts were saying, "There's something not right here. This lady is yelling, shaking her fist at you, wobbling, acting weird. I think I need to step in." Yet despite all that, he was trying his best to do what I told him to do.

I knew I needed to watch him, but I also had to keep my eyes on her. She might pull out a weapon—you never know. I had already called for backup, because anytime you are chasing down a runner, something is definitely wrong. So I knew another officer was on the way and I thought the worst that could happen is that Lex would break my command and hammer her, and then we'd all get sued.

When the other officer got there, he got out of the car and Lex looked him up and down. I could see he was making up his mind about the cop, so I said, "It's fine," and Lex instantly settled. Then I backed up and let that officer handcuff the woman and take her in, because I knew Lex had just about had enough. It was another one of those times where I knew right where the line was with him and managed to keep a lid on things. It's also a perfect example of how reliable and trustworthy he was, even under extreme stress.

Because Lex had a natural tendency to keep an eye on me and I had to keep my eye on him, we ended up knowing each other so well that it was almost like we each could read the other's mind. It happened with big things, like that traffic stop, and even with little things. For example, Lex needed a lot of bathroom breaks because of his irritable bowel syndrome. When I was out driving with him, I'd usually stop by an empty field and just let him run around unattended. He might be fifty or a hundred yards away from me, but the second I'd just *think*, "Okay, it's time to go," before I could even *do* anything, I'd look up and see that he was coming in. He'd go right to the car and I would never have to say anything.

We did a lot of night maneuvers in police training, and I definitely didn't like to boom out a lot of commands, so unintentionally, over the course of time, a kind of language developed between us that was just clicks and head nods and things like that. But you know, lots of dogs respond to cues that way. With Lex it went a step further. Sometimes in the course of an exercise I would give him a signal I'd never used before and then instantly realize, "Well, Lex is not going to know what the heck that means." But just as I was thinking that, he was doing it. It was like he was always a step ahead of me, like he understood my intentions. I have to admit, a lot of it was him. He just had an uncanny ability to almost feel what I wanted him to do. Honestly, it was a little bit spooky. Certainly, I never had that connection with another dog.

I remember once I was at a Schutzhund trial and Lex was a distance away from me and I needed him to come back in. All I did was just *think*, "Uh, oh, we've never done that exercise before," and he came right over and sat at my side. Another time, we actually lost points at a trial because you are supposed to give the dog clear verbal signals and we were communicating on another plane. I was supposed to call him to me, but I just did a kind of quiet "ssss" and he looked over. I briefly touched my left hip with two fingers and he burned a trail right to me and boom—sat perfectly in the heel position at my left side. It wasn't something we had ever practiced. Our own system of communication just kind of evolved between the two of us.

One of the big things I loved about Lex was that I had so much confidence in him because he was so reliable with me. I knew what he was going to do in every situation and that he wasn't going to screw up—ever. You can't say that about a lot of dogs. With so many, there's something they have to do in competition that they just don't like. You train it and train it, but when you get to the trial and the dog knows you can't correct him, he doesn't listen to half of what you say. Lex was always 100 percent. I knew there were things he didn't like to do, but we worked it out and I just knew that, when I gave him a command, he was going to do it.

The other part of that, though, was that I never felt Lex followed my commands because he had to. He *chose* to. He was such a personable dog with me, in that he didn't hesitate at all to roll over on his back and want me to scratch his belly. This would traditionally be viewed as submissive behavior, but Lex was not submissive with me. In fact, submissive behavior was totally foreign to him. It was just that when we were alone together, he was so relaxed and so confident that he didn't see any threat and could be my buddy.

I think people were surprised when they saw me with him, just the two of us, off to ourselves. Because he was such a monster on the field and at work, they never expected to see us lying down on the grass eating lunch, with Lex rolling around on his back like a little puppy and pulling on my hair in a playful way. The cops who knew him as a patrol dog were especially surprised to see that side of him. But there was still a dog in there; Lex was not just a thrashing machine.

It wasn't that Lex was aggressive and fought a lot. They were surprised more because he was really kind of unsociable. He didn't like or dislike other people—they just didn't mean much to him. Lex was a little bit of a loner in that way. He loved being with me, and then he liked being with Jill, one-on-one, but one of the few mysteries about his temperament was that whoever he liked, by golly he didn't want anyone else looking at them or talking to them.

When Jill and I lived out in the country, before the kids were born, I remember we had a really nice backyard. Jill was teaching at the time, so sometimes she would get home before me and take Lex out. He would roll over and they would play and he really had a good relationship with her. But when I came home, his focus always shifted to me.

I remember one time specifically, I came home and I walked out in the backyard. Jill and Lex were up on a swing we had by the pond on our property. He was on his back with his head in her lap and she was scratching his belly. It was a beautiful afternoon, with birds flying and the pond shimmering. I felt something tighten in my chest, just watching the two of them.

Of course, Lex got up to greet me. I went over and sat down next to Jill and put my arm around her. Lex had just spent all afternoon with her, as he did most afternoons, but you could see in his eyes that there was a conflict. He got up on the swing and wedged himself between us. He wasn't asking for attention and I could see he was actually uncomfortable there. I started teasing him a little bit, hugging Jill and saying to Lex, "Oh, don't get jealous." And he showed his teeth to her, just like that. As soon as he did it, I gave him a sharp correction. But I could tell he practically couldn't help himself. He was just too conflicted by the situation. After that, I didn't put him in that position again.

What Lex enjoyed most, what really relaxed him, were police scenario searches. These were situations we'd set up that were as close to real life police work as you can get. In a scenario search, the decoy runs and hides and the dog has to find him and engage him. I'd have somebody in a bite suit playing the bad guy, or somebody with no equipment on who we knew was going to be able to climb up somewhere the dog couldn't get to him. Sometimes we'd send the guy out an hour or more before we brought in the dog, because in real life the scent from a crime scene is not always fresh.

We'd change up the scenarios a lot, so sometimes the bad guy would be in a building, sometimes he'd go through a parking lot or through the woods or an area where a lot of other people have walked. We'd also switch between area searching, where the dog is off leash and is searching at his own pace, and online tracking, where the dog is on a long leash and is following a single person's scent. A lot of dogs would get frustrated switching from one to the other, but not Lex. He loved the challenge of the different scenarios. You could just see the tension spill off him as he did that sort of training.

In fact, Lex was a phenomenal tracking dog. He had a huge reputation as a predator and a wild beast, and that's what most people remembered about him. But the few trainers who worked side by side with me in searches got to see that he was one of the best tracking dogs I've ever owned.

Tracking was his favorite part of a scenario search because he loved to solve problems. A dog is really on his own when he tracks. I can't smell the scent, so I can't tell him what to do. He has to figure it out on his own. To give you just a little example, dogs track by following scent on the ground and by sniffing it in the air. Usually they do one or the other. But Lex was able to switch back and forth. When he lost a track on the ground or it was following a crazy path, he'd lift his head up and air scent until he got back to a good place to follow the ground scent. That's not something I could train him to do. He figured it out on his own. He made his own decisions about how best to tackle a problem.

Building searches are especially tough, because you get little pockets of air that swirl through a building in strange ways—ways we humans don't even sense or know—and it misleads the dogs. When high-drive dogs lose a scent, they'll keep searching and searching until they run into it again. That's different from a dog who steps back and says, "All right, what just happened here? I'm going to figure this out." Lex was always very clear-headed in those situations. He didn't search mindlessly and endlessly. He took a systematic approach and quickly ended up back on the right track.

A lot of trainers correct a dog for lifting his head when he's tracking because they don't realize they're discouraging the dog from actually figuring out the problem. That's where we get into the difference between trainability and intelligence. People put them in the same bucket, but they are not at all the same. For example, I think some of the smartest breeds are the sled dogs, such as huskies and malamutes. They are very intelligent and have great survival instincts, and are probably among the most independent and capable breeds out there. But they are also very resistant to training and a lot of times they are not good with obedience. That's because they figure, "Why am I doing this? I don't want to chase this stupid ball. I want to do my own thing." People need to understand that when we can't train a dog to do the people things we want him to do, it doesn't have any bearing on the dog's intelligence.

Lex actually had a good mix of both. He was very trainable and he had so much drive that he was a phenomenal, very flashy dog in everything he did—including formal obedience exercises. But he also was a very independent thinker. That duality was one of the things that made him so interesting. Most dogs are one or the other, but Lex could do obedience like a golden retriever, just glued to my hip, and was also very capable of being sent out on his own to search off leash over a long distance, where I had no communication with him.

Being such a good problem solver is a high-value commodity in my book because not many dogs are, and a police dog must be. You've got to have that ability to think independently. I'll give you an example of how that worked.

I used to compete with Lex in patrol dog competitions, which are just for working police dog teams. The year I won the National Patrol Dog Championship with him, the final scenario that day was that you had to search a mobile home. You didn't know if there was one suspect in there, two, three, or none. You just had to clear the building with the dog in a certain amount of time. They had set it up so there was a real active suspect in the back with a bite suit on who was pretty visible. The dog had to engage him, which means physically subduing him.

Almost everybody went through and saw the first guy, the dog did his thing, the handler called him off, and they walked out. Coming into that exercise, Lex and I were tied for first place with three other teams. We went in the mobile home, he got the guy, and then as we were coming out of the building, he alerted on the front door. I mean, he was eating that door alive. I almost corrected him off it because, like everyone else, I thought the exercise was over.

But it turns out there was a guy hiding behind the door. When Lex alerted, the decoy busted out from behind the door with a shotgun and Lex went after him and did his job. When I looked at the judge, he had a big old grin on his face. He told me, "You're the only ones who got that guy."

Everything I knew about Lex—his high drive, his rock-solid nerves, his warrior spirit, his ability to think on his own—came together for me soon after I started working him on the street. I got a call from my friend Mark Robertson. He was retired from the Shelby County Sheriff's Department and was now the top narcotics dog trainer in the county. There was a maximum security prison in Missouri that had been having a lot of problems with drugs being smuggled in, and they asked Mark to come in with a team of fifteen or twenty dogs and do a cell-to-cell search.

They way they did it, they would lock down a pod and put everybody from that pod out in the yard, then we would search all the cells and the common rooms for contraband. We had to go in with a lot of teams so we could hit every pod at once. This way, nobody heard about the search and had time to get rid of anything. We had to hit that prison fast and heavy.

We did a dawn raid, and let me tell you, it was super high-pressure intensity. All the inmates were screaming and hollering and trying to throw things at the dogs. I mean, these guys will do anything to get in there and kill you. They're lifers, and they've got nothing to lose.

The search took all day. Lex made two drug finds, and then he found an empty compartment under one inmate's bed that had obviously held something in the past. All the dogs had to take breaks throughout the day, because this is a really intense situation. By mid-afternoon, there were only about eight dogs who were really still searching. The other ones were just out of gas.

With that kind of pressure and the tension hanging heavy in the air, as a handler you have to try to keep your dog relaxed. But it isn't possible when you are in a maximum security prison, and that really saps the energy out of most dogs. Except Lex. Lex just absorbed all the pressure and spun it into high energy. Everybody noticed. He was amped up and ready to fight the monster all day long.

That night was one of the few times he was completely exhausted. I remember when we got back to the hotel room, he was on one bed and I was on the other. I was lying there watching TV and he jumped over onto my bed and lay down next to me—something he almost never did. He had this look in his eyes like, "Wow! We really did it today, Dad." He plopped his chin down and was looking at me with this goofy little kid's look. It was like he had really done his work that day and he was proud.

There were moments like that when we were alone and he would roll over on his back and I could play with him. I could get on top of him and kind of wrestle with him like a little boy with a puppy. He never saw that as a threat from me. With a dog as tough and as aggressive as he was, that's actually kind of an anomaly. I think there was just a little kid inside of Lex. But I didn't see it often. It was as if he knew he had to keep that warrior front up. It wasn't that he was afraid and had to put up a tough exterior to keep from showing his weakness. He just knew how the world worked.

Sometimes I actually wished he could dial that intensity back a bit. He could never simply sit down and watch TV with us. If we were hanging out in the house, he'd be wandering from room to room or pacing restlessly. As soon as I moved to get up, he was on his feet like a cat: "Are we getting ready to do something? That was fun, but I'm ready to do something." He was a working machine. I wished I could have said to him, "Buddy, just relax and take a day off." But Lex was all business.

It was almost as if Lex had an attention deficit disorder. He was such a thinking dog that he was always three steps ahead of what was going on. So while he sometimes looked distracted, in a flash he would refocus if he needed to take care of whatever was in front of him. But unless it was something he had to handle immediately, he had three or four other things he was thinking about. It was like, "Hey, you got a problem? Let me know. Until then I'm going to be over here smelling this and looking through this other thing." Of course, if the situation turned into anything he needed to confront, he could shake all that off and be focused in a heartbeat.

The flip side of that was he could also be dangerous in a heartbeat. Certain situations with Lex were about me keeping an eye on him to keep him under control so he wouldn't blow up. As a result, I learned all his little nuances—for instance, how his bark would change, where each bark would get just a little bit closer together and a little bit more intense. Most people probably never heard the difference, but I could. His body language would also change ever so slightly when I knew he was just about to say, "I'm standing here doing what I'm supposed to do, but I think I've had enough." Because I could see the blowup coming, I could always do something to diffuse it.

Mind you, Lex definitely let me know when he had enough of something. But when he blew up, it was more or less a temper tantrum, not a challenge for authority. In the heat of the moment, maybe if he was doing something he liked and I made him stop, usually he'd just turn around and—*rowf! rowf! rowf!*—talk to me. It wasn't something that happened all the time, and I didn't make a huge deal out of it, either. I mean, he definitely got a correction, but I also knew he was at a boiling point and I had pushed him past it. That was part of our mutual respect.

I have to say, there's something I like about an animal who carves out his own respect. And for sure, that was Lex. He made it clear, "I respect you, but you are also going to have to respect me and everyone around me is going to have to respect me."

I remember when he was five years old—that was in 1998—I was in McMinnville, Tennessee, at the Middle Tennessee Schutzhund Club, competing with Lex for his Schutzhund II title. Most of the people at that club had trained with me before and they knew Lex was a monster on the field—a really tough, aggressive, serious dog. When he was working, he wasn't out there with his tail wagging having a big party. He was out there doing serious things, and people recognized and respected that.

When the trial was over, the trial judge, Carole Patterson, a few other people, and I sat around in a little pavilion on the club grounds telling stories. One of the decoys told the judge about Lex's face-biting incident in St. Louis. Carole said there were a few dogs around the country that she had to be extra careful around and she knew not to get in their faces.

Right about then they announced the winners, and Lex and I had won the Schutzhund II division. There was a photographer taking pictures for a national Schutzhund magazine, and I didn't really want to do it because I felt Lex had had enough for one day. But I thought, "It's just a picture and it will be over quick." The typical pose for the winners is that the dog sits between the handler and the judge, and the trophy sits on the ground. I sat Lex down and the photographer said, "Hey, I'm getting a glare off that trophy, can you turn it?" And then, before I could do anything, Carole leaned right over Lex's face to move the trophy. Her face was coming down over the top of him, inches from his teeth.

Understand, at this point we had been competing in this trial for two days and Lex was at the end of his rope. I was working him as a police dog at the time, so we were doing a lot of scenario training and he was kind of keyed up about work. I really had to take him down a few notches to get through that Schutzhund trial, and he was sick of all the control work.

It all happened in a millisecond. He looked up at me with a look that said, "I'm getting ready to bite her in the face." I knew it was going to happen, and as I bent down to snatch him, he was starting to go off on her. He just turned around and was like, "Okay, if it's not going to be her, it's going to be you."

And it was. The way I remember it now, he bit me on my

right arm. But I was talking about this recently with one of the decoys who saw it all, and he said, "Don't you remember, you had that big tear in your pants? He punctured you on the leg and the stomach, too." So obviously those bites came first, because I know the arm bite was the last one.

Lex ended up locked down on my right forearm, just below the elbow. I quickly yanked his collar up with my left hand, so his front feet were off the ground. One of his canine teeth (the fangs) had gone in so deep that it was scraping the bone, and I remember feeling that and thinking, "This is going to be nasty if his feet hit the ground." That's because if he had been able to get his feet planted, Lex was a shredder. He would have been shaking his head and stripping the meat off the bone. The fact that he was locked on and compressing hurt like hell, but at least he wasn't ripping. It was lucky for me he wasn't a 120-pound dog. As it was, I remember later I could stick a pinky down the hole in my arm.

I was *really* mad at Lex and he was really mad at me. I have to admit, for me, a lot of it was my pride. I was so offended that he would bite me out there on the field in front of everybody. My left hand was up in the air holding his collar, and we were nose to nose, me cussing and him growling. Being up off the ground like that, he eventually started choking and had to let go of my arm. When he hit the ground, I was still cussing. I instantly hooked the leash on him and started doing some really fast obedience work. It put a quick end to the physical aggression and refocused him on something that reestablished the idea that we were going to do what *I* said. I was cussing the whole time, too. I heeled him around for probably less than a minute, then did a couple of downs and sits where I was really standing over him aggressively and popping out my commands. Then I heeled him on out, walked him over to my trailer, took his leash and collar off, and put him in the car.

There were no hard feelings after the fight. I understood why he went off and I knew how to get control of him. And, as I said before, it's not like we had this fairy-tale perfect relationship. We had our little squabbles and a few real blowups, but we were like an old married couple. You know how the other one is going to react and what buttons to push. And you know where the boundaries are. It was hassle-free handling, because that total familiarity made things really comfortable and easy.

The Hollywood version of Lex's story would be that he was transformed from a face-biting dog to a face-licking dog. But Lex was a real dog in the real world, and real life isn't like that. He started out in a situation that wasn't right for him, but when he ended up with me in a situation that *was* right for him, he was still basically the same dog. Lex was always Lex.

He turned out to be the greatest dog I ever had, but in some ways he always had the potential to be a face-biting dog. I just never let things get out of control, because I always knew he could escalate from zero to a hundred in the blink of an eye. It was kind of like if your best friend is an extreme cage fighter. He's a hothead, and if you take him to a bar you know that if somebody pushes him just a little bit, there's going to be a problem. Lex never stopped being that guy. He never shut it off and he never dialed back the intensity. That's what I loved about him.

Where I got to with Lex, that perfect conjunction of man and dog, would never have been possible without all the lessons learned from the other dogs in my life. That's what the rest of this book is about.

# 2

# Jack and Jill

Where I lived in Tennessee, most boys spent time hunting with their fathers. Hunting was one of those things all the men did, and when you were a boy, you really wanted to join in and be "manly." It was especially exciting for me because in those days the men of the house did "man things" and child raising was for the women, so hunting was when I got to spend the most time with my dad.

You go duck hunting in the middle of winter and it's cold, even in Tennessee, so the air feels sharp when you breathe in. For those of you who don't duck hunt, it's done from a blind, which is a flimsy little shelter designed to keep the ducks from seeing you. The blind is always near a body of water, because that's where ducks land. Ours was built up above a lake on stilts, and we had to take a little boat to get out there. The sun would just be coming up and mist would be rising from the lake, so taking our little boat out to the blind was like a mystical journey to another place. And in a way it really was, because when we went duck hunting, there was nothing else happening in the world.

Duck hunting was also my earliest exposure to working dogs and the kinds of relationships people sometimes have with them—relationships that are so close they are impossible to explain. The kind of relationship I had with Lex was, in many ways, like the relationship a hunter has with his once-in-a-lifetime dog, the one who seems to be able to read his mind. The first time I saw a man work with a dog that way, I was watching Jack and Jill.

I remember Jack Camp so clearly. He was a house builder, a carpenter, a master cabinetmaker, and a real funny storyteller. I went to the same school as Jack's daughter, Christie, so we grew up together and I knew him all my life. Jack was a classic: tall, dark, and handsome. Nowadays, he'd be the kind of guy you'd see on a television home makeover show. The women all loved him.

Jack had a black Labrador retriever named Jill. Jill never did have any formal training, but she was a great hunting dog. By that I mean Jack didn't send her to some fancy dog training school or anything like that. In fact, I think he barely trained her at all. Hunting puppies learned by watching hunting dogs, and from the reactions of their owners. I was six years old when we started hunting with Jack and Jill, and I didn't realize it at the time, but when I look back now at what that dog did, it's pretty miraculous.

The whole duck hunting thing was a kind of ritual: Everyone would drive to the diner for breakfast at four in the morning. It was still dark then, and I remember I'd be sleepy and excited at the same time. Jack had this big old blue Ford pickup with big tires on it, and when I was a kid, that was the neatest truck I'd ever seen. He'd drive around and pick everyone up to go hunting, and Jill would ride up in the cab with him. If we had too many people, he'd just tell her to jump in the back and she'd do it.

There was a thing with Jack and Jill that was something Lex and I had: Jack didn't tell her something to do and then watch her and think, "Okay, I'm going to see if she's going to do it now." It wasn't like he was giving a command; he just expected she would do what he said. I mean, Jack didn't even own a leash. Jill would sit in the truck while we were inside eating breakfast, and then we'd drive to the lake. Jack would open the door and she'd run around a little while the men were loading all the stuff into the boat, but she never ran off. When they were ready to go, they'd crank up the motor and Jack would say, "Come on," or she'd already be in the boat, because she knew from watching us when it was time to push off.

Now you have to imagine this: We're in a rickety boat, full of decoys and backpacks and duffle bags and gun bags and people, some of whom Jill had never met before, and everybody is piled in and the boat is shaking back and forth and it's twenty degrees out and dark—just think about how many dogs would be totally unnerved by that. But Jill would get in her little spot in the boat and settle.

When we'd get to the blind, Jill would be the first one out of the boat and she'd go to her special place. We would all be busy unloading the boat and putting out decoys and selecting duck calls and getting the guns ready, and Jack certainly didn't have time to stand over a dog to make sure she was complying. She just did.

By five-thirty there'd be a bunch of dads and sons in the duck blind. We'd stay there until lunchtime and cook and eat and talk. That was a lot of quality time. When I look back on that now, I appreciate it even more and it almost saddens me as a father, because I don't really do that sort of thing with my own kids. If I sat in a duck blind with them now, I'd have my cell phone and I'd be wondering if I could get any service out there. There was something to be said for being out where nobody could get in touch with you. There was a peace of mind about it; you could leave your world behind. I think nowadays we've lost a way to connect with one another, with the world around us, and with animals.

When you're duck hunting, the dog's job is to keep still as the ducks approach and watch where they fall when the hunters shoot them. That's called "marking the fall." When the hunters are done shooting, you send the dog off into the water to pick up the downed birds, and she's supposed to bring them back to you without chewing them up and just drop them at your feet. If the dog doesn't see where a bird fell, the hunter can send her to a specific spot to search using hand signals or a whistle. So hunting dogs have to work independently and at long distances, and you just have to have faith in them to do what you ask and come back to you. Nowadays, people who participate in competitive retriever trials spend years training their dogs to do this, but, like I said, Jack never really trained Jill in any formal, organized way.

Thinking back, I don't remember ever seeing Jack get on Jill or even reprimand her for anything. That kind of relationship was very contrary to the accepted wisdom at the time about how to train hunting and working dogs. The thinking was that they were not pets or housedogs; you were supposed to keep them in a pen and just bring them out to train or to work. The idea behind this was to really build the dog's drive to work. In dogs with a medium-level drive, that isolation would torque them up and then they'd bust out and really be ready to work hard. But the down side was that when the dogs first got out, they had a lot of pent-up frustration and they'd be running all over the place. I saw guys with those kinds of dogs yelling at them a lot, and the dogs never seemed to be able to settle, especially when we began the day, because they were so full of excess energy.

By contrast, Jack took Jill everywhere with him, including to work. She didn't spend her week cooped up waiting for the weekend hunt. As a result, what you saw with Jill was consistency in temperament. What I know now, and saw in Jill then, was that energy management is really the basis of behavior management. When we forget that, we end up spending a lot of time putting Band-Aids on specific problems and not addressing the excess energy question that's behind everything—digging, barking, jumping, destructiveness, and all the rest. Our dogs spend all day in solitary confinement, and then we wonder why they're hyper when we come home.

Anyway, Jack had a little spot set up for Jill on the platform with a little deck and a ramp that went down into the water. If it was really cold, she could come inside the shelter we had built, but when we saw some ducks coming in and he'd say, "Now,

Jill, get in your place," she'd go over and lie down on her deck. Of course, the ducks could see her outside (they couldn't see us humans in the little shelter—that's why it's called a blind), so she had to be really still. Sometimes if the ducks were flying very close she'd get a little fidgety and Jack would whisper, "Now be still," and that was it. She would just lie down and be still.

Sometimes we'd have five shooters in a blind and we'd shoot eight or ten ducks all at once. Jill would mark three or four of them in her head and then go out and bring them in one at a time without having to be directed or told until she got to the sixth or seventh one. They may have been floating a hundred yards away at that point, barely visible to us, just a little duck floating in the water that looks like the other couple of hundred decoys out there. But she'd swim right out to it and bring it back. Back then I guess I didn't give it much thought—that's just what hunting dogs did—but when I reflect back on it now, the abilities of that dog were amazing.

I remember one particular story about Jill that just blew me away, even when I was a kid. Jack was sitting on the edge of the duck blind and he had a Styrofoam coffee cup that was just about empty. The wind blew up for a moment and the cup sailed out over the lake and settled gently into the water. Jack looked out there and said, "Jill, go get that cup."

I can see this so clearly in my mind, even now. The cup was probably a hundred feet away, bobbing around between hundreds of floating decoys that must have looked to her like toys floating in the water. "Cup" is not a word Jill had ever learned, and retrieving a cup from a duck pond is not something she had ever been asked to do. When you think about it, there was no reason at all that that task should have made any sense to her.

Jill dove off the ramp and swam after that Styrofoam cup, heading straight for it between all those decoys. She brought it back. I remember even then, when I was six years old, I was completely blown away by that. But Jack didn't think much of it. He just stuffed the cup in our trash bag.

I thought it was something pretty special then, but now, as an adult who has worked with so many dogs, I am even more amazed. There is an enormous willingness on the part of good working dogs. They have to want to do it. When they are 200 yards away from you and there's no leash, you can't make them do anything. The good working dogs—they've got to have it in them. You can do things to build drive in a dog, but there are limits. The good working dogs are just born with it.

But there's more to it than that. Because for me, Jack and Jill are a great example of what a human-dog relationship should be all about. They were just a good match—a testament to some of the unknowns of that amazing relationship. There's a chemistry that creates a kind of synergy. As good as Jack was with dogs, he never had another dog like Jill. And I had hundreds of dogs coming through my kennel, but I never had another one like Lex.

Is it something in the dog or something in the man? I think it's something in both. That spark is on both ends. That's not to say you can't have good working relationships with other dogs, and certainly you love other dogs in your life. But sometimes it clicks in that incredible way and sometimes it doesn't. Most of the time it doesn't.

The tough thing as pet owners is, once you've had that, it's really difficult to give your heart away again. I've enjoyed all the dogs I've ever had, including Abigail. They're great dogs, every one of them. But thirty years from now when I'm sitting there in the retirement home having my nostalgic thoughts about dogs, I'm going to be thinking about Lex.

That's why people need to have reasonable expectations as pet owners. If you've had a pet like that—and often it's a childhood pet, because there is some naive nostalgia that goes along with having a pet as a child and you forget about the problems— you sometimes try to keep re-creating that experience. Maybe you have visions of your dog being just like Lassie or Old Yeller, and of course it just doesn't turn out that way. If that's what's happened to you and your dog, don't leave him to spend half his time alone in the backyard. Go out there and get to know him.

Another one of my dad's hunting buddies was Clifford Murchison. He was known all over our area for having great rabbit beagles. The fact is that my dad preferred duck hunting because it was more social, but Clifford and Dad used to jointly own a little ice company and they were really good friends. And in Tennessee in those days, men who were good friends went hunting together. Clifford's daughter, Shaney Mae, was my age, so I knew them pretty well. (By the way, today Shaney Mae is president of the Humane Society for West Tennessee and she has really turned their program around. Clearly, she learned to love animals from her dad.)

Basically, with beagles you let the pack out and you just kind of follow the dogs while they search for rabbit scent. When they pick up on a hot trail, the whole pack starts baying and they chase the rabbit.

Rabbits always take an evasive circular path, where they lead the dogs out a long way but then end up circling back to where they started from. This way, the rabbits don't get too far out of their territory and away from their rabbit holes; they kind of send the dogs on a wild goose chase. The rabbit hunters set up on the spot where the pack flushes the rabbit and starts to chase him. They spread out and wait for the dogs to come around full circle. It takes anywhere from five to thirty minutes. As you hear the dogs coming back toward you, you know the rabbit is a good bit ahead of them and he'll usually come running over the hill or around the corner.

I have to say, I found the dogs a lot more interesting than the rabbits. We don't have much opportunity anymore to observe dogs in a true pack situation, and you can learn a lot from it. What I saw with Clifford was that rather than try to train his beagles, he put the young dogs with the more experienced dogs so they could emulate them. That's how they learn best, because obviously a human can't run around baying and barking and tracking an animal with his nose. If you worked with a young dog individually, he might do a good bit of this naturally, but the mechanics of it wouldn't be as evident to him and he wouldn't grow up with the same savvy as a pup who gets to run with the big dogs.

In other words, young dogs see how it's done and then learn by example. And that's a technique I used later with my own dogs.

When I was teaching defensive behavior to a young dog, I often used Lex because he was so explosive. When we were training, one of the first exercises with a young dog was to have a guy get near him acting suspicious and trying to get the dog to show a little bit of an aggressive tendency. Now, if you have a dog who really doesn't know what to do, there's a whole bag of tricks you can use to bring out the aggression in him. But some of those tricks are kind of rough and can create a bad experience for the dog and cause him to shy away from protection work—in which case you've pretty much ruined the dog for that type of work. But what I found is that I could cut weeks off the training time and also make it very clear to the dog what he was supposed to do just by letting him watch Lex.

I'd stick the young dog on an agitation line, which is a six- to eight-foot cable fixed to a stationary post. The cable is spring-loaded, so the dog can lunge at the "bad guy" and put up an energetic fight without getting hurt. You don't want the dog hitting the end of the line on a lunge and getting a snap to the neck—that hurts the dog, and also seems to the dog like a correction for being tough on the line. And you don't want to correct a dog for being tough; the purpose of the line is to control the dog and build the aggressive response. I'd have Lex tied to another line about ten feet away. Then we'd have our guy kind of creep around and act suspicious, and Lex, who was so explosive in those situations, would bounce to the end of the line, snarling and barking with his tail up over his back. Usually, the young dogs would want to react as well, but weren't really sure if they should. When they'd see Lex go off like a bomb, they'd think, "Okay, when a guy acts like that, this is what you do."

You would see those dogs move ahead quantum leaps in training when they had an older dog to emulate.

Scent discrimination is another thing the young beagles learned from the older ones. A dog out in the woods is smelling a potpourri of scent all the time, and it's just as much fun to chase raccoons or deer as it is to chase rabbits. But those young dogs see the older ones chasing only the rabbits and they realize, "Oh, that's what we're out here to do." If there's a dog in the pack who starts running after deer or raccoons, the hunter will take him out very quickly because he'll start teaching the other dogs the wrong thing.

Most of the time when we are watching our dogs, we are also interacting with them, so we don't get to see them as I saw those beagles. But recently, I've had other opportunities to observe dogs undisturbed, and as a result, I've had to change some of my ideas about male dominance and territoriality.

I think nowadays very few people are able to observe dogs in this natural way, so we stick to what we see. And what we see is dogs who are typically restrained on leashes or in pens or behind fences. What we don't realize, sometimes, is that the way they react to other male dogs is not really natural. In fact, I think dominant aggressive behavior between males is not as pronounced as we think. Working with police dogs, I have been around a lot of bully-type dominant male dogs and yes, some of them really are dominant toward other dogs. But a lot of the aggressive behavior I see is the result of built-up frustration, and that frustration comes from the fact that these dogs are constantly on a leash or isolated behind a fence, in solitary confinement.

In fact, any good dog trainer will tell you that two dogs on leash are far more likely to have a go at each other than two dogs off leash. There are a couple of reasons for this. One is that dogs have ways of introducing themselves that include a subtle dance of body language and scent. There's a lot of sniffing and posturing back and forth that says "Who are you?" "I'm not a threat," "This is my spot," and things like that. But when we put one dog behind a fence or hold them both on leashes, we interfere with their ability to work all this out in their canine way. They don't have all the information they need, and that makes them tense. And that's when things can erupt.

But there's more to it. It's kind of like a bar fight. When you've got a couple of guys in a bar, especially when they have a bunch of friends around, a little insult suddenly turns into a big thing. And if the two guys are being held back by their buddies, the bravado level escalates even more. At that "let me at him" moment, if you could snap your fingers and suddenly the bar was completely empty except for those two guys, and there were no friends around they had to posture for, they'd probably snarl at each other a little bit and then end up laughing about it. Dogs are the same way. They act a lot worse when their owners are around because the dog has to defend the owner—and defend his own honor in front of the owner. The leash or fence, the owner, the territory—all those other components cause situations that are not very big to escalate into fights.

I learned an important lesson about that when we moved back to my wife's hometown in western Tennessee in 2005. It's a semi-rural area, and most of the houses are on a couple of acres, but there are about 300 undeveloped acres behind us. We've got a pack of anywhere from eight to fifteen neighborhood dogs whose owners let them out, and they kind of trail around together, crossing many territories of other dogs. None of the males are neutered, and the traditional way of thinking is that this is a recipe for dogfights—especially with the new dog on the block.

When I got Nord, the German shepherd I am currently training in Schutzhund, I was really worried about those dogs because we had just moved back there and I didn't want him getting into a brawl with the neighborhood big boys and getting hurt. Plus, I didn't want to take a chance on him getting hit by a car or causing an accident. So I kept him in a fenced area. The pack would come across my property and he'd be behind his fence, barking and acting like he wanted to kill them. It went on that way for months.

I wanted to have my dog out with me when I was in my backyard, though. So I came up with the idea to snap a leash on the dominant male in that pack, a spitz-husky mix, just to give Nord a chance to get used to being around him, because I knew I could control Nord. It turned out that spitz-husky didn't even have a collar on, so I took a twenty-foot cotton mesh line and tied it around his neck. Instantly, I could tell he'd never been on a leash before, and it just shut him down. We condition our dogs right from puppyhood to think a leash is nothing, so they end up being confident and cocky on the leash. But for this dog, it was total domination. He tucked his tail, lay down on the ground, and was completely submissive. This was a dog who bullied every dog in the neighborhood, and he was totally emasculated by a three-dollar leash.

Nord instantly started ignoring him. I thought, "Okay, I can work with this." I realized Nord did not have to fight that dog because I had done the fighting for him. I kept leashing that dog whenever he came into our yard, and told Nord to leave him alone. When I finally let Nord out to run up to him, it was just off our property so Nord wasn't defending our territory. I crossed my fingers and said to myself, "I'm just going to be passive. I'll be ready, but I'm not going to stand over him and tell him how to behave or put any pressure on him. I'm just going to let things unfold." And you know, they kind of growled around a little bit and squabbled, but then everything was fine. I found the more I let Nord out with those dogs, the calmer they all were. Sure, one of them would puff up a time or two, but that was it. It just wasn't a big deal.

However, even today, if I leave Nord behind the fence and he watches those dogs come by, he'll bark and snap at them through the fence and they'll kind of stomp and posture and pee on his fence post. His frustration builds up so much that if I were to let him out in the heat of the moment, he would run and just jump right on top of them.

There have been some pretty good studies done on wolves in the past ten to fifteen years, and one of the things they've found is that in a wolf pack, all-out brawls for dominance are infrequent. Sure, there are plenty of little squabbles, but they're not constantly fighting to determine who is in charge—which is what we used to believe. It happens once every few years, when the status of the dominant individual clearly changes. But mostly it's just subtle cues the dominant wolf uses to put the other wolves in their place. That raised head or withering stare, the little bit of snarling—the subtler things that reinforce the hierarchy all day—keep them from having the knockdown fight. The pack structure is just understood and worked out.

At home, all the little things you do every day also subtly reinforce the hierarchy. There are plenty of simple ways you can remind your dog that you are the leader. For example, sit on the floor and have a snack, and don't let your dog have a bite. Or make him wait for you to go up the stairs or through the door before he goes. This way, he's not always competing with you and he doesn't feel like he has to fight on your behalf when he meets other dogs. All these little things really do add up.

Wolves work things out with a minimum of fighting because they are in an environment that is not limited by humans. In the same situation, dogs would, too. Dogs running free have a minimum of frustrated energy. But while their natural tendency is to make their peace, letting all dogs run free is not possible in the real world. In close quarters, dogs are always reacting to our presence. As a result, I think we miss out on a lot of opportunities to learn about them.

Looking back, I think watching those hunting beagles and Jack working with Jill was about as natural as it gets with people and dogs. Because a big part of what dogs were born to do is work with us. It's something that's in their genetic makeup. Most dogs don't work anymore, but they still have that genetic imperative to do things with us. If we step back and stop intervening at every moment of their lives, if we don't work quite so hard at directing their behavior, they tend to figure out on their own ways they can be part of our lives. I think that's why Jill didn't need much training and yet was the best hunting dog I've ever seen. Jack let her figure most of it out on her own, and just gave her direction when she needed it.

This genetic hardwiring to cast their lot along with ours is a big part of the difference between domesticated animals and wild animals. Dogs and humans evolved together, working side by side. It's why that wordless, almost mystical connection with dogs is possible. It's in their genes. It's in ours, too.

# 3

# Predators and Prey

The squirrel crept closer to me, maybe an inch at a time, pausing after each step to scan the yard, then stand up and sniff the air. He looked at me and then looked around and then moved forward just a tiny bit more. I was sitting on Granddaddy's back porch with a peanut in my hand, and I wanted that squirrel to come just ten feet away from me before I tossed it to him.

Squirrels are prey animals and being out in the open is dangerous for them. So is approaching animals as big as humans—even seven-year-old boys. With each step closer, he had to reassure himself that I presented no danger, so he'd stop and check me out, then make that little gesture squirrels do when they point to themselves as if to say, "Who, me?" He never took his eyes off me, but at the same time I could see that he had a sense of what was going on in the whole yard.

It had taken almost an hour for him to get from the bottom

of a big old oak tree at the other end of the yard to within about twenty feet of me. Almost there. I was trying to make myself look as small and harmless as possible. I was sitting kind of hunched over, with my body sideways to him, and I had my outstretched hand resting on my knee and my eyes a little down and to the side, so I wasn't looking right at him, because predators look at their prey straight on.

That squirrel was so close now that I wanted to get a better look. So I shifted my eyes up, just a tiny bit. And, bam! He was gone across the yard and up a tree before I could finish exhaling. Behind me, Granddaddy chuckled, "He caught you looking."

Nonverbal communication is the world of animals. I couldn't have trained any dog, let alone police dogs, without an understanding of how that works. There are now all kinds of charts and videos you can study that explain how when a raccoon flicks his ears a certain way it means one thing and when a squirrel stands up on his hind legs it means something else. But no matter how many pictures you look at, you're never doing more than memorizing. The only way to get a feel for this kind of thing is to experience it.

I call it active observation. I know people who hunt or hike or just take a picnic into the woods and come home and say they didn't see anything. I don't really know how that's possible. You need to just sit still—I mean *really* still—and try to take it all in and ask yourself some questions. Why is that squirrel doing this? Why is he walking this way? I've seen squirrels in this place before but now their behavior is different. Why is that happening? Is the weather different? Is it the breeding season? Is it the season babies are born? Are there motherless babies?

It's like being a private investigator.

I remember so clearly the first time I went deer hunting—like it's a movie running in my head. You have to be dead quiet so you don't scare off the deer, and I sat there and watched the world come awake. Because I was so silent and still, I was a part of it. It's like I became a tree or a rock. I'd never experienced anything like that before, because even if you walk quietly in the woods you are constantly interrupting whatever is going on around you. But when you are sitting still in a deer stand, you can just become part of it and see things undisturbed and naturally.

When the deer do come, I'm always amazed at how such a large animal can move around so quietly. Sometimes you've just been sitting there watching the same patch of woods in total silence for an hour and then all of a sudden you look back around and, just like a phantom appearing, there stands a big deer.

Dawn and dusk are especially interesting times because they're transitions. You see some of the animals winding down while the others are waking up. Sometimes early in the morning you see an owl cruising around, getting ready to call it a night, or a raccoon or a possum. It's like a changing of the guard. I found it fascinating.

I was ten years old the first time I watched the world wake up from a deer stand. They have an event in Tennessee called a juvenile hunt that's held the middle week of November, so kids under the age of fifteen can hunt with a gun (normally you have to be eighteen). I had to be old enough to be able to sit in the deer stand by myself out in the woods in the dark and not be afraid, and by ten, I was. So my dad took me out on the four-wheeler and dropped me off at the stand in the dark at four-thirty in the morning.

A deer stand is a kind of camouflaged platform in the middle of the woods, and the idea is to sit as still as you can and wait for the deer to come by. Now, deer are shy animals because they are prey, so they are always on the lookout for predators. And that means you have to be very still and quiet and very patient.

If you've never done it before, you might think sitting silent in the woods for a couple of hours could be pretty boring because nothing much is going on. But it's not like that at all. In a small patch of woods you can see fifty feet in every direction, and if you just focus on that and really think about what is going on, it's like watching a circus. I remember seeing the birds awaken. The bugs in the tree started coming out from wherever they were deep inside the trunk and going up and down, carrying things back and forth. Then the birds started trying to eat the bugs before they got back inside their holes. I realized that everything has its life cycle, and it just starts to unfold in front of you.

Once I watched a mama coyote and her three little babies running around in a field. The farmer had just cut the hay and baled it up into long rolls. The pups were probably twelve to fourteen weeks old, and they were romping around, kind of playing hide and seek. As they spread out, they kept looking back and checking with their mother. Suddenly she stiffened, raised her head, and pricked her ears forward. It was as if an electric shock wave ran across the field. Every one of those puppies took notice of it and stood up and looked in the direction she was looking—although she had not made a sound. Then they immediately started going back toward her. It turned out to be nothing and they fanned out again, playing little puppy games in the field. But I watched that same thing happen twice more, where every reaction she had was read instantaneously even from a hundred feet away. It didn't matter where the pups were in the field or how far they were from her; they *felt* it. It was all about her presence and her body language.

Reading body language is an instinct for animals, and eventually it became an instinct for me, too. And a lot of that came about from just watching. When I really think about it, I realize that while dogs are predators, I've learned a lot from watching both predators and prey. In fact, the techniques I use to bring out certain traits in young dogs and test their courage without breaking them down, I learned from watching prey animals like squirrels.

When I started training dogs professionally in my early twenties, the police dog world was an old boy kind of network. Until about 1990, police patrol dog training in America was stuck in the 1950s—which certainly limited what people could do with the dogs. Those old training methods developed out of the military dog training used in World War II. The idea was to dominate the dog completely and correct every mistake he made—emphasizing what the dog was doing wrong, rather than what he was doing right. It was definitely not a confidence-builder for the dog.

A lot of those old guys had been doing the same things the same old way and had mixed results. Still, they were not ready for a twenty-year-old kid to come in and start teaching them a radically different, softer, less physically overpowering way—a way I learned from the squirrels in Granddaddy's backyard (something I would never say out loud in a police dog training situation!).

My grandfather lived about a mile from us and his backyard was a canopy of huge one hundred-year-old oak trees that were filled with squirrels. Granddaddy never tried to take a baby and raise it and make it a pet; that wasn't the point at all. Feeding those squirrels was just something for him to do. My grandmother had passed away when she was really young and Granddaddy was the local postmaster for a long time. He was done with work every day at four o'clock and had plenty of time on his hands, so he started going out into the yard with shelled peanuts and seeing what it would take to get a squirrel to grab one out of his hand.

As a kid, I liked the challenge of it. And now, as an adult looking back, I liked the patience it taught me. Because the squirrels, being prey animals, were so cagey that you really had to turn inward and monitor everything you did. Every action you took just seemed to be amplified: your posture, if you stood up or sat down, if you shifted your eyes (as I found out the hard way). You had to sit down low and make sure your body was not facing the squirrel and try to be as small and unthreatening as possible.

Granddaddy and I would talk in low voices. He taught me that talking and having to think about a conversation was better than silence, because with silence, you get these pregnant pauses or feelings in the air that animals seem to pick up on as tension. It also helped to divert my mind a little bit, because when the squirrels started getting really close to me I'd get excited and that would change my body language in ways they could sense.

Dogs really pick up on this, too. When I do dog bite prevention programs, the first thing I tell people is that if they are nervous being around a dog, the best thing to do is carry on a conversation. Having to refocus your mind on what you are talking about takes that tenseness out of the air and helps you focus on something else. Which is just what Granddaddy used to tell me about those squirrels: "Daydream and put your mind somewhere else, because if you are thinking about them, they know it."

He also taught me that taming is a very long, patient process. Each squirrel responds differently, and some are easier than others. It's not the kind of thing where you walk outside and say, "Okay, I am going to teach that squirrel to come take peanuts out of my hand." Sometimes it can take three months, six months, a year, and sometimes it never happens. We'd start out with the squirrels twenty feet away or even farther, just getting them used to coming near the porch and getting peanuts; we'd be inside then, looking out the window. Then we'd get them used to us sitting on the porch, so they'd come down out of the trees while we were sitting there and pick up peanuts we'd left in the grass. Then we'd start putting those peanuts closer and closer to the porch. It was never Granddad's goal to touch the squirrels— he just wanted to see if he could get them to take a peanut from his hand.

It took him two years to get the first one to do it, but it was interesting to see how once one or two squirrels ate from his hand, it was a lot easier to get the others, because they were learning by example. While the old ones never really took to it, the young ones who were impressionable would see and think, "Johnny gets peanuts easy. He doesn't have to work all day because that big animal over there gives them to him. So I'm going to suck up my guts and go over there and do the same thing."

Granddaddy had a little call that he did. He'd come out in the afternoon and stand on the porch and do his little squirrel call and shake a peanut in the air. During those years when he had several that were pretty tame, they'd come almost falling out of the trees. Some would even come inside the house. He'd leave the door open and they'd walk right into the kitchen and get a peanut off the table, or he'd sit outside and they'd get them out of his hand.

In the winter of 1976, though, it all went too far. I remember this so clearly because it was the bicentennial year and Granddaddy, because he was the postmaster, got us all the bicentennial stamps. We'd spent a lot of time working with the squirrels that year and had gotten a lot of them to where they would come up to us.

All Granddad ever gave anybody for Christmas was shelled pecans, so he'd get these bushel bags of pecans in October and sit down every evening to shell them. He had a foot sheller, and you'd stick the pecan between two plates and then step on the lever and crack it open. Then you'd have to peel all the shell stuff away. It was the most tedious thing in the world, but I loved doing it.

One day we were sitting in the kitchen shelling pecans and he noticed that the squirrels were at the door. We'd been hand-feeding them peanuts outside a little earlier, but we'd quit to come inside and shell pecans. They were all sitting at the kitchen doorstep, and Granddaddy said, "I'm going to open this door and see if we can get these squirrels here in the house." That sounded great to me.

He put away the shelled pecans, then opened the door, and they didn't move. So he set a peanut almost right in the doorway and one squirrel had the guts, came up and grabbed it, and ran off a couple of feet. Nobody got killed, so the next one came along. Over the course of a couple of hours, he had them coming in the door three or four feet and they would grab the peanut and run back out. Well, the next day we did it again, and over about three days they got to where they'd come in the kitchen as soon as he opened the door. And then he got one to jump up on the table. After a few days, there were about four of them that would come right in when he opened the door, jump up on the table, and take a peanut.

And then one night, Granddaddy forgot to put the pecans away. We had them stacked up, out of the shell, on the kitchen table, and one of those squirrels saw them and was like, "Eureka! This is the motherlode." And he ran over there and grabbed some. Then another one ran over there and grabbed some. Then a big fight broke out in the middle of the kitchen, and Granddaddy jumped up and pulled me to the side, because I was sitting right next to them and he didn't want me to get bit.

Well, him jumping up and grabbing me created pandemonium, and one of the squirrels took off from the table and hit the cabinets and the countertops; it seemed like he was bouncing off the walls like a super ball. He ended up in the light fixture over the kitchen sink, so that started swinging like crazy, and then these two others were fighting over the pecans. . . . I mean, it went from this beautiful Audubon moment to total animal chaos.

Granddad was trying to shoo them out the door, one was trying to get out the window—except that it was closed—and to me the whole thing looked like a cartoon. One squirrel ended up in the living room, and it took us the rest of the evening to get that guy out of the house. When we finally got them all out, Granddaddy just looked at me and said, "Maybe we shouldn't do the kitchen thing."

That kind of chaos only happens with hypersensitive animals. But not just prey animals. If you can manage to figure out how to make yourself small and unthreatening to a squirrel, the dog part should come pretty easily. A good example is a female German shepherd named Sascha who was sent to me from Germany in the mid-90s. She was actually a Schutzhund III-titled dog, but she had very shaky nerves in certain situations. Schutzhund offers three levels of titles, with increasingly difficult exercises at each level. Schutzhund III is considered the master level. For a dog to attain that title is a phenomenal accomplishment, but the fact that such a nervy dog could do it proves how circumstantial things are with dogs. Sascha could fall to pieces on you when she was off the competition field, but she was fine on it. Dogs just don't generalize; everything is situational with them. So when Sascha was on the competition field doing a routine she had trained to do a hundred times before, she seemed like a real tough girl. But novel situations exposed her for what she really was.

Sascha had been raised by a woman in a houseful of girls, too, so she was not that great around men. Eventually, she was shipped to a guy who was a pretty tough handler. It was a bad mix all around, and on top of that, she was not a good traveler. So when I picked her up at the airport, she was in a corner of her crate, shaking.

I got her to my house and she would not come out of that crate for anything. I knew she had to go to the bathroom, but when a dog is cowering and scared to death, I am not stupid—I am not going to reach into that crate.

So I warmed up some really great-smelling beef, put the crate on one side of the room, sat down on the floor on the other side, and turned on the TV. I sat sideways, in a spot where she could see me through the open crate door, and started watching a TV show. I ate a little bit of the beef, then set out a plate where she could see it and get to it without having to come near me. She still wouldn't come out, but she was thinking about it. Then she started whimpering a little bit in a way that I translated as, "I'm too scared to come out, but I'm reaching out for help." So I lay down on my back, making myself even smaller and less threatening, and I spoke to her in German, saying her name and "good girl" in a total belly-up position—as submissive as I could possibly get. I crept over to her on my back, talking softly the whole time, and slowly reached inside her crate. She finally stood up, and very slowly I put a leash on her. As soon as I did that, she came out of the crate. I stayed on my back as she walked around and smelled me; I didn't try to pet her at all. Finally, she went over and ate the beef off the plate. And that's the way we started.

Now, I could have gotten frustrated when she wouldn't get out and just picked the crate up and dumped her out on the floor, the way a lot of people do it. But she was already damaged; why make it worse? It took me an extra hour to really gain her trust, but it was worth it.

Understanding how prey animals see the world taught me a great deal about how we, as people, make ourselves threatening or non-threatening. And those skills really helped me a lot with dogs like Sascha, and when I was learning to be a good training decoy for protection dog work. I knew how to bring out strong or aggressive behaviors in dogs or apply a little bit of intimidating pressure, and I could recognize exactly where a dog's threshold was and when we had reached it. When you are confronting a dog, the difference between standing there square on and turning your shoulders thirty degrees and your head slightly is tremendous, and I learned about that by feeding squirrels.

You can put this knowledge to work in a lot of different ways. For example, if you adopt a dog from a shelter who has been abused and she's very intimidated by men to the point where she might just cower and pee on herself when she sees them, then the best thing to do is to tell the man in your household to approach that dog by getting low to the ground. Maybe he can offer the dog food but not pressure her to come get it and not look directly at the dog. The two of you can engage in some conversation so the dog doesn't feel like she's being scrutinized. That's how to start a relationship in a way that the dog can mentally and physically handle.

The flip side of this is knowing how to make yourself intimidating if you need to. I would venture to say that probably less than one out of twenty working police dogs on the street, when confronted full-on with a bad guy who understands aggressive behavior, would actually engage him head-on. There are a lot of cops who I am sure want to argue with that, but I've proven it time and time again. Dogs may do well working with decoys in bite suits, but when they really have some pressure put on them in a street situation, many will hesitate. A lot of it has to do with body position, because those same dogs may run around behind you and snag you from behind or pop you in the back of the leg. But if you keep them in front of you, that pressure of your presence is very intimidating and it seems to almost build a wall that the animal feels he can't penetrate. The problem is that turning to the side even a little bit will kick in the dog's predatory behavior, because it suggests that you are turning to run, which gives the dog a shot of confidence and the courage to come on in there and try to take a bite.

This may seem like a long way from you, but it's not. If you were walking down the street and a dog confronted you a bit aggressively, you could apply the same principle. You stay in front of the dog and look as big and intimidating as possible. You stand your ground with that dog and speak to him in a hard tone. If he tries to circle around and get behind you, you just spin and circle, too, so you stay in front of him. Honestly, there are very, very few dogs who will ever make contact with you in that situation. They might circle around a time or two, but when they don't see an opening, they'll be thinking, "Okay, I'm not quite ready for that kind of confrontation," and they'll be on their way.

And that, of course, brings us to the predators. I learned about them up close and personal when I adopted Rascal, a four-day-old orphan raccoon. In the summers, we always vacationed at a resort called the Cloister at Sea Island, on the south coast of Georgia. I wasn't big on going to the beach, but I liked the fishing and especially the crabbing, because I loved setting up the crab traps.

The guy who ran the docks, Frank Meade was his name, was one of my fishing mentors. He would let me do little things for him and pay me a couple of bucks. Like when they came in from charter trips I would help unload the boat and clean it up for him. I did it just to hear the fishing stories, especially the ones about sharks. I was nine years old that summer, and totally infatuated with sharks.

Anyway, one of the maintenance guys came over to Frank one day and told him they had been trimming some of the palm trees around the main hotel and had come upon a nest of baby raccoons, and one of them had fallen out. They put the raccoon back in the nest and a couple of hours later somebody called the hotel and said there was a baby raccoon on the ground; the mother had come back and tossed it out because it smelled like humans. They asked Frank what to do (everybody knew he was an animal guy) and he said there was no way that baby could survive without round-the-clock care. So they figured they'd put it out of its misery.

"I'll take it," I said.

I knew what I was getting into—sort of. One of the veterinarians who was kind of a mentor to me back home was Dr. Ben Lifsey, and he had raised some raccoons when I was about five or six. Dad and Ben were hunting buddies, and I had gone out to his house and met Rascal, a raccoon he'd raised since she was a baby and eventually released into the wild. Dr. Lifsey lived way out in the country, and Rascal would still come back around to his house sometimes. I was totally blown away by her; it was the coolest thing to see her come right up onto the porch. She was huge. You couldn't really touch her because she was pretty wild at that point, but she loved to play with Dr. Lifsey's dogs.

So I thought, "I'll take that raccoon and I'll raise it just like Rascal, and I'll call Dr. Lifsey and he'll tell me what to do." I have to give Mom credit. Most moms would be saying, "We're on vacation at the beach, you are not bringing a four-day-old raccoon in here." What she said was, "Okay, but you are going to have to take care of it and I'm not going to do anything. It has got to be on you. If you don't take care of it, it's going to die and it's all going to be on your shoulders." Agreed.

So we called Dr. Lifsey and he told me what to do. To start, we ended up having to drive all the way to Jacksonville, Florida, which was about an hour and forty-five minutes away, to find a place that sold veterinary baby formula. Then I got a box and a kid's little doll bottle, and Mom got me a cooking timer with a ringing bell on it, because I had to feed that baby every four hours, twenty-four hours a day. And I did it.

I pretty much gave up my whole summer vacation to take care of this raccoon (whom I instantly named Rascal), and I thought it was the coolest thing. She was just a little blob when I got her, and by the time we left Sea Island three weeks later and I took her home, she started to open her eyes and she would chirp and chatter and kind of cling to my clothes. A far cry from a predator. In fact, it was going to be my job to teach her how to become a killer.

Predators learn what food is and all the skills they need to catch it from other predators of their same species—mostly, their mothers. So I was going to have to stand in as a raccoon mama. My first teaching task came when Rascal was about six or eight weeks old and she started wanting to climb. Dr. Lifsey told me climbing up a tree is instinctive to raccoons, but they need to be taught how to get down. How do you teach a raccoon to climb down from a tree? It sounds like the first part of a joke, but the answer is deadly serious to the raccoon. They need to be up a tree for safety, but they need to get down to hunt.

The first thing a baby raccoon tries is backing down the tree. But generally they're not comfortable with that, so they turn around with their head facing the ground. Except that doesn't feel right either, so they just kind of panic and sink their claws into the tree and freeze. Or they fall. Or they skid down.

The problem is raccoons don't trust their claws when they are babies. What you have to do is get the raccoon flat on the tree and then hold your hand over the top of her body and press a little bit so she gets the idea that she has to cling to the tree. You can't support her too much or else you become a crutch, so in the beginning I kind of held behind Rascal's head and put a flat hand out so if she fell, I had her and could just stick her back on the tree before she started falling end over end. Eventually, Rascal learned to pick up one claw at a time and anchor herself as she climbed down—the reverse of what she was doing when she went up.

Rascal was living in our house and basically had free reign. One night Mom had a little dinner party for about ten of her women friends. I remember Rascal was around four months old then, about the size of a pug. I kept her in my room during the party, but after the ladies went home, my brother and I were in the kitchen helping to clean up. Now, whenever there were dinner plates in the kitchen, Rascal was usually there. But this time we couldn't find her. I whistled and she didn't respond. And then . . . I will never forget this . . . I turned the corner from the hallway into the living room and there she was, on top of the coffee table with her head completely buried in a wine glass. She was hugging that glass, drinking it dry. I looked around and saw that most of the scattered glasses were already empty (although, to her credit, she hadn't tipped over even one). Rascal was hammered.

I freaked out; I knew enough about animals by then to know how dangerous her situation was. We called Dr. Lifsey, and he asked, "Can she walk?" Just barely. "Keep an eye on her and make sure there's no more wine around. If she makes it through the next thirty-five or forty minutes, she's going to make it. But she's probably not going to feel good and she'll be a little crabby tomorrow." And boy, was she ever! A raccoon with a hangover is not a pretty sight.

Dr. Lifsey told me that at about four months of age I would start to see Rascal act a bit more wild. Before then she had been almost as friendly as a puppy. But now the wild was coming out more and more, and it started with strangers. Where she used to be inquisitive whenever anyone came into the house, now when she heard the door open she went flying out of my lap and dove in between the pedals of our player piano and into the body of it. It was a big old player piano with a stand-up box, and Rascal loved to hide inside it. You could hear her walking around in there—every once in a while a couple of the keys would tinkle, too. (About four years later, when we moved to Texas, the moving men picked up that piano and it sounded like somebody had poured a big bag of coins into the box. We undid the back panel and it was full—I mean jammed full—of coins and paper clips and spoons and all kinds of shiny things that Rascal had obviously snagged and hid in there. We also found several pieces of my mom's jewelry, including some gold necklaces and a diamond ring that was a family heirloom and that Mom thought was lost forever.)

The next phase of turning on the wild in Rascal was teaching her how to be a real predator. Dr. Lifsey warned me to be sure to teach her to catch food that was easy to find in our area. So I settled on crawdads. At the time, our family had a cabin over in Arkansas, on the Spring River, kind of up in the Ozarks. I took her up there with me one weekend to a spot with lots of little tidal pools next to the rapids and waterfalls, where I had been catching crawdads for years. I sat down next to a pool that was about as big as a coffee table and about five inches deep. I'd pick up a rock, find one sitting there, and just be real slow and easy and try to snatch it. I was demonstrating for Rascal, and she was watching and playing around, obviously loving the antic part of it. Then I caught a crawdad and set it down on a flat rock next to her. She started pawing at it—raccoons' hands are super sensitive—and it pinched her. She shook her hand and the crawdad went flying off.

I caught another one, and this time I pinched its little claws off. Then I put it up to my mouth and pretended to eat it. After a few "bites," I held it up to her mouth. She took a little crunch, then jerked it away from me, took about five chomps and swallowed it whole. She had this look on her face like, "I've been searching for that my entire life!" Suddenly, she forgot I was there. She was just hands everywhere, reaching into the water, and finally, after about twenty minutes, she caught a crawdad herself.

That was it for the rest of the trip. I'd let her out of the cabin and she would run over to that spot and sit there for hours, feeling under every rock. Sometimes the crawdads would pinch her and she would let them grab hold of her and pull them up that way. Then she would rip them to shreds and eat every last little bit as if she hadn't eaten in two months.

That was when I could sort of see the wild animal light turning on. When we got home, Rascal started spending a lot more time in the trees outside in the backyard. Dr. Lifsey suggested that we start getting her used to sleeping outside at night. But we wanted her to be protected from dogs and other, bigger predators, so he gave me a cage to put her in. He told me to hang it from a tree and set a little two-by-four with some notches in it against the cage so she could climb up. At first I closed the cage door every night (and put a lock on it, because raccoons are notorious for undoing latches). After a couple of weeks, I started leaving the cage door open and she just decided to stay up there. I'm sure at night she would come out and venture around though—after all, raccoons are nocturnal.

At the same time, she had gotten really selective about who she let handle her. It was pretty much me and my mom, and mostly me. She wasn't as cuddly anymore, either, wanting to crawl up in your lap all the time and snuggling up like a baby. She was six or seven months old at that point and she was reminding me that, after all, she was a wild animal.

I had no problem with that. I knew she'd never be my pet and I had spent almost eight months playing raccoon mama precisely so she could go out on her own. A lot of people who want to get a wild animal buy into this myth that if they bring them up like a pet, they will be a pet forever. But when Rascal was still a baby, Dr. Lifsey was constantly reminding me that she was going to change from a cuddly little thing into a wild animal, and that there was nothing I could do about it. As they start to mature, wildness takes over in every animal who is not truly domesticated.

Domesticated animals have been selectively bred over hundreds of generations. But when you take something from the wild, no matter what the environment, that animal cannot be a pet. Domestication is a genetic change, and it doesn't happen over one generation. Zoos are full of tame animals who are still not domesticated, even after many generations of captive breeding.

Anyway, I couldn't let Rascal keep living in our neighborhood because it was too populated and she wasn't sufficiently scared of dogs and cars and people that she could be really safe. I talked it over with Dr. Lifsey and he said, "Why don't you bring her out here to my place, because I can keep an eye on her a little bit. Plus, all the dogs I've got here were raised with my raccoon, so when they see one they are not going to chase it."

So we took the cage she was already used to spending at least part of the night in and put it about a hundred yards from his house. Then he started feeding her every day, twice a day. He left her locked in the cage for the first two or three days, then began opening it and letting her come up on his porch—although he never let her in the house. She slept in that cage the first winter, and when spring came along she went on her way. She visited Dr. Lifsey's house every once in a while, but not that much. And by the next winter she had her own place.

Now, Rascal was huge for a raccoon. I had kept feeding her that baby formula long after she was eating solid food, because I thought her size would give her some advantage when she was out in the wild. So she was the biggest raccoon I had ever seen. But still, I always wondered if she made it. I got my answer about two and a half years later, in the spring. Dr. Lifsey told me he was sitting out on the back porch one evening and Rascal came right up, bringing two babies along with her. I was so proud!

When I look back on that time, I realize my experiences with wild animals shaped my approach to dog training in many ways. I come at dog training from a different angle, and that has always helped me—even though for a long time I didn't really understand where it came from and I didn't speak about it. My method is more intuitive.

I think with Rascal probably the best lesson for dog training was that it gave me a healthy appreciation for genetic predisposition. I don't ever try to fight that concept. I see young trainers who think they can overcome anything, train their way out of any behavior. But you have to accept the limitations of how much a person can influence any animal's behavior.

Just recently I was watching a guy in the local PetSmart with a young dog obedience class. I could tell he had a genuine love for animals. He also had a solution for everything: With the proper training there was no feat that couldn't be done. To me, that just screamed inexperience. And I know someday he'll realize that what he was saying is not true, because every dog is an individual.

It was a big advantage for me that, even in my early stages of doing police dog training, I never had to swallow that pill because I had swallowed it early on with Rascal and the other wild animals I encountered. It was never a stretch for me to understand that dogs as a species have some very specific limitations, as does each individual dog, and you just have to work *with* them instead of trying to work against them.

You've got to take a look at what you've got, strip it down to its naked form, and see where you are. To me it's just not smart to skip that step before you start any training program. And this gets back to what I said way at the beginning of this chapter about active observation. It's hard to *really* watch your dog without trying to influence his behavior in any way, but if you can discipline yourself to do it, you can learn a lot.

For example, have your neighbor come over and ring the doorbell, and just sit there and watch how your dog reacts. Is his first reaction fearful or aggressive or passive? The answer will tell you a lot about a dog's basic character. Now let the person in and watch the dog again. Does he react the same way to men and women? Does he shy away from one particular type of person? Does your dog initiate contact with new people or new animals, or does he let people come to him? Is he indifferent to meeting people and animals? Is he fearful? I think particularly when an animal is fearful, indifferent, or aggressive in this kind of situation, it can be a predictor of a lot of other behaviors.

Whether it's meeting other people or meeting other dogs, the doorbell ringing, strange noises, unfamiliar places—if you know how your dog is going to react, you can be prepared in advance to deal with it. If your dog tends to react in a way you don't like, the next question you ask yourself is, "How can I modify this situation to better fit our life?" Sometimes you can, sometimes you can't, and if you can't, you need to come up with a game plan for dealing with the dog's behavior. That makes you more confident, and that confidence transfers to your dog. I believe one of the reasons Lex was such a super dog was that I knew what his reaction was going to be to just about anything, and that gave me confidence. Even if I knew he was going to react in a way I didn't like, I anticipated what was coming and was prepared to deal with it.

But instead of watching their dogs, I find people are watching a particular training method or watching the results a trainer gets with one particular dog. They don't think about how that might apply to their own dog, and they end up setting the bar too high and setting themselves up for failure. When that failure comes, they don't say, "Let's wipe the slate clean and start over with a different approach." They say, "Well, that training stuff obviously doesn't work," and they give up. It's like somebody saying, "I'm going to go buy a bunch of clothes for my husband, but I'm not going to take into account how big he is, or whether he likes to wear suits or shorts and T-shirts or a tuxedo. I'm going to just go buy some clothes and hope they fit him and that he likes them."

You always have to start by assessing your dog, and the more detailed your observations, the better you are going to be able to match the training to your pet. There are a lot of trainers out there who have developed a training method and now say, "This is 'the' method, and if it doesn't work on your dog it's because you are doing it wrong." That's something I have been battling against my whole career, because I believe there's no one method that's right for every dog.

A company recently approached me about doing a set of training videos they planned to call The Harrison Method. I told them, "That's exactly what I am *not* going to do." If I limit my training to one set of techniques, then I'm saying one size fits all and you are obligated to do everything that one way. But the truth is that approach just doesn't work. Any single method may be great for a couple of dogs, or even most of them, but there's always going to be a big percentage for whom that approach doesn't work.

My training method is the anti-method. You need to be open to every method and throw your preconceived notions out the window. Understanding dogs and their behavior is a never-ending process. It's like building a library: If you want to teach a dog to sit, there are twenty different ways to get there and each way will work well on at least one dog you're likely to meet. And when somebody shows you the twenty-first way, you've got to be open-minded and stick it on your library shelf, because you may need to pull it out one day. To me, that's what a good dog trainer does.

# 4

# Sabina

It's a little known law of nature that when a boy needs a dog, a dog always finds him. The opposite is also true: When a dog needs a boy, a boy always turns up. That's how it was with Sabina and me. She needed a boy, I needed a dog.

Strictly speaking, Sabina was not my dog. She belonged to the family who lived across the street, the Townsends. Improbably, she was a Belgian Tervuren—perhaps the only one ever to be seen in my little town of Jackson, Tennessee. The Townsends had a big old mutt named Levi who had been hit by a car. They wanted another dog who looked just like him, so they sat down with an issue of *DogWorld* magazine and looked at all the ads in the back from breeders until they saw the Tervuren. That's how they got Sabina.

But about six months after she arrived, their oldest son went off to college and their younger one went to boarding school, and Sabina ended up in a five-foot-high pen in their backyard.

The Townsends were old, retired people, and they fed Sabina and otherwise didn't do much with her. But Sabina was a high-drive, young, exuberant dog. She had no boy, and she started escaping almost at once.

I got my first pet when I was five and a half—a fifty-four-inch corn snake sitting under the Christmas tree. I named her Ginger, and I used to walk around the house with her wrapped around me. I was fascinated by that snake, but you can't take a snake outside and teach it to chase squirrels or play army men or secret agent. By the time I was seven or eight, I was also already hanging around at the Oak View Kennels, a local boarding and training kennel owned by Mr. Only. He was a high school principal, and he'd trained dogs for the Marines in World War II. He was a tough old bird, but he was super nice to me and I really loved being with his dogs. I started out doing little things like filling the dogs' bowls and cleaning the kennels. When he decided that I could handle the dogs pretty well and I wasn't afraid of them, he'd let me bring out specific dogs for training. It was sort of a gradual thing where I went from gopher to advanced gopher.

Next door to the kennel, his son, Mark, ran a pet store with all kinds of animals, both ordinary and exotic, including a six-foot python named Elsa who was the store mascot. So when school was out, I often spent my mornings in the kennel and my afternoons in the store. Mark was the exact opposite of his father, a free spirit with not a trace of tough guy. He instantly got it that I really loved animals, and he spent a lot of time answering all my questions and teaching me what he knew.

My work with Mark made me realize that there's something

interesting about every single species. My work with Mr. Only made me realize how much I wanted a dog. But Mom was not so keen.

When Sabina started running around the neighborhood, I naturally called her over to me and started playing with her. From the get-go, there was something special between us. We really understood each other. In the beginning, she played with everyone and let all the kids pet her. But as she matured and we spent more time together, she became more and more bonded to me. The turning point came when Sabina was almost a year old. I was wrestling with another boy, and Sabina jumped up and body-blocked him and showed her teeth. After that, the neighborhood kids started being a little more leery of her when I was around. As we became closer, she distanced herself from the other kids. As it turned out, Sabina was a one-boy dog.

She spent the whole day with me, from the time I came home from school until I went to bed. After she was about eighteen months old, the Townsends didn't even bother putting her back in the pen. They would just leave the door open and put food out for her. So she slept outside in their yard and spent her days with me.

Although she never was, I certainly thought of Sabina as my dog. It's another little known law of nature that a one-boy dog belongs to that one boy. And I've never disobeyed the laws of nature.

Everything I know about dogs—bonding, nonverbal communication, body language, drive, and instinct—I learned first with Sabina. The games I played with her laid the foundation for the scent discrimination, tracking, and protection work I did later. And, after Lex, Sabina is probably the dog I had the closest connection with—that silent bond. Because kids don't worry about reading up on the latest training methods; they just figure out how to communicate with the dog. That's the same way dogs figure out how to communicate with us. Which is why there's nothing closer or more natural than a boy and his dog.

The neighborhood we lived in was made up of tree-lined streets with huge antebellum homes on either side. There were big old magnolia trees that must have been planted back before the Civil War. They were real easy to climb, because their branches were spread out and straight and went all the way to the ground. Sometimes we would play a little game of hide and seek where I would tell Sabina to sit in the backyard and then I would go off and climb a tree and hide, then whistle for her to come find me. Of course, back then I was amazed by the fact that she could find me 300 feet away and up in a tree.

From my perch in the tree, I could watch her work out where I went by following my scent on the ground. I was still a kid playing, so I certainly wasn't thinking about observing her scent discrimination skills, but my mind was recording the whole thing and interpreting anyway, because I was fascinated by what she was doing. I remember that as she got better at it, I had to make the game harder. I knew enough about hunting to know that the higher you get off the ground, the more your scent goes over an animal's head and swirls around. It will confuse a deer, and it will confuse a dog, too. So on a windy day I'd see how Sabina would end up going to a tree twenty or even a hundred feet downwind from me and have to work her way back to where I was.

In retrospect, the best thing about that game is that I was able to see a dog totally using her natural, untrained abilities. Later, that became very important when I was working with dogs who were trained to track. I realized there is a learned way and a way that's natural for them, and a lot of times those two are different.

I remember a particular dog named Nanto with whom I worked when I was in my late teens. He had an FH3, which is a heavy-duty tracking title from East Germany. (FH stands for Fahrtenhund, which just means "tracking dog." Like Schutzhund, there are three levels of Fahrtenhund titles.) A bunch of trainers were looking at him when he first came over here, with the idea of buying that dog. I remember watching him work with one guy who was testing him as a tracker and thought he knew just how to handle him. The guy didn't have a good feel for the dog, though, and was manhandling him around the track. I knew in my gut Nanto wasn't responding the way he could. This trainer was dragging him around on a prong collar and correcting him every time he raised his head. Finally, I said something and the guy basically told me to shut up. I did, but I thought, "As soon as he leaves I'll figure this out on my own."

When he left, I took Nanto out myself. Because he had been in such a tense situation minutes before, we just played ball for a few minutes and then I had him lie down and watch me lay a very simple track. We followed it kind of like a game, and I could see his body language change. Then we moved on to something harder, and he tracked like a champion for me. I had that gut instinct because of Sabina—because I already knew what a dog looks like when she's figuring out a problem totally on her own, unrestricted by a leash or even by any training.

I used to love playing army man and secret agent kinds of games with Sabina. Sometimes I'd bury something on top of a hill and then we'd have to fight our way up the hill (against an imaginary but fierce army) and she'd find the things and dig them up. We also used to do a lot of stalking and sneaking. The year Sabina and I became dog and boy, I got a BB gun for my birthday and we began squirrel hunting. We started doing something that I now recognize as almost wolf pack behavior, where the pack splits up and stalks from different angles. We would see a squirrel and Sabina would start going around one way and I would go around the opposite way like we were circling it, always staying in visual contact. She just knew what I was doing and I knew what she was doing. I look back on those games now and realize that she was mimicking me a lot—seeing my body language and my quietness and the tension of creeping up on something. I'm sure she had a lot of natural instinct to do that, as well. In the end, though, I think we each acted a little bit more like the other.

I remember thinking at the time, "Man, this is cool!" I watched a lot of *Wild Kingdom* back then, and I'd seen wolf packs where they would split up and everybody had a job. Sabina and I started doing that, too. I never used any commands, because if I said anything, the squirrel would run off. We'd just look at each other as we watched the squirrel and then we would get on either side of it. Then my body language would go "pow!" That was her signal to go after the squirrel.

The first time I actually shot a squirrel down and it hit the ground, Sabina grabbed it and ate it. I could see the lightbulb go on over her head: "Okay, if I chase things, my boy brings them down and I can have them."

Getting off the topic a minute here, you may be wondering how I could sit for an hour over at my granddaddy's house with a peanut in my hand, trying to tame a squirrel, while I was shooting them in my own backyard. Well, in our neighborhood it was not discouraged to harvest a couple of squirrels, especially if they were the ones who were getting in and out of your attic. We actually had a fire that almost burned our house down because of all the squirrels in the attic chewing on the wiring. So the squirrels were considered to be rats with bushy tails. But then I would walk less than a mile away to Granddaddy's house, and we were taming them and treating them like royalty. I think little kids respond to what the adults around them do and don't think too hard about stuff. Anyway, I would never in a million years have thought to shoot one of *those* squirrels. Those were the *tame* ones—it was two separate worlds. And just so you know, I certainly didn't make a dent in the squirrel population in our neighborhood, because there were plenty of them.

Squirrel hunting brought out an aspect of Sabina's personality that I hadn't seen before. She wanted them, and if I went to take one she would show her teeth and snap. Even at that early age, though, I knew I couldn't let this kind of behavior get out of control. So when she got possessive, I would stop the game and stand up straight, change my whole body language and my tone of voice, and say, "All right, give it to me." And I'd make sure she did. In the end, although I'd let her work off a lot of energy, it was clear I was in control.

How did a seven-year-old figure out, "Okay, we can growl and we can roughhouse a little bit, but I'm going to set the limits here"? That's a fair question. I don't exactly know the answer, either; I just knew in my gut that no matter how much fun we were having, I couldn't let Sabina push me around.

From a behavioral standpoint, it's not a lot different than playing an intense game of tug-of-war, where the dog is pulling and growling and you are tugging and growling back and he's locked down on the toy. Lots of people do that with little dogs, big dogs, all dogs. In that situation, as with Sabina and those squirrels, the dog is allowed to exhibit aggressive behavior without being punished for it. But he also learns that the game has a structure and that there are limits.

I know a lot of dog trainers who say you should never play tug-of-war or let your kids wrestle with a dog, and I don't discount this out of hand. I think if you are giving broad, general advice, it's the right, safe way to go. I don't personally follow it, though, because I know how to structure those games and where to draw the line with my kids and my dogs. Now, occasionally are you going to get scraped by a tooth or a toenail? Definitely. But that's also true if you allow your kids to wrestle and roughhouse with each other. Sometimes the dog will get overexuberant and someone will get popped. And that's why if I was sitting in a court of law and I had to give an answer, I would err on the side of safety and say, "Don't do it."

Still, I have to admit this is another case of "Do as I say and not as I do." Because I think rough play is essential to dogs. If you've got two dogs (or if you take your dog on regular playdates with other dogs), those dogs engage in a lot of rough, high-energy play between themselves. But dogs who do not have regular opportunities to let that energy out eventually become a powder keg of frustration. Those are dogs who are never allowed to express much emotion, and it's going to come out somewhere: digging up the yard, chewing up the furniture, barking, pacing, chasing his tail, doing something destructive that he shouldn't be doing.

So the question becomes, how can you let that energy out safely with your family dog? Well, you need to find a game he enjoys that burns off a lot of energy, and then play it with him several times a week. I also really recommend taking dogs to places where they can get together with other dogs and just hang out and be who they are—provided, of course, that your dog is friendly that way.

Sabina and I played wrestling games that would scare the dickens out of my mom. Sabina was lightning fast and scary looking. I'd get down on all fours and show her my teeth, and she'd growl back, showing every tooth in her head. Then she'd pounce on me and mouth my neck and I'd roll out of it, get her in a headlock, and put my hand up in front of my mouth as if I had a long muzzle like her, then use that hand to grab her by the scruff of the neck and shake her a little bit, then hold her down and she'd twist out of that and roll, because we were actually about the same weight. Sabina enjoyed playing that game and it was fun for me. I'd end up with slobber all over my head and neck and arms and little tooth imprints on my forearms and shoulders where she'd grab me, but I loved it. I remember one time we were wrestling on the floor in the playroom and Mom walked in and started yelling. "That dog's getting ready to kill you." I knew I was totally safe, but when you're seven years old, how do you explain that?

The fact is, I learned a lot from Sabina that kept me from getting bitten later on when I was working as the decoy "bad guy" training police dogs. A big part of doing decoy work is understanding the mechanics of presenting opportunities to bite while gaining leverage and staying on your feet, and Sabina taught me a lot about the kinetics of how dogs move and how they throw their weight and use their bodies. You have to know how the dog is going to be pulling or pushing and what his limitations are, and I had a gut understanding of all that because of the way we'd wrestled.

I'm very comfortable being really close to an aggressive dog—almost more comfortable having my hands and my body on him than I am from about four or five feet away. If a dog is getting aggressive with me and I'm chest-to-chest or chest-to-thigh with him, full contact like that, I feel safer. I know that sounds crazy, but a good analogy is snake charmers. You see those guys sitting and playing the flute with a cobra coiled right in front of them, inches from their face and well within striking distance. They know that when a cobra is upright and hooded out, he can only strike down at about a forty-five-degree angle or more. So they can literally have their face five or six inches in front of a cobra's face and he can't bite unless he raises up higher and strikes down. The mechanics of it are impossible. That's why those guys look so crazy, but they know they are not going to get bit.

It's the same with dogs. When you feel a dog put his shoulder against you and really start trying to bowl you over, how he braces himself to do that, how weak he is when you get his legs out from under him, and so on, you really learn exactly what dogs can and can't do. I once had a rottweiler from Czechoslovakia who was a bully. I'd had him for about a week, and one day we were sitting together on the ground by a pond on my property, quiet as can be. When I started to get up, he stood up real fast and leaned on me. It was kind of aggressive, even though there was no growling; he was shouldering me, which was his way of telling me, "You sit down, I don't want you standing up over me." It's a precursor to something more aggressive. Often these kinds of situations escalate and get out of control because people don't recognize the signs. When you are sitting in a chair and you start to get up, the dog might put his front paws on the chair, lean into you a little bit, and keep you from getting up, or lean against your legs—those are all precursor signals that you are going to have a problem if you don't address it.

I certainly wasn't going to let this very large rottweiler make me sit there, but he really had me at a disadvantage. So I just reached over to pet him so I could get close to him. As I got up on my knees he stiffened a little bit. But I already had my hand under his neck scratching him and I was turned to the side and I had gotten my knees under me. I was scratching him under the chin, almost to the opposite side of his cheek, so my arm was already across his chest and under his neck. My other arm was free, and I started scratching him between the shoulders. And then, just like that, I had him in a hold and I got close to him and then he really got stiff and knew something was wrong. I started standing up and he started growling, and I reached under and hooked that front leg with one arm and had his head hooked with the other, and I just rolled over on top of him and made him lie down. He was trying to bite me, but there was no way he could. I was real calm, too. I wasn't fighting him or rolling him or throwing him on the ground. You shouldn't get into a fight with any dog, because you won't win. The way I had him, it was just a very passive way of saying, "I'm in control here."

I actually petted him once I got my body on him and my left hand came free. When he really started growling, I said, "Ah, stop that," real quietly. And then he started calming down and after a minute I could feel his body give in. Some people get on top of a dog and start yelling at him, but a dog is not going to go down without a fight. This dog didn't feel a need to defend himself because I wasn't fighting him. When I heard him sigh and saw the tension come out of his body, I slowly sat up and petted him, gave him a down command, and told him to stay down. I stood up but I didn't loom over him, then I just said, "All right, let's go." And that was that. I never had another problem with that dog.

It never came to that with Sabina. We just knew each other too well.

I never actually trained Sabina to do anything, but she knew how to do everything. Including take care of me. I remember one time I was walking back from the candy store through a pretty rough area. I couldn't have been older than nine. Sabina came along, but she didn't exactly heel so you couldn't always see that she was with me. There were some kids who were probably thirteen, fourteen, fifteen years old, and as I came around the corner with my little sack full of candy bars, they confronted me and started saying stuff like, "Hey, kid, what you got in that bag? Give it here." Before I could get five or six words out, Sabina was between me and them and was showing her teeth and snapping. I hadn't even called her—she just knew. Well, the kids started backing up, saying, "Hey man, put a leash on that dog." But of course, Sabina never walked on a leash a day in her life. So I just said, "I don't have a leash. Y'all better move out of the way." And they did. I was thinking, "This is the coolest!" As I walked away, Sabina was right beside me, although I had never taught her to heel. She just knew what needed to be done in that situation and did it.

I was never one of those little kids who got picked on a lot, but there's no question I felt safe when Sabina was around. I remember the winter I was nine years old, it snowed about eight or nine inches in February. That was totally unheard of for west Tennessee, and we got out of school for a whole week. It was one of those great wet, heavy snows that packs really well. My brother and some of my cousins started making huge snow boulders, and then we stacked them up and built an igloo big enough that we could put seven or eight people in it. I could stand up inside, being the youngest and smallest. We added on a little wraparound tunnel that snaked all the way around the bottom of it, so there was no wind coming in. Then my brother cut a little hole in the top and to the side, like a chimney.

I wanted to sleep in the igloo that night, but nobody else would do it and I was afraid to sleep out there by myself. Sabina slept outside anyway, so I decided to see if she would sleep with me. She stayed there the whole night.

I remember lying on my side in my sleeping bag with my

back against the wall of the igloo. I had one candle burning, so I had a little bit of light, and she put her back up against my chest and pressed herself into me. I had my arm over her and I remember just lying there, my face kind of in the top of her neck. I felt safe and like there was nothing to be afraid of because I knew she was with me. I slept like a baby and hardly ever woke up at all.

That was the first time I *really* had a dog. I mean, it was like the movies, where the dog nestles up to the kid who's freezing to death and keeps him warm. Even though it was just the side yard of my house, it was this big ice man adventure to me. And I had my dog there with me.

But Sabina wasn't my dog. And when I was eleven, that became painfully clear. My parents got divorced, and my mom decided to move us to a new house across town. I was already spending some nights with my dad, and when I wasn't around, Sabina just stayed in her own backyard and the Townsends fed her. But if we moved . . . well . . . Sabina wasn't ours to take. I'm sure if I'd gone over to the Townsends and knocked on the door and asked for her, they would have given her to me. But Mom said, "Listen, we're moving to a smaller house and she'd be in a strange place. She'd have to stay in a fenced-in yard, because that's the way everybody lives in that neighborhood. But those fences are three feet high and we already know a five-foot fence won't hold her. So how are we going to keep her in? And what is she going to do when you're away with your father?"

Everything she said was true. But in retrospect, I realized Mom was also taking the opportunity to cut our ties with Sabina. The fact is, she was terrified of German shepherds and all dogs who looked like them, because when she was a kid she was attacked by one. Sabina was already spending some nights in my room, and Mom knew that if she came to live with us there would be weeks at a time when I'd be at my dad's place and she'd be alone in the house with Sabina. She just couldn't handle that.

To be fair, I don't think Mom ever understood what the bond was like between Sabina and me. All our adventures, all the time we spent together, were just between us two. Mom never saw that. Looking back, probably in Mom's eyes Sabina was just a neat neighborhood dog who I liked and who I brought in the house occasionally and who used to hang out with me outside. Sabina had been with me about three years, and that probably didn't seem like much to Mom—although three years is forever for a kid. Mom was in the middle of dealing with her divorce and working on her own life, too, and I think she couldn't understand the magnitude of the things I shared with that dog.

So we moved away, and I never saw Sabina again. Years later, when we had moved to Dallas and I was about seventeen, my mom and I were talking one night and she told me she had been in touch with the Townsends and knew what happened to Sabina. The people who bought our house had kids, and after school Sabina would always be at their back door moping around and looking for me. After a few months, the Townsends decided to give her to some cousins who lived about thirty-five miles away. She was just five years old and still needed plenty of exercise, so they thought it would be best. But the second or third day they had her, she destroyed the pen they were keeping her in and disappeared.

She turned up about a month later at the back door of my old house, fifteen pounds lighter and looking terrible. She'd had to make her way through an entire city and downtown area and a suburb, through a bunch of rural areas, then another town and a suburb and then country again. Now, thirty-five miles to a dog in the wilderness, just kind of loping across the woods, is not that significant a range, but it is when you consider that miles and miles of that was just neighborhood after neighborhood after neighborhood of houses built close together and interstates crossing all those neighborhoods. How did she get across I-40? The Townsends ended up keeping her, and she never stopped coming around to our old house, looking for me.

Mom didn't tell me that story until so many years later because she knew it would just wreck me. I would have probably done something crazy like gotten on my bike and gone back to the old neighborhood to get her. I guess on some level I still carry a lot of guilt about Sabina. I feel like I abandoned her, even though I didn't really have much control over it at the time. I felt horrible. I still feel horrible. I mean, it's hard enough not to get choked up just telling it thirty years later.

Of course now, as an adult with some training skills, I'd give anything to have her back, because I realize what a high level of trainability she had. But it wasn't just that. She was a phenomenal companion. We got each other on some very deep level. I really loved that dog. She was my dog. I was her boy.

# 5

# PJ

PJ stood for "Praise Jesus." PJ was not particularly reli-
gious, but the man who sold him to me was. In fact,
I'd have to classify PJ as a sinner—but a lovable one. He was
Dennis the Menace personified, and you just couldn't stay mad
at him for very long. PJ was also responsible for a genuine miracle:
He turned my mom and my stepdad into dog lovers.

PJ was an American Staffordshire terrier. I guess he was my
consolation prize for moving to Dallas. After my parents got
divorced, my mom started dating a great guy from Dallas named
Lee. They finally decided to get married at the end of my eighth
grade year. My older brother was already in college and I was
getting ready to start ninth grade. I had to transfer from a private school in Jackson that I had gone to since kindergarten,
where there were ten students in my class, to a supersize school
in Dallas where there were more than 1,000 kids in each class.
Big jump.

Lee was building a big house for us right next to a golf course. He was fifty-one at the time and had never been married. Lee was not a dog lover, but I really wanted a dog and everyone was trying to appease me because I was moving without protest.

When Lee said okay to the dog, I think he imagined we meant a Chihuahua or a nice little house pooch. But I had my heart set on an Am Staff.

When I am interested in something, I research it obsessively. So I pulled out all my old copies of *DogWorld* magazine and started calling the Am Staff breeders who advertised. I was about thirteen at the time, and I'm sure they could tell from my voice that I was a kid. But they'd answer my questions and some of them even sent me pictures of their dogs. So by the time Lee said yes to a dog, I knew about some of the top bloodlines in the breed.

I also knew I didn't want a puppy. Puppies can raise hell in your house, and I thought that level of destruction would be too big of a shock for Lee. Plus, raising a puppy takes a lot of work and time. And with me in school, most of that would have fallen on Mom. That would not have gone over well. So we needed an adult dog.

There was a guy outside of Philadelphia named Larry who owned the Prizer Kennels. He was a big show-dog breeder and at that time was the hot guy in the breed. His dogs were cross-registered with the American Kennel Club and the American Pit Bull Terrier Association, because back then, in the early 1980s, the Am Staff and the pit bull were pretty much the same dog. In fact, PJ's generation may have been the last of the dual-registered dogs. By 1985, the breeds were starting to differentiate and nobody was doing it anymore.

I spoke to Larry a couple of times, and he told me he had nineteen adult dogs who all slept in his house. This was really unusual, because back then a lot of Am Staffs were still pretty gamey, meaning those dog-fighting genes hadn't yet been watered down. As a result, a lot of the breed had problems with dog-on-dog aggression. And even at age thirteen, I knew enough about genetics to know I didn't want a dog from a kennel with aggression issues.

Larry told me he was serious about stamping out this kind of aggression in his bloodlines. He said, "When I have a litter of puppies, I don't ever sell them until they are at least sixteen weeks old. Meanwhile, I watch all of them and if I see any unusual levels of animal aggression in them as young puppies, I don't care if they could be the next Best in Show dog, I put them down." I know nowadays that sounds very harsh, but I understood right away why he said it. If you're breeding hunting dogs and you've got a few pups who clearly are not going to work out in the field, you can sell them as nice family pets. But when the problem is that the pup is too aggressive with other dogs, you can't sell him to anyone because that makes him dangerous—and *that* would be unethical. And meanwhile, you don't want him in your breeding lines. Even today, when Am Staff lines are considerably less gamey, having nineteen adult intact males and females living in a house together is a significant accomplishment. I thought, "Wow, that guy is choosing quality over trying to make a dollar. He's that serious about trying to make some changes in the breed."

Larry told me he had a male who was one of the most beautiful dogs he'd ever produced, but he had an undershot jaw—his lower jaw hung out past his top jaw—which is considered a flaw in the show ring. I ended up talking to Larry for months, and in the end, he probably sold me the dog just to shut me up. The dog was a year old, had some show training, was very well socialized with other dogs, and Larry was willing to let him go for $500.

Larry was also a serious evangelical Christian and all his dogs had biblical names. The one he had for me was registered with the American Kennel Club as Prizer Lion of Judah, but over the phone Larry referred to him as PJ. "Is that for Prizer Judah?" I asked. "No," he said, "it's for Praise Jesus. Hallelujah!"

I remember so clearly the look on Lee's face when we went to get PJ at the Dallas Airport. We picked him up in his crate at the cargo terminal. I opened the crate right away, and out walked a magnificent mahogany, black, and gold brindle dog with a little bit of white on his chest and neck. It was a rich red mahogany, almost the color of an Irish setter. He was really substantial, too—massively muscled and about eighty pounds. Lee was speechless. Honestly, I think he was terrified. This was no Chihuahua.

A lot of pit bulls are clowns. They end up being in trouble half the time but they're so adorable about it and they do so many good things that you start to think of them as the mischievous little brother who you love but who always pisses you off. There were housetraining issues, and PJ went through a destructive phase, as well. We had this brand-new half-a-million-dollar house (that was a lot of money for a house in 1982), and here's this dog who was a marking machine. He would eat things, too. He'd get cassette tapes off the desk and chew them up and swallow them. He chewed anything that was on the floor, and ruined several pairs of shoes. It got to where we would do the little "PJ" task before we left the house—making sure there was nothing on the floor for him to destroy.

When I think about PJ's first year with us, I wish, wish, wish I could go back, knowing what I know now, because I made a lot of dumb mistakes. We did a lot of great things with him and he was spectacular, but there were a lot of problems I didn't recognize as a thirteen-year-old that would have been easy to correct.

To start with, we let him have free run of the house when we were gone. He was housetrained about 90 percent of the time when we were home, but sometimes we left him for too long and he would pee somewhere. In retrospect, I'm thinking, "Hello, dummy! Stick him in a crate or put him in the utility room instead of leaving him loose in the house"—which would have been fine with him because he was a lazy pit bull. But nobody talked much about crate training back then. There were probably times when Lee woke up thinking, "What have I gotten into with this dog? He's going to ruin this house and make us crazy." I think PJ would have endeared himself to Lee and Mom a lot sooner if I'd known what to do that first year.

One of the things I did finally figure out was that PJ was bored. He came from a pack of nineteen dogs, with all the exercise and interaction that implies. And now he spent six to eight hours a day at home by himself just waiting for me to come back from school. No wonder he got destructive! So as soon as I got home, I always took him for a long walk. It gave us both something to look forward to. For me, as a thirteen-year-old, he was such a manly dog. I wasn't really looking for a macho tough dog, but there was certainly nothing to be ashamed about when I was walking around with a huge pit bull on a leash. And he was a head-turner; I mean, that dog just oozed confidence and personality.

Still, I knew how much he loved to run because he was so athletic, and I hated walking him on a leash all the time. So I used to take him out running at night. We lived in a brand-new subdivision, and there were still about 200 undeveloped acres plus the eighteen-hole golf course, so at night I would take him out to the edge of the subdivision and cut him loose. He loved that, and so did I.

He also slept in my room. This wouldn't have presented any problems, except that PJ was a roller. If he found a manure pile from another dog or a coyote, or a few cow flops, he had to throw himself into them. He was especially partial to horse manure. I can't count how many times I let him off the leash at night and, when I'd whistle and he'd come back, as I'd reach down to clip a leash on him I'd smell this horrible stink. Fortunately, I had a large walk-in shower with a tiled seat in the back, so I'd just open the shower door and tell him to get in. He'd go jump on the seat and let me wash him.

By age thirteen I had already learned a lot from all the other dogs in my life—especially Sabina—but PJ was the one who started teaching me about living with dogs and all that entails. I'd seen a lot of hunting dogs at work, and Sabina was definitely my dog, but she didn't really live in my house. PJ did. I began to understand how much you need to think about how the dog is experiencing the world, because so many behaviors that we consider to be problems are really just normal behavior for dogs.

Early on I learned that you've got to pick your battles. You don't want to let a dog run over you, but at the same time you've got to be smart about things, put the odds in your favor when you want to correct an undesirable behavior. For example, PJ loved to sleep on the furniture, and while it was okay for me to have him on my bed, Mom would not allow him on the couch. When he'd go where he wasn't supposed to, if I wanted to pull him off, he'd growl. There was no way I was getting into a contest of strength and will with an eighty-pound pit bull, and I quickly figured out that if I started to pull him off, he might snap at me. But I could outsmart him. I would act like he hadn't done it, just walk away, and go get a leash and clip it on him. Then I'd stand five or six feet away and give him the "get off" command just once. If he didn't comply, I'd yank him off the couch. Pretty soon, when he saw me coming with the leash, he'd get down on his own.

PJ's occasional crustiness taught me about what I call flashpoint confrontation. There are a lot of dogs, especially small dogs, who will turn around and bite if you are touching them. Very, very few will travel a distance of five or six feet to bite. Coming toward you to take a bite is a whole different world for a dog—it takes real hard aggression to make a dog go after you like that. I hear about this problem all the time in one form or another. "Oh, that's his pillow and when he gets on it, there's no getting him off or he'll give you a nip." Or, "Once he's on that chair, you'd better leave him alone." While a dog like that might snap at you if you are pulling him by the collar, if you put a leash on him, very few—probably less than one in a hundred—would ever come off the couch, up the leash, and actually pop you. It's a personal space issue. When you're six inches from them, you're in the dog's space. Six feet away is a different world. Now, this also tells you a lot about a dog who will come up a leash for a bite. If it's your own dog, you've got some major issues you need to get control of.

I guess, in hindsight, the main thing I learned from PJ is that every dog is going to have a set of issues and you have to keep working with them. It's just like a marriage: There are going to be good days and bad days, but if it's the right match, the good ultimately outweighs the bad. Like I said, the first year with PJ was a whole lot of trouble. But it was the kind of thing where you would yell at him and then you'd have to step around the corner and cover your mouth from laughing.

There was just something about PJ's personality. His face was capable of so much expression, and you could see everything he was thinking. Plus, he was an attention hound. If you didn't pay attention to him, he was going to make sure you did; he was not going to be ignored.

Sometimes when he did something I was really angry about, he'd just stand there and be like, "Yeah, what are you going to do?" But most of the time he'd go into his snake act. His belly would hit the floor and he'd lay his ears back and crawl over to me or simply crawl away. He'd give me that "Oh, poor pitiful me" look, and I'd just start laughing, because usually it was over something ridiculous.

He knew how to put on a big show, too. If there were people

in the house, he'd strut in and bring his bone and throw it up in the air and catch it, or toss it against people's legs and then pounce on it. He would never just sit back and be a wallflower. He had to stand in the middle of the room and do something. I remember at Christmastime when we were all focused on opening our presents, he'd stand in the middle of the floor and start barking ferociously, as if he was saying, "Quit looking at that stuff! I'm here! Why isn't anybody looking at me?"

Mom reminded me recently that PJ also loved to terrorize the UPS guy. It wasn't that he disliked the guy, but it was all part of PJ's big show. Our house was U-shaped, and the front door was in the middle of the U. PJ would be in one end of the house or the other, and it was almost like he could feel that truck drive up. I had a floor-to-ceiling window in my room that faced the front of the house, and he would run to my window and stand there barking like crazy. Then he'd sprint down the hall and start pounding on the front door, just slamming his body up against it.

Mom was always a little bit scared by that, because she was afraid PJ was going to attack the UPS guy, so she'd hold him back. Of course, now I know that when you hold a dog back, it's called loading, and that's the last thing you want to do if you're trying to quiet him down. It's like when two guys are squaring off in a bar. If one guy tries to hold his buddy back, that guy just gets more aggressive and starts screaming, "Let me at him!" By restraining a dog and letting him lunge over and over, you're loading up his aggressive response. The thing to do is to train him in a reliable "sit," and then make him hold it in those situations. Hindsight is always 20/20.

So, predictably, when Mom held PJ back, he'd put on an even bigger show. She would just barely be able to contain him while she cracked open the door to get her package. The UPS guy would slide the little slip through and she'd sign it, and then he was out of there. The thing was, as soon as the guy left, PJ would kind of chuckle like, "I showed him! Boy, that was fun." I think if I ever actually let him out, he would have barked some and then come right back in the house. He just loved playing the game.

PJ could sure put on a show, but he didn't ever bite anybody. Never even came close. He was a people lover. In fact, that was one of the things that made him so funny. He was an enormous dog; I mean, when he was in his prime, he was more than eighty pounds of solid muscle—just a brick wall. But all that mattered to him was getting in somebody's lap.

Now, when we're talking about the bull terrier breeds (and that includes Am Staffs and pit bulls), there's something I want to make sure you all understand. These dogs were bred to fight other dogs. They were not bred to fight humans or to bite humans. In fact, they would get all worked up in the fighting pit and then have to switch gears instantly when their human owner took them away. So that genetic inclination to bite is there, but it has to do with other dogs and not with humans.

People still call in to my radio show and say, "I've got this dog on my block who ran after another dog or chewed up my neighbor's Chihuahua, and now I'm worried about him around my kids." I always explain to them that aggression toward animals and aggression toward people come from two different places in a dog. In fact, in my personal experience there's almost a seesaw effect: A couple of the most people-aggressive, hardcore Malinois I've ever seen lived with cats and birds and let the cat stomp all over them and were great with other dogs.

With the bull terrier breeds, the ones who fought professionally in the late nineteenth and early twentieth centuries, a prized trait was a lack of people aggression. In real pit fights, those dogs were handled by their owners in the middle of a fight, when they were locked down on an opponent. Any dog who would turn around and snap at his handler in the middle of a fight was a problem and they wouldn't breed him. The true pit bull had plenty of gaminess but no people aggression.

Another trait that was highly prized, for obvious reasons, was a high tolerance for pain. I remember one time Lee was carrying a stack of patio blocks that he was going to lay in the backyard. PJ would get under your feet sometimes, and he jostled Lee, who accidentally dropped about ten bricks on PJ's head. It knocked the dog to the ground and one of the bricks cracked right in half. But PJ just popped right up, shook his head, shook the bits of concrete off him, then looked up at Lee and started wagging his tail, as if he was saying, "I'm not sure I like this game, but I'm still here."

That combination of having a really high tolerance for pain and a history of being under control around humans actually makes well-bred pit bulls pretty good dogs if you've got kids around, because kids are always making mistakes. I saw a perfect example of that when PJ was about four years old. Lee had a cabin up in Hardy, Arkansas, where we used to spend weekends in the summer. His cousin Bob had a place up there, too. At the time, Bob was a district attorney in Memphis. He was prosecuting a very high-profile case in which an elderly woman was mauled and killed by two pit bulls who were owned by a Memphis police officer who lived next door. It was a big case and got a lot of attention in the press, and this was right around the beginning of the movement to ban certain breeds that were perceived as dangerous. Because of this particular case, Bob would spend his week going over reports that pit bulls were dangerous as a breed, and on weekends Mom and Lee would be up from Dallas with PJ.

At the time, Bob had three kids: a newborn, a four-year-old, and a two-year-old. PJ was great with them, but Bob had been reading so much information about how dangerous pit bulls were that he was starting to feel a little uneasy. Bob and his wife had margarita hour over on their deck every afternoon, and Mom and Lee always brought PJ. One afternoon, Bob took Mom aside and admitted that he was kind of nervous around PJ, although he still wanted us to come by.

Meanwhile, Neil, the four-year-old, picked up a nacho chip and asked his mother if he could feed one to PJ. She said, "Sure, if he wants one," and Neil, being awkward the way little kids are, jammed a big jagged Dorito right into PJ's eye. PJ went "mrmff" and shook his head. His eye socket was bleeding and everyone caught their breath for a second to see what he would do. He just turned around and laid his head in Mom's lap.

After Mom pulled the chip out of PJ's eye and dabbed him with a napkin, Bob stood up and said, "Wow! That's incredible. I think *I* would have bitten a kid who did that to me." He had to reevaluate everything he was doing regarding pit bulls.

The thing about PJ was that he'd come from a bloodline

where sociability was emphasized. He grew up in a house full of dogs and he was always okay around other pets. But as I got older and learned more about dogs, I realized you can't completely extract 200 years of selective breeding in a few generations. Genetics is just not that simple. I warned Mom and Lee to be careful with PJ around other dogs, because there was always a possibility that if a dog jumped on him, he might take it for a few moments, but if he unleashed that inner pit bull, things could get ugly.

And one day they did. There was a family down the street who had two German shepherds, a male and a female. Those dogs had gotten out a couple of times and had bitten somebody every time. Now remember, Mom was already afraid of German shepherds because she'd been attacked before, so she was always uneasy going by that house. One night she was walking PJ and out from under the shadow of a streetlight came these two German shepherds, making a beeline for her. Mom was terrified and panicked, which really got those dogs going. PJ, reading Mom's fear and seeing these dogs coming at them like torpedoes, reacted exactly as his forefathers had been bred to react: He grabbed the male dog under the chin and slammed his head on the sidewalk. PJ had a neck like a telephone pole (it was twenty-two inches around), and Mom said it sounded like a cantaloupe hitting the pavement. The dog was out cold; Mom thought he was dead. Then PJ turned his attention to the bitch, who was growling at Mom. He jumped on that dog and threw her down. When Mom got him off the bitch, that dog ran away. The other dog came to and also hightailed it out of there.

PJ was seven at the time and had never been in a fight in his life. But those genetics are always there. I was afraid that fight had woken up a monster in PJ and that he'd get very gamey, but he never did. Still, he was always a little wary around other dogs. And for some dogs, one fight is all it takes to turn those long-dormant genes back on.

You may remember that in 2006 a bull terrier won Best in Show at the Westminster Kennel Club dog show in New York. Ch. Rocky Top's Sundance Kid, known to family and friends as Rufus, was the first bull terrier to win it, and he got a lot of press as a result. Now, Rufus was a show dog all his life. At Westminster, the dogs spend all day on display in an overcrowded area in the back, with people pressing in to see them and other dogs all around. In the show ring, they trot around practically nose-to-butt with dozens of other dogs. Show dogs are extremely well-trained, well-socialized animals.

About a year after Rufus's big win, I was at a swanky black-tie dog fanciers' event in New York City. There were a lot of show dogs in attendance, including Rufus. I know his owner, Tom Bishop, so I was talking with him. Everyone wanted to see Rufus, and we kept getting interrupted by people with little yipper dogs. I noticed that as Tom talked to them, he turned very subtly and stood in front of Rufus and blocked him a little bit. Finally, I asked him, "Man, what's going on?" He shook his head and said, "You know what? I'm glad Rufus won Best in Show because I think I'd have to retire him anyway. I don't think I can show this dog anymore."

Then he told me the story. His wife was keeping an American bulldog for a relative of theirs, and those are big old hundred-pound dogs. One day the bulldog went after Rufus. Nothing really precipitated it. Rufus tried to avoid the fight, but he finally had to defend himself. And something just turned on in him. They got into it, and quickly it became an all-out death match. Rufus tore the bulldog's ear off and seriously injured him. Rufus himself still had scabs and puncture wounds on his neck. This happened three weeks after Westminster, and fortunately, Rufus's press tour was finished by then.

"That dog is eight years old and he's never been in a fight in his life," Tom told me. "But it was like turning on a light switch. From that point on, the dog-fighting genes bubbled up to the surface. Just watch him eyeball the other dogs in the room." I looked and it was true. You could see it in his eyes, the locked-in focus on the other dogs. That one fight had unearthed the genetic skeleton in Rufus's closet.

It's really important to understand that dog behavior is about 75 percent genetic and 25 percent environmental. And I think this is even more true for particular bloodlines than it is for breeds as a whole—which is why Larry, PJ's breeder, was so ruthless in developing his bloodlines. You've got what you've got when it comes out of the womb. You can shape and mold a dog within those parameters, but you cannot sidestep a dog's genetic heritage. I had a caller on my radio show recently who told me his dog's barking was driving him nuts. It turns out he had a schnauzer, so I asked him, "If you can't stand barking, why would you buy a schnauzer?" With so much good information on the Internet, there's no excuse anymore for not knowing what your dog is genetically predisposed to do.

With those kinds of hardwired behaviors, people always ask me, "Can you change it?" Yes, you probably can, but you're fighting such a battle against genetics that to get the result you want, you're breaking down something so primal in the dog that you're going to end up with other problems. That's true of beagles chasing things, malamutes pulling on a leash, and pit bulls fighting with other animals. People fool themselves into thinking, "It all depends on how you raise them." And I'm not saying that how you raise a dog isn't important. But you can't think that if you raise him right you're never going to have a problem. You're just more likely to be able to get that problem under control sooner.

Of course, when it comes to genetic heritage, there's a good side as well as a bad. The bull terrier breeds, for example, have a high tolerance for pain and a bred-in tendency not to be aggressive with their human handlers. In fact, my very first experience with bite training was with PJ. And it's lucky for me that it was.

Larry had told me PJ needed a lot of exercise and advised me to find something he likes to do that expends a lot of energy. While I was researching the breed, I spoke to an Am Staff breeder who lived outside of Dallas and trained all his dogs to play tug-of-war using a thick karate belt. I remembered him telling me that it exercises the dog's powerful neck and gives him a chance to really bite down hard—which uses up a lot of energy and gets a lot of frustration out, too. That was the first time I'd heard about using training as a way to dump a dog's drive onto something and take the edge off a high-drive dog. It's a concept I have used ever since.

By then I had been studying martial arts for a few years, so I started with an old karate belt because they are heavily stitched. I folded it over several times and held it and we would play tug-of-war games. This was something PJ was not allowed to do in Larry's house, because when you get that many dogs together, if one starts acting aggressively, even if it's a game, the others will jump in and you'll end up with a big fight. But it was just me and PJ, and I'd push and pull and growl and get in his face. He loved it.

Then I started doing bite work with him. I'd roll up a bath towel and let him come and bite that, then I taught him to do it from a distance. I'd make him sit at one end of the hallway and I'd sit at the other end and say, "Okay, get it!" and he'd run and jump through the air and hit it and I'd let him swing through under my arms. After a few months I started wrapping the towel around my arm and securing it with duct tape.

When I think about that now, it's a wonder I didn't get hurt. PJ just knew how to limit himself. If I had enough towels on me so that he had a full mouth of fabric rather than my padded arm, he didn't adjust his bite—which would have broken my arm. He'd still bite and hold on, but he would just end up tearing the towel to shreds. (Mom was always buying new bath towels.) Within a year I had PJ to where I could wrap a towel around my arm, put him in a down-stay and walk away. He would be lying there quivering with anticipation. Then I'd say, "Okay, get him," and he would run up and fly through the air and slam into me. I could get him to let go on command, too.

I can't believe I did all that, but at the time I didn't know how dangerous it was. I ended up learning a lot about bite training through trial and error. There was no pressure on either of us and it was all fun. Now, when I look back at that time, I realize how much of my training philosophy I came to on my own, long before I started working with the big trainers. When I started formal work, everyone still thought you had to put a dog into defensive drive to get him to do bite work. But I knew from working with PJ that you didn't need to put all that pressure on the dog.

That sort of thing was heaven for a teenage boy, but it scared the heck out of Mom. She and Lee loved PJ's clownishness, but he was basically my dog and I did what I wanted with him. That changed during my junior year in high school. I had grown up in Jackson, my dad and all my friends still lived there, and I couldn't imagine not going to high school there at least some of the time. So my junior year I went back and lived with Dad, and left PJ with Mom and Lee.

It was amazing how fast he worked his way deep into their hearts. They were the only ones left who could feed his insatiable need for attention. And he demanded more and more of it—but by being silly and sweet and letting them know he just couldn't live without them. Lee was semi-retired by then and he and Mom traveled a lot. The first time they went away after I left, it was just for the weekend. They put PJ in a boarding kennel and he was a big drama queen about the whole thing. He pulled the saddest mopey face you've ever seen when they left him, and it tore Mom up. They brought his favorite sleeping bag and his regular food to the kennel, but when they came back for him he'd torn that sleeping bag to shreds and hadn't eaten one bite of food the whole weekend. Mom was really upset, and Lee said, "We're not going to do that again." So they started hiring house sitters.

That Christmas, they were supposed to go to a resort in

Mexico. But at the last minute their regular house sitter had an emergency and couldn't come, so they canceled the trip. I think Lee lost more than $5,000 on that trip that he could never get back because they cancelled so late. But he just said, "Forget it, we're not leaving the dog alone."

When Mom called and told me that, I remember laughing and saying, "Lee is love struck, whether he will ever admit it or not. He and PJ are it."

And they were. Lee would come home from his office at 2 p.m. and he and PJ had this special routine. It didn't matter if other people were around or not; they did the same routine every day, seven days a week. Lee had a big reading chair with an ottoman, and he would sit down and start reading the *Dallas Morning News*. PJ would lie on the floor next to the ottoman grinding down his big old Nylabone and making a lot of noise. This would go on for ten, fifteen, sometimes twenty minutes. Now that I look back on it, PJ showed a lot of patience, because typically when a dog gets enjoyment out of something he'll start fast-forwarding the cues to get to the good stuff. But PJ waited awhile before he would put his bone down, stand up, and start growling at Lee. He'd start off with a low growl and show his teeth a little bit. Lee would keep his paper in front of him and pay no attention. Then PJ would turn his head sideways and get that crazed dog look with the widest eyes. He could put on this incredible display where he'd foam at the mouth and start these deep breathing growls. (PJ was a great actor.) Lee still wouldn't pay any attention to him.

Now remember, Lee's legs were out in front of him on the ottoman. So next, PJ would walk between the ottoman and the chair and gently put his lips right up against Lee's knee or thigh. Then you could hear a clicking sound as PJ started taking tiny little bites. He'd keep pressing his lips a bit closer and you could hear those teeth clicking, until finally he pinched a little piece of skin. When he did, Lee would throw the paper up in the air and yell "Ay!!" and jump up. PJ would start running around the house and Lee would chase him.

We had a hallway that wound around the whole house, and sometimes Lee would chase PJ and sometimes PJ would chase Lee. PJ did this little scoot run where he would run with his ass down, so we called him Scootch the Wonder Dog. When they finally got back to the big open room where they started, Lee would stand there with his hands out and be like, "I'm going to get you," and PJ would just be growling and snapping the air and running around the room. It always ended up with Lee getting down on all fours and PJ diving on him to attack. They would be pawing at each other and snapping and fighting, and you'd hear these guttural snarls and gnashing of teeth. Lee would grab PJ's head, and PJ would start mouthing Lee's bald head. PJ would be foaming at the mouth and Lee's head would be covered with slobber. Sometimes they would get into it pretty heavy and Lee would have little scabs on top of his head where PJ would accidentally scrape a tooth on him. It looked really terrifying if you didn't know what was going on.

After about five minutes Lee would just stop and say, "Okay, buddy, I've got to finish the paper." And it would be like throwing a light switch with PJ. He'd go back over to his spot and calmly start chewing on his bone.

They did this every day at about the same time. If there were people in the house, they would be shocked and think the dog had rabies. If they already knew the routine, they'd just laugh so hard they couldn't breathe. PJ never missed a day—and neither did Lee.

Lee sat in that chair to watch TV, too. Then PJ would crawl up into Lee's lap. He'd lie on his back with his head up against Lee's stomach, his spine running down in the middle of Lee's outstretched legs, and all four feet in the air. Lee would watch the news and scratch PJ's chest, and the dog would lie there and start snoring. Lee would have to tell him to be quiet. PJ could lie there like that for hours, and he was so heavy that Lee's legs would fall asleep. But Lee loved having PJ sleep on him, so he never disturbed the dog.

I was back in Dallas for half of my senior year of high school, but went off to the University of Tennessee in the fall of 1987. PJ stayed behind with Mom and Lee, because by then he was really their dog. Mom took him everywhere with her—and remember, this was the late 1980s and she was going around with a pit bull. She used to take him to the salon where she got her hair and nails done, which was in a very hoity-toity part of Dallas. Mom would stroll in there with PJ and he'd go make the rounds, greeting everyone. Then he'd lie down at her feet and they'd all give him treats and pet him and make a fuss. They just loved him. And believe me, he loved the attention. He was so full of himself that when he got home he could barely fit through the door.

Mom really liked him to ride in the car with her, and he was great about it. She would crack the window halfway down and he would sit in the seat behind her and stick his head out the window. Everyone in our neighborhood got to know him because they saw him drive by with his head hanging out. He loved it so much that Mom eventually bought a car just for him—one where the armrest was exactly the right height so that he could sit comfortably with his head out the window. It was a really nice Volvo, and a few years later when she went to trade it in, the car was in pristine condition except for the armrest on the driver's side back door. It was completely worn down and ripped up from PJ putting his feet on it.

PJ was definitely a celebrity in our neighborhood, but he wasn't the only one. Herschel Walker, the running back for the Dallas Cowboys, lived a few doors down. He had a rottweiler named Big Al who was famous because he had saved Herschel's life. The football player almost died from carbon monoxide poisoning in his garage, and Al was the one who barked like crazy and woke Herschel's wife up. The dog ended up being on the cover of *Sports Illustrated*. Herschel definitely loved Al, but he had grown up with pit bulls in Georgia. So when he'd see Mom out with PJ, he'd put Al inside (Al was not particularly friendly with other dogs) and come play with PJ.

Mom and Lee threw a lot of parties, and PJ entertained at all of them. He loved to be the center of attention and would do anything to get you to look at him. There just wasn't anybody who didn't like PJ. Of course, there were people who didn't know him and were afraid because he looked like a big scary pit bull. But he'd do something silly and pretty soon they'd be all over him. He was one of those dogs who everyone remembered. There was no dismissing or ignoring him. He was a walking eighty pounds of pure showmanship.

The funny thing was, although he looked like the ultimate tough guy, PJ could be the biggest baby in the world. If he didn't want to do something or was a little bit timid about it, he would lay on the drama. Imagine a pit bull drama queen! He just had to have people fawning over him.

When we'd go to our cabin in Arkansas, there was a spot on the river PJ loved. He couldn't swim (too much muscle and not enough fat for him to float), but he loved to run through the water in this particular place where there were rapids and falls and the water was just four or five inches deep. The water rushed over the rocks, which I guess he found interesting, and a lot of people went wading there, which fed his insatiable need for attention. You had to take a canoe to get there, though (motorboats were banned on the river), and PJ hated the canoe. To be fair, most dogs would. I mean, it was a metal canoe so it made a lot of noise, and there was no flat spot in the bottom. A canoe shakes, and if a dog is nervous or unsteady, he digs in with his claws. But there was no way he could dig into a metal canoe.

Instead of refusing to get in, PJ would go to the edge of the dock and stand there and start whimpering and shaking. Then he'd lie down on his back and roll over on his belly and tuck his little tail up between his legs with this look on his face like you were standing over him with a hatchet getting ready to kill him. It was totally for dramatic effect. We'd just stand there laughing. Then Mom or Lee would call his bluff. They'd say, "Oh, get over it," and he'd jump up and get into the canoe.

Up at the cabin, Mom and Lee spent a lot of time just sitting around on the porch reading, and PJ would get into a big lounge chair with one of them and snooze. None of the working dogs I had later was ever able to dial it down to be that kind of dog, and I have to admit, I miss having a more mellow canine relationship. But by then, PJ wasn't my dog anymore—he was theirs.

By the time I was a senior in college, I already had my first true working dog, Kazan, and was starting to do some work with the Knoxville Police Department, so I was keeping other dogs to train. I was living on a big piece of property in Knoxville, about ten minutes' drive from campus in an old farmhouse that had been beautifully renovated. It was in the middle of a thick stand of trees, and you couldn't even see the house from the road. A developer owned it and the thirty-five acres around it and was planning to eventually knock it down and put up new construction subdivisions. He wanted to let the housing market get higher before he started, though, so for now he just wanted somebody to stay at the house and keep people off the property. I was living there with my friend Alan, and, in terms of college housing, we were probably the two luckiest guys in Tennessee.

I had also bought myself a wolf, Diablo (you'll meet him in the next chapter), and if anything was going to keep the neighborhood kids from building bonfires in the woods around the house, it was the notion that I was patrolling with a wolf.

By this time, PJ was almost ten. He'd been living the easy life with Mom and Lee, and they'd let him get a little porky. I really wanted to bring PJ to Tennessee because I thought he'd love the chance to run around all day and because he needed to trim down. And he certainly did love it. I'd drive around the property in my four-wheeler with all the dogs running alongside, and PJ turned into a rock-hard, svelte eighty-pound pit bull. He was also the only dog I had who established any kind of relationship with Diablo. They became a very odd couple: the pit bull who wasn't dog-aggressive and the wolf who was afraid of every dog I had except PJ.

PJ came up to live with me in August. That December, he was out running around near the house with a neighbor's dog who sometimes came by, and I was sitting on the porch keeping an eye on them. I went inside for a moment to answer the phone, and suddenly Alan came running in, screaming, "PJ's been hit by a car!" My heart just stopped. PJ had run up to the road— something he never did—and Alan said he heard the squeal of car brakes and then a big thud. He looked up and the other dog came running through the woods with PJ behind him dragging his right back leg.

I ran outside and PJ was standing there on the porch with his leg kind of twisted around behind him. It was horrible to see, but I thought, "Okay, broken leg, fixable." Then I got a look at the white part of his belly and there was a big tire tread mark. When I saw that I thought, "Internal damage. Not okay." I could tell PJ was kind of freaked out, but he was just standing there as if to say, "Let's do something."

Right at that moment, my friend Joelle pulled up in her car. I grabbed PJ's crate and ripped off the top half, then put the bottom half and a blanket in the back of her car. I lifted PJ up in there and he was hurting, so he growled at me a little. I understood and tried to be as gentle as I could.

We rushed him to the veterinary clinic and the vet took a quick look at him and said, "Well, obviously, his leg is broken at the hip." But I saw where his eyes were looking—that big tread mark across PJ's belly. At this point PJ was starting to go into shock, and the vet said, "We need to know what his insides look like." He took a lot of X-rays, then went into another room.

PJ was lying there on the table and I remember the way he looked up at me, as if he was saying, "Please help me." All of a sudden I realized, this could be it. I mean, he's about to die on this table. Every memory of our lives together was flooding through my brain at a thousand miles an hour. I was just torn up. Each breath he took, I was waiting for it to be his last.

Then I thought, "How am I going to call Mom and Lee, after I begged and pleaded for them to let me keep him for a couple of months—which they obviously didn't want to do? Now here he is, about to die from getting hit by a car. That's the ultimate in irresponsibility. This dog has been through thick and thin with me and he's getting ready to die right now."

As it turned out, the internal injuries were not serious. PJ survived, but the broken leg turned out to be a bigger problem than I could ever have imagined. The vet put a metal pin in his leg, but it never healed right and his hipbone never fused to the stub on his femur. So for the rest of his life he just dragged the leg around like so much useless baggage. The vet told me to keep him thin to minimize the stress on his joints while his body adjusted. But the pin kept working its way up and it finally broke through the skin. The veterinarian he was seeing by then said we had to just leave it open, so every time PJ took a step, this metal pin shot up about an inch through a hole in his hip.

I remember having to call Mom and Lee after the accident to tell them. That was absolutely the worst phone call I have ever made in my life. They were in shock and said almost nothing. When I took PJ back to them, he had lost a lot of weight and I think Lee almost died.

PJ ended up living to be thirteen, and that's a long life for a pit bull, but those last three years were tough. He never complained, though, and he was never a mopey, whiney dog. On his face PJ was still the same old happy-go-lucky guy. He spent his last days going to the cabin in Hardy and to the store with Mom and all the other things he loved to do—just on three legs instead of four. It was a struggle at times, but he tried hard not to let that leg slow him down. His resilience was amazing.

Mom and Lee sure weren't going to let him live with me again, and I wasn't ever going to ask. And it was the right thing for him, because PJ needed that retired setting. In Knoxville he was still trying to run with my dogs, and that was a problem. So instead, he spent all day with Lee.

Ultimately, it was cancer that did PJ in. Lee and Mom finally had to make the painful decision to put him down. After PJ died, Lee told Mom he was going to be gone for a while. He packed a bag and went to Palm Springs for two weeks and didn't talk to anybody the whole time.

When I was working on this book, I wanted to ask Lee about some of his memories of PJ. But he had a hard time talking about it. He never got another dog, either. When a dog gets into your heart, the loss hurts forever. Amen.

# 6

# Diablo

Nobody really knows when it happened—when the first wolf walked into an encampment of humans and, instead of making off with some easy prey or scavenging for leftovers, sat down by the fire and started making friends. Scientists have long thought it happened about 10,000 to 14,000 years ago. Now there's some new but still controversial evidence that it was more like 100,000 years ago.

Whenever it happened, scientists do agree on one thing: Today's dogs, from Chihuahuas to Great Danes, all descended from wolves. Dog behavior comes out of wolf pack behavior, so for me it's the foundation that builds the house. I was always fascinated by wolves and had a huge curiosity about wolf pack behavior. I was also at a time in my life when I wanted to push my limits as a dog trainer, to learn more. It seemed to me that a wolf was the perfect way to do that. Could I influence his behavior? Could I socialize him? What effect would he have on me?

I got Diablo in the spring of 1989. I had just moved to that beautiful country property in Knoxville where PJ would eventually come to join me. At that time in Tennessee, there were a lot of people who were breeding wild animals for sale—everything from monkeys to big cats. I had heard about a guy named Danny who sold animals to a lot of zoos. He had a reputation for having real wolves, as opposed to wolf-dog hybrids, and his facility was only a thirty-minute drive from my place, so I decided to go have a look.

When I drove up the gravel driveway to his place, I saw a sprawling facility with lots of little concrete buildings and small pens. He had a lot of monkeys housed in groups in indoor-outdoor pens, screeching and hopping around. He raised a lot of big cats, too, and I saw pumas and jaguars pacing back and forth restlessly in ten-by-twenty-foot pens with concrete floors, separated by chain-link fencing. Just looking at them made me feel sad. Danny was certainly not into constructing habitats for his animals; he was in it for the profit.

All the wolves were housed in pairs in pens—each pen next to the other, which went against their natural instinct to form packs. And there was something else about them. They looked—I don't want to say downtrodden, but they were real lethargic. They just sort of stood there. There was a certain dullness about them, like they had given up. I saw a sad resignation in their body posture and their eyes.

Danny had a pregnant gray-and-white Minnesota timber wolf pacing around in a small pen. He'd had a couple of litters out of her before. Nearby in another pen was the father of her litter, a McKenzie Valley timber wolf from Canada. He was jet-black without a white hair on him, and he had the yellowest eyes—almost like one of the big cats.

I was glad to be able to see the father, because then I could make sure the cubs weren't hybrids. No matter how wolf-like the dog you mix in, there are definitely telltale signs. The main one is eye color: Hybrids lose that yellow eye gene. Their overall look is different, too. Even if a cub is just 25 percent domesticated dog, the coat and legs and bone structure are not the same as a pure wolf. Wolves also don't have the kind of domed crown of the head you see on a husky or a malamute—or a hybrid. A wolf's head is long, the top is flat like a big diamond, and the muzzle is a lot broader. It's more like an alligator's face.

Wolves carry themselves differently from any other animal, as well. They're very leggy; they almost look like they're on stilts. And their movement is rangy. Instead of running and bounding, it's as if their upper body and the top three-quarters of their legs stay almost still and the lower parts of the legs do all the moving. It's probably an evolutionary adaptation that minimizes body movement while the feet do the work. That conserves energy and also enables the wolf to travel through brush without making noise.

In retrospect, I didn't really know what I was getting into with a wolf. But I definitely knew what I did not want to get into with a hybrid. I think it's the most dangerous combination you can put together. What tempers all the wild ferocity and explosiveness of a wolf in captivity is that it comes with a terrifying fear of people. When you mix in the domestic dog, yes, you do water down the explosive ferocity somewhat, but it's still there. And meanwhile, you have also watered down his fear of the unfamiliar—the thing that was keeping him in check. So you end up with the worst of both worlds.

When people tell me they want a wolf hybrid, I keep asking them why until they finally *always* admit it's about having something they think is cool. They want to be able to say, "I own a wolf." Other than that ego factor, there's no basis for wanting a wolf hybrid. Putting that wolf wildness into a dog means you can't do much training with him, and hybrids are not socially reliable as pets. So what do you want out of it that you can't get from one of the 300 domestic dog breeds? Nobody has ever been able to give me a good reason for having a wolf hybrid—because there isn't one.

Anyway, having satisfied myself that Danny was selling 100 percent pure wolves, I put down $250 in cash as a deposit. This was in March, and the cubs were expected in early May. Danny said he'd give me a call when they were born and that I'd have to bring another $500 when I picked one up.

The call came right on time. There were six cubs, and Danny said I had to get mine in the first five days if I wanted to have any chance of the cub bonding with me. To understand why, you need to understand the difference between a tame animal and a domesticated one. Domestication changes the appearance and behavior of an animal at the genetic level. It's evolution at work. A domesticated animal is a different species from a wild animal. That's why a wolf is not a dog and a tiger is not a house cat.

Now remember, we pass on our genes to our offspring. So domesticated animals pass on their domestication. That means puppies born to dogs will all be domesticated dogs—naturally inclined to live closely with people. But wild animals just pass on their wildness. The process of taming gets a wild animal used to the company of humans, but there's no change in the fundamental makeup of the animal. Genetically speaking, he's still a wild animal—which means all his offspring are wild, too. So you have to start from scratch with every generation and tame them again. The sooner you start, the easier it is.

I drove out two days after the cubs were born. Danny had already taken them away from their mother, so I could see them all squirming around in a separate pen. It was tough to choose from among the cubs, because at two days old there's not much difference between them. I wanted a male, for no particular reason other than that I have always liked male dogs. So I pointed to a little silvery black one. Danny sent me into the house and came in a little while later with the cub in his hands.

I was surprised at how much he didn't look like a dog puppy. He had sharp, angular features, not like a puppy's round baby face. His eyes and ears were closed, so smell was the primary way he understood the world. That's how wolves bond with their sire and dam and the other cubs in their litter. Knowing that, I'd brought a cotton shirt with me that I'd worn for a couple of days so it was all nice and stinky. I put the shirt in a box and wrapped the cub in it, so he'd get used to my scent. I put the box on the front seat next to me and drove most of the way home with my hand on the cub to keep him warm.

A two-day-old cub needs round-the-clock care, so I was the acting wolf mama. It was Rascal all over again, and if I could be a raccoon mama as a young boy, I could certainly be a wolf mama as a young man. To do that, I kept him up against me a lot. If I was sitting down at night and watching TV or something like that, I'd put the cub in my lap. Sometimes I'd lie down on the couch, take my shirt off and put him up against my chest so he could feel the warmth. Or I'd tuck him under my armpit so he could snuggle up against my bare skin and really smell my scent.

The big difference between raising Diablo and raising Rascal is that I knew right from the start Rascal would never be a pet and I always intended to release him into the wild. The jury was out on how much I could socialize my wolf, but I had a lot higher hopes of having a dog-like pet. Looking back now, I'm not sure why I thought Diablo could be a pet when I knew Rascal could never be one. I guess I was just figuring that since wolves had evolved into domesticated dogs and raccoons had never evolved into domesticated anything, the possibility was there.

At about four weeks old Diablo's eyes and ears opened, and he was in love with the world. His eyes were an opaque baby blue, almost like glass marbles, but I knew they'd change color when he got older. He'd play with toys for hours on end, ripping the squeakers out of plush puppy toys and shredding the rest. He was a destructive little machine, cute but fierce. His coat reminded me of a raccoon's—very coarse and stiff, with no flow to it, just sticking up like a bristle brush. His big paws were way out of proportion with the rest of his body.

The first five weeks, Diablo was similar to a dog. Mostly, he just ate and slept and was very needy. But there were a couple of interesting exceptions. First, he almost never yelped or whined. He whimpered a little when he needed something, but not like a puppy. Baby wild animals are generally quiet, because if they're not, a predator finds them and they get eaten.

I fed him canine milk replacer from a bottle until he was about eight weeks old, because I wanted him to have plenty of nutrition. Then I started making a mixture of milk replacer and dog food. And he grew enormously fast.

Raising Diablo was a lot like raising a litter of high-drive working puppies, like those I trained for police work. Regular domestic puppies at seven or eight weeks old might chase you and grab your pants leg for fun, but then they quickly run off to find another game. But high-level working puppies, like Malinois, will hang off you like ticks as you walk through a room because their prey drive is so strong. Diablo was the same. The difference was, when most puppies get tired they'll just go somewhere and lie down. Not him. When I was with him, there was no sleeping or lying around. He was usually off-the-charts playful or showing me intense submissive behaviors, such as rolling over and urinating on himself. And he would *never* settle down. Sometimes he'd wear himself out to the point where he'd just lie there panting, but if I got up he'd be right with me. He was like a hyper, clingy kid.

When I think about that now, I feel kind of sad because he really needed the kinship of his littermates. We know that singleton dog puppies miss out on crucial canine socialization with their littermates. They learn important social lessons from their mother, too, so we try not to take pups away from their home before eight weeks. And the pack instinct is even stronger in wolves than it is in dogs, so I can only imagine how much Diablo was missing out on. When he was young, he was just starving for more attention, although at the time, I didn't recognize it for what it was.

When Diablo was a bit older, my roommate's girlfriend would take care of him when I was out of town. She loved him, and Diablo really loved her, too. She was tiny—about five-foot-one and a hundred pounds—and he would maul her with affection. That's what he did if he liked you—he'd push you down and lick you all over. I thought it was kind of crazy, but now I realize that there's a lot of physical touching and licking and closeness in wolf packs and he desperately wanted that.

Diablo had another distinct wolf characteristic that always amazed me—an unbridled feast-or-famine response. He ate about eight cups of food a day, compared to the four or five cups a day I feed a working German shepherd. But no matter how much food I gave him, it was never enough. And by three months old he was already guarding his food with a primal passion. He'd splay his legs around his bowl, crouch low, and snarl explosively as he ate, gnashing at the air, rarely pausing even for a breath. If a dog of mine was doing that, I'd quickly correct him, because guarding is one of those dangerous behaviors that you can't let slide in a dog. But I knew I was never going to be able to change Diablo, and I just left him alone when he was eating.

The insatiable food thing drove me crazy. I kept thinking if I fed him regularly and well, he'd get over it. But he never did, because that impulse to gorge was absolutely not a learned behavior. It was pure genetics saying, "I've got to eat everything. I've got to eat even if it's to the point where I'm so engorged I can't really stand up and I'm sick. I have to eat because I don't know when my next meal's coming." I see voracious eaters in my training practice and I have people call my radio show and tell me that their dog will just keep on eating if there's food available, but that's almost always a competitive impulse, not a starvation response. That "hungry" dog has another dog around while he's eating, so he's protecting his resources.

Diablo, however, would eat to the point where he couldn't walk. Once, when he was just five months old, I gave him more than ten pounds of dog food in one sitting. I just kept doling it out and he kept eating until his stomach got so bloated I was worried about him, so I stopped.

All that food made him a big boy. By the time he was a year old, he weighed almost ninety pounds and was thirty-four inches tall at the shoulder. He was the size of a female Great Dane, although he certainly wasn't shaped like a Great Dane; it was all bone. He was just big, leggy, skinny, long, and tall. His silvery black fur was quickly shed and he ended up totally black with banana yellow eyes.

For such a big animal with no formal training, Diablo was surprisingly easy to manage. A dog with his athleticism might have run off and been tough to catch, but something in him knew to stay near me, like he would have with the leader of his pack. He'd spring to my side and lie down every time I got next to him. It wasn't something I had to teach him, like I'd have to with a dog. Actually, I didn't teach him any formal commands. His mind could really only process very black-and-white ideas—feast or famine, leader or follower, safe or unsafe. Training commands made absolutely no sense in his world; his mind didn't seem hardwired to process anything other than what came to him instinctively. There wasn't a need for training anyway, because the submissive part of him was so potent that I could take complete control of him with a glance.

I did get him used to a collar at first, but getting him used to a leash was impossible. Pressure on his neck must have felt similar to the bite correction he'd get from another wolf, which would mean, "Don't you dare move." So having a leash on him just shut him down into a position of total submission and he'd freeze. If I started to pull him, he'd squeal and whine like I was hurting him. He didn't need that kind of restriction anyway; if I was there, Diablo was at my side.

This clingy behavior was based on his instinct for pack harmony. When I needed him to come to me, he just came because we had an understanding. The reason this worked with him is that his life with me was a little bit like a real pack setting because we didn't have a lot of confusing issues going on. If you have a pet dog at home, you've got maybe five family members who all interact with the dog in different ways—which means there are a lot more ways for the dog to mess up and get into trouble. But Diablo and I had a closed system. He lived outside in a large pen, and we frequently went walking together in the woods. When he was out, he was with me and just me. I knew enough to keep it simple.

As close as wolves and dogs are, dog packs and wolf packs have some key differences. Yes, dog pack behavior developed from wolf pack behavior, but most dog packs don't have to survive the way a wolf pack does because dogs are mostly scavengers. Real wolf packs have to organize cooperative hunting and cub-raising activities, where each member of the pack has specific tasks. So the pack as a whole is functioning at a higher level.

I think one of the reasons wolves can perform these complex functions as a pack is that they lead very simple lives. You have leaders, you have followers, you eat, you breed, you feed and raise cubs, and you survive. We think our dogs have got it so easy because they don't have to worry about getting food. But we fill our dogs' lives with a confusion that wolves could never handle. When you're out in the wild, you don't have to worry about riding in a car or going to the veterinarian or meeting dogs you've never seen before at the dog park or performing tasks that make no instinctive sense to you, such as rolling over on cue. Wolf life is raw and wild and simple. Food, sex, survival—that's pretty much it.

The food drive is handled by the pack leader. He says when the pack is going to go out and hunt, and they follow his lead. Young wolves learn how to hunt in the pack by circling prey and working cooperatively, but the alpha wolf—the leader—pretty much leads that whole entourage. Male wolves spend about 75 percent of their awake time in search of food, so the follower wolves have a very clear idea of what they're supposed to do most of the time.

The survival instinct, which goes hand in hand with the denning instinct, is mainly the job of the females. They need to raise their cubs in a place that's warm and close to food and water, and that they can protect from other predators. Nothing complex there.

As for sex, usually it's just the alpha pair (the top male and female) who mates in a wolf pack, so if you're not at the top of the hierarchy, you just don't get any. Simple!

But for our pet dogs, nothing is that simple (except, if they are spayed or neutered, the sex part). We stick them into our family "pack" and we've got all these complex family dynamics. If you have a big dog, the dog senses in himself, "Well, I should be leading them, but then my human leader says no, but he's not always leading me." That's pretty confusing.

Wolf packs don't change much, either. Yes, over time pack members die and new ones are born, and young males branch out and find new packs, but you don't have wolves who casually wander into the pack's territory for a playdate or little wolf cubs bringing their friends from another pack home for the afternoon or visiting wolves who come over for summer vacation. For our pet dogs, though, there's a constant ebb and flow of people and dogs in and out of their lives.

Wolves spend all their time in their own territory, too. A wolf pack's territory can be large, but it's finite. They don't go on trips far away and they try not to encroach on the territory of other wolves. But our dogs are take-along pets. Some adapt and some don't, which is why you have dogs who act very differently when they're in their home territory than when they're far from home. Dogs who have not been well-socialized to new environments, or nervy dogs, have their identity closely tied to where they are. You take them somewhere else and they're kind of lost for a while. Just like wolves, dogs are comfortable in structured environments. Routine is everything to them—it's comforting, it's cozy, it's recognizable.

Luckily for us, domestication has given dogs a flexibility to adapt to changing environments that wolves will never have. But their adaptability is not endless and we make a big mistake by undersocializing our dogs and then expecting them to be fine when, after they've spent their whole lives at home, we take them someplace really unfamiliar and they fall apart. (That little Yorkie we met in the Introduction is a good example.)

We also make a mistake when we refuse to acknowledge the pack order they have established among themselves. It's always best to let the dogs work things out on their own and then follow along. That's true whether you have several dogs yourself or whether you take your dog to the dog park or doggie day care or for regular playdates. Most of the time, dogs who see one another often just naturally figure out who is on top and who takes the various subordinate roles. If we recognize their hierarchy and follow some simple rules, there's pack harmony. But we interfere, either because we don't recognize the hierarchy or because we somehow want to boost up the lower ranking dog.

A lot of times I see people who have several dogs, and when they leave them alone in the backyard, they get along pretty well. But fights explode when the owners are around. Maybe they feed one of the lower-ranking dogs first or give him the better toy or simply pet him first. The alpha dog sees that and says, "Hey, it's my job to correct this; I've got to go over there and correct this right now." And he does. So you create aggressive behavior between your pets by not following the rules that they've worked out among themselves.

There was no confusion like that for Diablo. I was Diablo's mom and dad and pack leader and everything. In the beginning, I had dreams of teaching him more domestic kinds of behaviors, because I pride myself on being very skilled at conditioning dogs to think for themselves. But it didn't work out that way. Most things were completely outside his comfort level. For example, after about three months it became clear that Diablo wasn't going to be a house pet. He began to get spooked by being in the house and he'd pant, shake, and slink around, crouching low like he was trying to be invisible. He was skittish about noises, too—just the quiet sound of a door shutting made him jump or run under a chair. He never had a bad incident that scared him, he was just a wild animal and human stuff gave him sensory overload.

I set up a big eighty-foot-square pen for him outside with a few poplar trees in it and an old cinder block well house with a stone floor and a capped well. I put some hay down as a bed and scraped off as much of the chipping white paint as possible. I closed off all of the openings to the well house except for one small door, to give him the security of a wolf den. He didn't really like that house, but he'd go inside if it rained. He liked to be out in the elements. He'd sprawl in the weeds at the back of the pen, farthest from the house, and watch the world go by.

When Diablo was six months old, he wouldn't step foot on asphalt roads or a gravel driveway. He knew they were "human things" and would avoid them. I couldn't get him to cross a road, so I kept our walks to the forest. Wolves are basically nocturnal animals, so I also started letting him roam at night, with the roads around the farmhouse and the woods as natural barriers that I knew he wouldn't cross. The first time I let him out, I camped out in the backyard with him to make sure he didn't run off—even though I knew intellectually that he wouldn't. It wasn't in his nature to leave his den and his leader. He just wanted to explore.

He came and went, but he never went too far or for too long.

Eventually, I got to where I was feeling secure about it, and I'd let him out and then get myself to bed. Diablo was always in his pen in the morning when I got up, waiting for his meal. He was nothing if not predictable.

Often, late at night I'd wake up with a chill down my spine to hear Diablo somewhere deep in the woods howling his heart out, a haunting vibration that carried for miles. Wolf howling is a very complex thing and it can have a lot of different meanings. Diablo's was mostly loneliness. He was howling, "Is there somebody out there who will be my friend?"

Diablo taught me a lot of lessons in posture behavior. I had to be ultraconscious of my body language and how I played with him, because I had to send really clear signals that I was the leader and he was the follower. I couldn't get down on the ground with him too much or roll over on my back in play because he might read this as weakness. Even at six months old, he was a large presence, and though I would have tangled with him if necessary, I didn't want him to challenge me. I had to be steady but determined, so it was always clear I was in charge.

People don't often think about posture and body language with their own pets, but they should. Dogs have an inherent ability to recognize body language and even the kind of energy you give off. And that ability is magnified in wolves. Diablo was so in tune with my body language that if we were outside and I changed my thoughts from "we're out here just relaxing" to "we have to go now," he would *feel* it and he'd be at my heels, waiting for direction.

By the time Diablo was seven months old, I felt we had established some real bonds of companionship. But the other dogs I kept never took to him at all. He had an intangible wild element that they felt threatened by. Domestic dogs, even those who are a world away from being wolves, like shih tzu, are highly instinctual creatures. They know the difference between wild animals and domestic ones. A neighborhood cat, for instance, might be able to cross a dog's yard with nothing more than an alert glance, but that same dog might never let a raccoon out of there alive.

Dozens of dogs came in and out of my kennels during the time I had Diablo, most for training and police work. These dogs were well socialized to other dogs and would run up and greet each other and posture or invite play. But it was different when they saw Diablo. They'd viciously attack him through the fence around his pen—even while Diablo was on the other side exhibiting completely submissive behavior, on his back, whining, urinating all over himself. With two male dogs, once one of them shows submissive behavior the fight is generally over, or else it never gets started. But my huge, lanky, Great Dane-size wolf rolled over like a puppy and the male dogs still went after him.

Everything with Diablo was so over the top, and it just seemed to elicit extreme behavior from them. When he would go to greet other dogs, he would get up under them and pee all over himself and kiss them all over their faces with this desperate "please play with me" attitude. It was really sad to see, and it seemed to bring out the worst in the dogs. They sensed a wildness in him, and they were scared of it. And the truth is, if he'd acted even a tiny bit aggressive, they'd have turned and run. But instead, what they saw was a strange wild animal who happened to speak dog. And what he was saying, amazingly, was, "I'm afraid of you." Which opened up the possibility that they could eliminate the thing they feared. And they tried to—every single time.

The aggression I saw from the police dogs I trained surprised me, but these were, after all, high-drive dogs. It got very strange, though, when I kept my friend's Labrador retriever, Charlie, for a few weeks while he was out of town. Charlie was a fraternity house dog, super socialized around people and animals, a smiling, friendly politician. But the second he saw Diablo he launched a full-on aggressive, fear-based attack. As usual, Diablo rolled over on his back, but Charlie ran toward his pen, snarling and barking, spittle flying. I'd never seen him act like that.

The one exception was good old PJ. I didn't expect much from that relationship, but PJ was his usual tolerant self with Diablo. The first time they met was the day I drove PJ up to Knoxville. I got him out of the truck and walked him over to Diablo's pen. The wolf was there waiting for me. PJ trotted right up to the fence, sniffed Diablo, and then lifted his leg and peed on him through the fence. I almost laughed out loud. Diablo panted and whined and paced back and forth until I let him out. PJ stood all of twenty-four inches at the shoulder, but when he approached Diablo, the big wolf crawled to him on his belly and licked him all over in a blatant display of submission. PJ sniffed him and then walked away, Diablo at his heels.

PJ was the first dog who didn't attack Diablo, and, even better, the pit bull actually played with him. I don't know how much of it was because PJ was so in tune to me that he recognized how much I wanted him to be friendly. Whatever the reason, he was really good with Diablo. Now, he didn't totally love him, but he did tolerate him, and eventually the pair started romping around together, PJ acting like the big old tough guy. Diablo loved him with something like hero worship.

I loved taking Diablo out into the woods and watching him in his natural element. The farther we'd get from the house, the more relaxed he'd be. Sometimes I'd climb into a deer stand in the trees and watch him while he played and investigated the forest floor. He would grab sticks, flip up leaves, and chase butterflies—all kind of adolescent dog behaviors. He loved to nose around under fallen logs, discovering various scents. And watching Diablo, who was bigger than a German shepherd, run through the woods was almost like watching a video on mute. He would float. Not even the leaves rustled under his feet. It was eerie.

Seeing him like that, I realized that Diablo was missing some important aspects of wolf life by being with me. For one, a wolf isn't a freeloader, he's a hunter. I had to find a way of bringing out that predator part in him. I managed to teach Rascal how to hunt, so I thought I might be able to teach something to Diablo.

I couldn't chase and catch a squirrel, but I thought if I could present him with a squirrel he might be able to make the connection on his own. So one sunny spring afternoon I walked him far out into the woods. I brought a BB gun with me and, as we walked, I scanned the trees for squirrels. When I saw one in range, I aimed and shot. The squirrel fell, and Diablo went over to investigate.

So far Diablo had eaten nothing but dog food, so I had no idea how he'd react. He smelled it, then licked it. There was a little blood on the body, and when he licked that part, he turned into a completely different animal. It was like a keg of dynamite exploding. His whole body posture changed. He went into a very aggressive guarding stance over the body and then in probably less than three seconds the entire squirrel—including the fur and tail—was gone. He had turned into a predator right before my eyes.

Nothing was the same after his first taste of blood. I remember the first time I let him out for a walk after that. Usually, I'd open the gate and he'd come out and greet me and piddle around waiting for me to give him direction. Now he headed straight for the pine woods where all the squirrels were. He'd smelled squirrels a hundred times before in the forest, but now he immediately knew they were prey animals. He was up against those trees, nose up and down, looking . . . stalking . . . creeping . . . sniffing.

He never did get another squirrel (not that I saw, anyway), but he caught rabbits. I saw him flush one from a woodpile once and he was on it in a second. It was the ultimate example of the term "wolfing it down." He was seven months old when he started hunting, still in that adolescent gawky phase, but when he was hunting he could move like lightning and with the agility of a gazelle.

Once, around that time, a friend of mine shot a deer. He took the meat he wanted, and as an experiment, I tossed the carcass into Diablo's pen. He devoured the entire animal—skin, gristle, innards—then crushed all the bones to dust and ate them, too. It was a savage display—like watching a horror movie. He was ripping and crushing and growling with every bite. He even ate the teeth. I watched in complete awe. It was one of those times when I said to myself, "He's not a dog *at all*."

I loved seeing Diablo in those moments when he was all wolf—wild and completely comfortable within himself. But in my more painfully honest moments, I had to admit that I didn't see them very often. I was warehousing him—feeding him and giving him some attention—but I wasn't fulfilling him. The wildness was also coming out in him more and more as he got older, and it was getting a little spooky. There was no doubt in my mind that Diablo regarded me as top dog and would not go after me, but I had roommates and was in college and a lot people came and went from my place. Sooner or later, there was bound to be an incident. Diablo was a big wolf and somebody was going to get hurt.

The last straw was PJ's accident. Besides me, PJ was Diablo's only friend. When I took PJ back to Mom and Lee's house in Dallas, Diablo was devastated. His pack numbered just two members again, and I became his only source for the companionship he craved so desperately. When I was around, he couldn't get enough of me, constantly touching me and walking by my side, looking up at me with those piercing yellow eyes. Dogs need packs, but they can get the companionship they require from humans. Wild animals are different. Diablo needed to be with other wolves.

I knew I didn't want him to end up in a zoo, and I also knew he'd be no better off at another place like Danny's where each wolf was kept in a pen with nothing to do but occasionally breed. There were not many options, and although I knew I should find another place for him, I was also determined that it must be a *much better* place than the one I was offering. That's what he deserved, and I wasn't going to settle for anything less.

Reluctantly, I started calling wolf breeders I found in the classified sections of *Outdoor Life* and *Field and Stream*. I knew my standards were going to be high, and I didn't really think I'd ever find the right place. I ended up talking to a lot of people, and they all seemed to be warehousing their animals. They'd have taken a pure-blooded wolf in a second, but I turned them all down. I was ready to keep Diablo forever, rather than send him to a place like that.

Finally, I spoke with a guy named David who had a big spread near Raleigh, North Carolina. He was a third generation wolf breeder. His grandfather started the pack, his father took it over, and now David had it. The pack had been in the family for fifty years. The first time we talked, there was a lot of skepticism on both sides. He got calls every day from people who had gotten hybrids and were told they were wolves. The animals were not very manageable and their owners were looking to dump them. I was very skeptical of him, too, based on all my previous phone calls. I knew what I wanted for Diablo, and the way he described his place, it seemed like what I was looking for. But how much can you tell from a phone call?

Finally, we both agreed that we needed to see what the other had. I told him I'd arrange to drive out there with Diablo so he could have a look at the wolf and I could have a look at his place. It was just a look-see for both of us—no promises.

I underfed Diablo for two days and then, on the morning we were leaving, put hamburger meat in the back of a very big crate. Of course, he still wouldn't go inside, so I sort of shoved him in. Surprisingly, he didn't freak out; instead, he shut down. He struggled for a little while, but then he just settled down and panted heavily and salivated, feet splayed to each corner of the crate, terrified. I loaded the crate into the back of a pickup truck and pulled out of the driveway.

The drive was seven hours, and I could see him through the rear window stressing out the whole time. I'd stop and give him little treats, but for Diablo it was like a trip to another planet. The trucks rumbling by and all the movement were terrifying. He kept throwing up in the back of the crate. We drove Interstate 40 all the way, and once we got past the mountains it was flat terrain, just me and the yellow dividing line on the highway, and I had a lot of time to think. I pretty much expected to find the setup unacceptable, but I was willing to give it a shot. However, I wasn't going to leave him there unless the place was perfect.

We finally pulled into David's place just before dusk. He had an old single-story ranch house on the property, which was mostly gently rolling hills and green pasture gone to seed. He had a lot of acreage. I saw some big fenced-in areas out in the distance with a little pack of wolves just left to be themselves.

I unloaded Diablo's crate and David peered inside. My wolf was cowering in the back, scared, and David couldn't see much. "Why don't we let him out?" he suggested gently. I reached in and pulled Diablo out. He unfolded himself out of the crate and, as he did, David gasped. "Wow! That's a magnificent animal." He knew right away that Diablo was a pure wolf from his eye color. He also couldn't believe how massive Diablo was—just over a year old and already 105 pounds. Even so, he was still all bones and legs; we both knew he was going to get even bigger.

Poor Diablo was glad to get out of the crate, but he was exhausted. He just stood there beside me, trying to take everything in. He was a little shaky and it took him a few minutes to get his legs steady and to breathe normally.

On the phone, David and I had discussed Diablo's bad experiences with dogs, and he'd told me about Olive, a female who was half wolf and half German shepherd, whom he called a transition animal. She lived in his house and acted as a kind of bridge between the human world Diablo had been living in and the wolf world I hoped he was moving toward. He suggested we take Diablo to meet her in a little enclosure behind the house, but I was reluctant because I didn't want my wolf to have yet another bad experience. "Olive will take care of him," David reassured me. "She'll be okay with him."

As soon as Diablo saw Olive, he perked up. I let him go and he started sprinting over to her. She saw him and trotted his way, and he skidded to a stop almost at her feet and began his submissive act. The poor guy! The whole world was above him on the ladder. He put his head down and rolled over on his back and urinated all over himself. I held my breath waiting for Olive's reaction.

She came over and licked his face. Then she sniffed around him and did a little dog play jump, the way a puppy would. Diablo rolled up onto his side with a look of amazement on his face, like, "You mean you'll really play with me?" I was very excited and so was he. They kind of popped around for a few seconds and then she took off in a playful run and he followed. She

didn't turn around and bowl him over, and I could see those
dark clouds of stress roll away from him. He looked back at me
just once, as if to say, "Hey, look at this! I'm getting to play here.
Can you believe it?" Then he and Olive were off in their own
world.

Diablo looked like a real wolf, magnificent, breathtaking. I
had such a rush of mixed emotions watching them play. It was
exciting—kind of like a dad on the sidelines watching his kid
play football for the first time. I knew how happy he was to
finally be accepted, but just seeing that look on his face that said
"this is all I've ever dreamed of" was like a kick in the stomach.
I knew then for sure that I'd cheated him, and I felt a terrible
guilt about it.

David, meanwhile, was still taken with how beautiful Diablo
was. Then he said, "You know, he seems very well adjusted."
That surprised me, because all I could see was the anxiety in
him. But David was used to seeing wolves who had been in set-
ups more like Danny's where they were caged and treated like
wild animals. Diablo had seemed so wild to me because I was
comparing him to dogs. To David, he seemed remarkably easy
to handle.

At the time, his only breeding male was an old McKenzie
Valley timber wolf who was getting up in years, so he said he
wanted to breed Diablo. He asked softy, "How much do you
want for him?" I took a deep breath, then said, "You can have
him. I just want the first right of refusal if something happens.
Even if I can't take him back, I want to be able to call the shots
about where he goes." David said that was no problem.

There was a huge tangle of feelings pounding away in my

chest and I didn't want to get all emotional in front of David, so I didn't stick around there much longer. As I pulled out of his driveway, I started to cry. They were tears of happiness and sadness and joy and heartbreak, all at the same time. I was happy for Diablo that he was finally in his element. I was sad to lose him because I had spent so much time raising him and trying to do right by him. I was wracked with guilt for seeing how much he had been missing out on that he really, really needed. I was comforted that he was finally in the right place and that I'd done the best possible thing.

If this sounds like the end of a Disney movie . . . well . . . in a lot of ways it was. I kept in touch with David for a while and I knew Diablo lived happily ever after with a wolf pack on a ten-acre spread where he could be with his own kind and act like himself. He had great genes and ended up being highly sought after as a stud wolf because he reliably passed on his jet-black coat to his cubs and because his social skills made him slightly more like a dog than a wolf and therefore easier to handle. He fathered cubs every year on that farm and lived to the ripe old age of fourteen.

As for me, I'll never forget watching him play with Olive, completely relaxed and himself for probably the first time in his life. It was the last reminder I would ever need that you can never deny the wildness of wild things.

# 7

# Ivan the Terrible

When I first met him, he was just Ivan, the most beautiful German shepherd I had ever seen. He was red with a black saddle in deep, rich colors. He had a finely chiseled head and a massive neck. He was definitely eastern bloc—heavy and thick-boned—but he also had the height and elegance of Rin Tin Tin. I immediately fell in love with him.

Ivan was also massive for a working dog—about 105 pounds—but perfectly proportioned. When we started doing a little bit of testing with him, I saw right away that he was extremely powerful but worked like a seventy-pound dog—quick and agile. If I'd had to give him a nickname that day, it would have been Ivan the Magnificent.

After college, I started importing police dogs from Europe and moved to Atlanta to start my first kennel for training family and estate protection dogs. The kennel quickly became a police dog training facility, and by the early 1990s we were doing pretty well. I had a guy working with me part-time named Karoly Mazeros, a Romanian, who went by the name of Charlie. Charlie was tall and tough and looked a little bit like Dracula—jet-black hair, pale skin, and light blue, almost gray eyes. I'm sure he speaks better English now, but at the time you could barely understand him. He smoked constantly, even when he talked and when he was working the dogs, and always had a cigarette precariously clinging to his bottom lip that I expected to come flying out at any moment.

Charlie was becoming fairly famous at the time as a Schutzhund trainer. Nobody really knew who he was, because he didn't join any of the big Schutzhund clubs and he trained alone. The famous guys who competed at the top levels also put on seminars and sold videotapes and made appearances, but Charlie would just show up at a trial with an Eastern European dog from bloodlines nobody had ever heard of and blow everyone away. He won the national championship a couple of times that way, and he was getting a reputation as someone who had very, very good dogs.

But that wasn't the best thing about Charlie. The best thing was that he had connections in Eastern Europe. Everybody wanted dogs out of the eastern bloc countries, because they were phenomenal police dogs. We had been importing mostly from Germany, but because Schutzhund was becoming so popular over there, the German dogs were getting kind of sporty—not serious about the work because it was never real. The dogs from Eastern Europe had better street temperament—more of a natural balance between prey drive and defensive or fight drive. Sporty dogs have crazy prey drive, which makes them easier to train and to handle, but they don't have a lot of basic fight instinct. Plus, the demand was driving up the prices and a lot of the better German dogs were becoming too expensive for police departments.

Meanwhile, the Czech and Hungarian and Russian dogs really had a better temperament for serious police work. And they cost less, too. The problem was that a lot of the guys in those eastern bloc countries were not entirely honest. Police dogs have to be really healthy: The teeth, hips, eyes, heart all have to be sound before you even get into the whole temperament side of it. The dogs would be X-rayed and examined by a veterinarian before any sale, but sometimes these dishonest brokers would forge the records or show you the X-rays of one dog and then send you a different one. A lot of people who jumped on that eastern bandwagon got taken, because when they had their dog reexamined in the United States he might have a bad hip or two broken teeth, but he was already here and paid for and you could never get in touch with the seller to send him back.

That's where Charlie came in. He had a bunch of buddies over in Romania who were picking out the best dogs and sending them to him. One day he brought over a batch of dogs from Russia, and Ivan was among them. He was so beautiful and had such drive that I wanted him right away. And then Charlie told me he wanted just $1,200 for him (which was very cheap—in those days a green, untrained police dog was going for $2,500 to $3,000 wholesale). I couldn't believe it.

I know what you're thinking: too good to be true. Ivan looked like a $10,000 dog and Charlie couldn't have gotten that great of a deal. But he was a magnificent dog and I *really* wanted him.

He also *loved* to ride in the car. I didn't think anything of it, because lots of dogs like to go for car rides. But one day Ivan jumped into Charlie's car when the door was open and I said, "Charlie, get that dog out of the car. We're going to put him in the kennel because I have another dog I need to work with." And Charlie said, "Well, I need to run to the store real quick. I'll let him come with me and I'll be back in a minute." So he left and came back, then got Ivan out and put him in the kennel. He was only gone about five minutes though, and somewhere in the back of my mind I was thinking, "Wow, that was a quick trip to the store."

A friend of mine, Dave Taylor, who also trained with me, picked up on it and one day he said to me, "Charlie acts a little weird around that dog. What's the story?"

A few days after that, all three of us were going out to lunch. Charlie had his pickup truck and said he'd drive. I had Ivan out, and before I could put him in the kennel, he jumped through the open window into the truck and just sat there like, "Where are we going?" There wasn't enough room for the three of us and the dog, so I said to Charlie, "Get that dog out of there. Come on, let's go." Charlie hesitated and said something half in Romanian and half in English that sounded like, "This dog has a little problem."

And then Charlie reached in the cab to clip a leash on Ivan and the dog was nothing but teeth. He pulled his lips back and was growling as if he was saying, "Don't touch me or I'll eat your heart right out of your chest." Charlie started sweating and said, "Let me just drive him around for a minute." So he got in the car, drove Ivan around for five minutes, came back, opened the door, and said, "Come on out." Ivan got right out and lay on the ground. It seems he had this little quirk: If he got in a car, by God you were taking him somewhere or there was going to be a fight. Think that's how Ivan got his nickname? Guess again.

Years later, Charlie told me how he really got Ivan. That dog had so many weird behaviors and had chewed up so many people that the Russians he dealt with basically told Charlie, "If you buy these other dogs, we're going to give you Ivan for free."

But that was many years later. At the time, even with his car quirk, I was sure I could work with Ivan. A few days later, I took him into Atlanta with me. I was going to PetCo to get one of those barriers that you put across the backseat of your car and crank open so the dog can't jump into the front seat and bother you while you're driving. It was about a forty-five-minute drive, and I put him in the back of my SUV. I left the leash on him and just shut it in the rear door so he couldn't jump over into the front.

As the trucks passed, he started getting wound up and barking at them. Ivan was such a big, heavy dog that the car shook when he barked. I yelled at him to quit barking, and all of a sudden I felt this strange motion in the car. I was going seventy miles an hour down a six-lane highway, but I could feel the car moving in a whole new way. I took a quick look in the back and saw that he had gotten so wound up that he just clamped down on the seat in front of him. I mean, full mouth, bit the top of that seat down to the springs and started shredding the upholstery. By the time I could pull over to the side of the road, he had shredded about three feet of the bench seat in the back. That car was never the same.

When I got back to the kennel, they asked, "Well, how did that barrier work?" I said, "It worked great after I put it in."

Ivan had a mysterious and probably abusive past. Charlie told us some pretty rough stories about the training and treatment a lot of those border patrol dogs had early on. From the beginning, we'd all say, "If that dog could talk, he'd have crazy stories to tell." He reminded me of a war veteran who didn't want to talk about what he'd seen. There was a puzzle to be worked out with Ivan.

One of the things I did know was that he had nightmares. Very few dogs have them, but Ivan would thrash and snarl in his sleep. If you woke him up during one of those dreams, he was liable to leap up and attack you full on. Ivan was definitely wrestling with demons.

There wasn't much I could do to comfort him. But he did find a way to comfort himself. Sometimes he'd lie down, curl up, and stick his rear leg in his mouth, almost like he was trying to chew it off. Except he didn't chew at all. He just whined in a real low whimper and sucked on it like a pacifier. Then he would fall into semi-sleep and suck on it with an intensity that worried me. I would wake him up and check everything, feel all the bones. But he never did hurt his leg, and I could get him to snap out of it pretty easily. When I did snap him out of it, though, he wasn't really back to himself. It was like he was a puppy again and he'd kind of clown around and act goofy.

The behavior seemed like a regression for him. I'd heard that a lot of those big Russian border patrol training places had hundreds of dogs. They basically kept them in a warehouse, and when they weren't being trained, they were just stuck in a box.

So I think sucking on his leg like that was an outlet for his stress. He did it till the day he died. And I never could figure out how to make it better for him.

At the time, police departments wanted dogs who could do narcotics detection work. But the dogs all had some protection training before they came to the United States, and I believed (and still do) that for all working dogs, the more types of training, the better. So we started doing protection work with Ivan. What they were really trying to stress in training for police work was bite and hold dogs. In other words, if the dog did bite, they wanted him to take a nice grip and just hold his man. But that was not Ivan. He was a battle warrior and if he bit somebody, they got hurt. During training, I got a couple of puncture wounds and some deep bruising. But that's not how Ivan got his nickname, either.

Ivan ended up partnering with a police officer named Robert. Robert worked in the city of Lilburn, which is one of those little towns that has been swallowed up by metropolitan Atlanta. Lilburn had 13,000 people and one K-9 police officer whose dog was getting ready to retire. Robert was an experienced K-9 officer and a tough guy. He was about thirty years old, five-ten, 220 pounds, and pumped up. He was serious about his job and intense about his dogs—not a time-card-punching kind of guy. Robert loved Ivan because he was so beautiful and because he had such drive. I worked with him for a little while until I was convinced he could handle this quirky dog, then I sold Ivan to the Lilburn Police Department.

Despite his quirks, I wasn't all that keen to let Ivan go. He was just too spectacular a dog, and I knew someday I'd want to breed him. But he needed to be working. I also knew Robert well and he lived nearby, so I could continue training with Ivan. And I had the department sign a buy-back agreement, which meant when they were done with Ivan, I had the right to buy him back.

I rode around with Robert and Ivan the first two weeks they were on patrol, just to make sure everything was okay. Certainly, I knew there were going to be some problems Robert had to work through. One of them, of course, involved the patrol car. Ivan rode in the back of the car and there was a sliding window that separated him from Robert. Usually, Robert had the window open and Ivan would ride with his head in the opening, resting on Robert's shoulder, and Robert would scratch his chin while they were driving. But when it came time for Robert to shut the window, if he tried to push Ivan back, he'd get bit. Ivan just wanted to keep getting petted, but the bite still hurt. So Robert learned to stick the butt end of his flashlight against Ivan's forehead to push him back. They managed to work it out.

K-9 units of all types—police, search and rescue, military, and the rest—do ongoing training with their dogs, and setting up those sessions was also part of my business. I was in my early twenties then, and I have to admit that a lot of those older cops didn't take very well to some young kid telling them how to train dogs. Especially a kid who wasn't a cop. So I always had to be very diplomatic and learn a lot of tactful ways to teach them things by showing them rather than telling them.

We were doing a multi-jurisdictional training night, which meant we had all the Gwinnette County dogs, which were the best in northeastern Atlanta. They had an active K-9 department—maybe twenty-five dogs. This was about a month after I'd sold Ivan to Robert and they were both there. We were finishing up the narcotics training with Ivan, and in this session we were teaching him to alert to the presence of drugs by scratching when he smelled them. With narcotics training there are two ways the dog can indicate the presence of drugs: passive, where he just sits down calmly, and aggressive, where he scratches at the source of the scent. You teach the dog to do one or the other. The passive indication started with bomb sniffing dogs, because you don't want them scratching at explosives. But nowadays it's prevalent for narcotics dogs, too, partly because of liability issues. A dog can scratch up a person who is carrying drugs on their body, or cause property damage scratching at a hiding spot. Of course, if you find drugs in that hiding spot, there's no longer any liability. But I know of cases where a dog tore up a car indicating a place where drugs had been hours ago. In that situation, the car owner can't be arrested—and can sue the police department.

Passive indication is a stepchild for a working dog, because it's a lot more fun for the dog to do training exercises that keep him excited, and that means he works better. Plus, with an aggressive indication the dog can pinpoint *exactly* where the drugs are. Anyway, in those days they wanted a more aggressive indication. And that suited Ivan just fine.

You keep the dog's intensity up in these scratch drills by using a ball or a toy to get him excited. Then you throw the toy under an overturned milk crate and let the dog go. You praise the dog for scratching at the crate, and when you feel like you've gotten enough scratching out of him (and before he gets frustrated), you pop it open and let him get the toy.

Nobody else wanted to work around Ivan because everybody was already afraid of him, so Robert was holding him and I held the milk crate. I was teasing Ivan from a distance with a tennis ball and then I told Robert, "Let him go," and I tossed the ball under the crate and stood on top of it. Ivan came flying from about twenty feet away and was going at that crate like a boxer on a punching bag. All the time I was petting him and telling him, "Good boy!" But Ivan got frustrated quickly, and finally he just reared back and let out this scream, sort of like a pig. And then, bam!—he locked down on my foot.

The force of it knocked me off the crate. I was lucky that he bit it from side to side, up around the ball of the foot, because I had on steel shank boots and his teeth went into the steel plate. Otherwise, he would have crushed my foot. The problem now was that he was locked down and we could not get him off. I started unlacing my boot, but soon realized he had bitten so hard that he bent the shank and I couldn't get the boot off.

Let me set the scene for you. I was lying on a concrete floor with a 105-pound German shepherd clamped to my foot. Everyone around us was yelling but didn't dare get near Ivan. Robert was almost lying on top of him, verbally correcting him and trying to pull him off. And Ivan had just blocked everybody out. He had gone into his own world, squealing like a little dog and holding me in a vise grip. He wasn't attacking me—he was just venting his frustration about that tennis ball.

I quickly realized all the commotion was making things

worse, so I said, "Robert, ease up; he's about to blow up." Robert gave me Ivan's leash and I sat up to think. Ivan was standing there quivering and continuing to crush my boot in his jaws. I petted him a bit and told him to settle down. That's when my foot really started to hurt and I realized the whole shank was about to give. I grabbed the tennis ball from the crate and put it on top of his nose, hoping he would unclamp my foot and go for the ball. And for a second, his eyes cleared and I almost thought he would. But then he decided, "Nope," and he was back in the twilight zone.

By now a couple of minutes had passed. I was afraid he was going to make a quick little adjustment in his jaws, and then he'd get my boot from top to bottom where there was zero protection except for a little leather, and my foot would be crushed. I told Robert, "You've got to be ready. If he adjusts his grip, you've got to get him off me quick." But that kind of little adjustment happens in a millisecond, and the chances were good that I was going to end up with some broken bones.

Finally, I decided we had to choke him off me. I tossed my end of the leash to another guy, who attached it to a line and slung it over a metal bar. Then Robert pushed the collar right up under Ivan's chin and they lifted him by the leash until his own weight made him light-headed and dizzy. Believe me, this is not my favorite way to handle a situation like that. But I just couldn't see any other way to get him off me.

When I finally got that boot off, the steel shank was so badly bent that I had to throw the thing away. This is not, however, how Ivan got his nickname.

You may be wondering why Robert kept working with a dog

who could not be called off in a high-intensity situation. But the truth is that frustration training is nothing like what happens in real life. If it was a real situation I could have gotten him off me quicker, but it probably wouldn't have been as neat. Because despite the danger, the trainer in me still didn't want Ivan to have any negative experiences with his training. So we took him off with a minimum of rough stuff.

Certainly, Ivan was no fun to work with in a bite suit, because he was so big and powerful and intense. When you're wearing a bite suit, your hands and feet and face are exposed. Still, most dogs see a guy in a bite suit and they know it's a training situation. So they bite when they're told and they let go when they're told, and they keep their bites on the equipment. But Ivan never really had a lot of fun doing bite work; he preferred a fair fight. So there were a couple of times when he came off a bite on the suit and tried to bite someone in the face. A lot of dogs are able to recognize the unreality of the situation and choke back the throttle a little bit during training. But for Ivan, all fights were real. Whether you had a bite suit on or you were standing there in street clothes, he was going to give 100 percent.

In my opinion, back in those days police departments actually needed more dogs like Ivan. They trained with equipment all the time and didn't do any of what we call civil training, which means you do the work in a more realistic setting. They'd end up with dogs who looked great and were well trained, but they'd get out on the street where lives were at risk and the dogs would run up to somebody and be looking for the protective sleeve or the bite suit. When they didn't see it, they would just stand there and bark. That happened thousands of times.

With civil training, you work the same scenario in many different ways. You put a dog in a muzzle and have him attack a guy who is wearing regular street clothes, so the dog learns he's got to try to bite somebody. The good thing about this kind of training is that you can bring out a lot of real dominant aggressive behavior in a dog in a fight, because you can get down on the ground and let him maul you when he's got that muzzle on. You have to be careful, though, because a muzzled dog soon becomes frustrated. So you must quickly spin the dog around, pull off the muzzle, and let him bite someone in a suit. The dog comes away thinking, "Okay, when he tells me to go after somebody, whether they've got street clothes on or not, I've still gotta go get them."

We also have what are called civil suits. They're really thin, tight-fitting sleeves, so you can put a regular jacket over them and let the dog bite that a few times. But with a dog like Ivan, you never had to do any of that. When he was going to get somebody, he was going to get them whether they had equipment on or not. It didn't make any difference to him.

I don't mean to imply that Ivan was out of control. On the contrary, when he got into working mode, he was very reliable, temperament-wise. He did good bite work and he did good narcotics work. He got frustrated real fast, though. If he didn't get what he wanted when we were doing those narcotics drills and other training work, he needed a real reward fairly quickly or else he'd get pissy. And pissy in a 105-pound German shepherd is not something you want to see. So when he got that way, we'd divert his behavior to something else he could bite on.

Ivan was so exceptional in every other way. Plus, he really

liked people and was good around them. He just had a few triggers or quirks that could quickly turn him into a very dangerous dog. Robert knew what they were and avoided altogether any situations that could cause problems. He was completely realistic, and because of that, he was one of the few people I trusted to work with Ivan.

Ivan was gaining a reputation among the police departments in the Atlanta area, too. He was known to be well-mannered and incredibly tenacious, and he was called in to work in tough situations. The local police departments admired and respected him. But Ivan really earned his fame as a street warrior in April 1992, during the riots that followed the acquittal of the police officers in the Rodney King case.

People were sitting in their living rooms watching the riots unfold in Los Angeles on live television. It got some people really fired up, and little mini riots were sparking up all over the major cities, including Atlanta. Somebody had made a false call from the local housing project, asking the police to come and deal with a domestic violence situation. Robert and Ivan responded, along with another officer in a patrol car. Robert left Ivan in the car and the two officers went in.

The housing project was laid out in a U shape—just one way in and out. The address of the call was the last building at the end of the little cul-de-sac. When the officers went to the apartment, though, nobody was there. When they came out, a crowd of about 150 to 200 people had gathered and some people were throwing rocks and bottles at the police cars. The cops were on heightened alert at the time because of what was unfolding in

Los Angeles and all across the country, so they called for backup and stayed inside the building.

As the officers watched, the crowd started rocking the police cars, trying to tip one of them over. Robert was really afraid for Ivan, who was out in the car. He and his partner tried to push their way through the crowd to get to their cars when somebody threw a brick and hit Robert in the head and knocked him down. Most K-9 officers carry an automatic door release that they activate when they leave the dog behind in the car. It's a little radio device that opens the doors of the patrol car so the dog can get out. The device has a level in it (like the tool you use to find a straight line on the wall), so it automatically opens the doors if the officer goes horizontal. It's a way his K-9 partner can protect him. When Robert was knocked down, his release popped the doors and let Ivan out in the middle of that melee.

In the end, they checked eleven people into the hospital for dog bites and Ivan was the only dog there. And they pulled a seven-inch shard of glass from a bottle out from between Ivan's shoulder blades. He had been cut on the foot and kicked and beaten, and he was still fighting when they got him under control.

Most police dogs go their whole career without ever having a full-blown street fight, so for a dog to be in a riot situation and put eleven people in the hospital—well, there's not one in a thousand working police dogs who would have stayed and fought like that. It earned him enormous respect in the law-enforcement community.

And that is how he got his nickname. The *Atlanta Constitution* wrote a story about the riot, and they called him Ivan the Terrible. They did not mean it as a compliment.

Soon after, Ivan's short career as a police dog ended. The department decided he was too much of a liability. He was eight years old at the time (possibly—those Russian documents on dogs were not worth the paper they were written on) and had worked for three years. I remember Robert called me and said, "I've got little kids at home and I just can't keep him as a house dog." So I picked Ivan up and brought him home. I was living by myself at the time and Jill and I had just started dating. Ivan proved to be a great house dog. He was friendly and silly and Jill loved him. But we started discovering more of his strange quirks.

Ivan loved clothes—underwear, T-shirts, and things like that. He'd go into the laundry room or my closet and get something and walk around with it for a while. Then he'd stand up, step on it with both of his front paws, and use his mouth to shred it into little pieces. I remember one time I was on the phone and he walked into the room dragging one of my T-shirts in his mouth. He bent down and started to rip it up, so I yelled, "Hey, quit that." He whipped around on me in a millisecond and body blocked me in the chest and was all teeth, like, "Don't do that."

Bottom line: Ivan could sometimes be a punk. "I want what I want and I'm going to throw a tantrum if I don't get it." But him throwing a tantrum meant people getting hurt. He was like a little kid when he didn't get his way, rather than the tough, elegant dog he was when he was working. When he'd act out, like the time he was shredding my underwear, it was like a five-year-old throwing a fit when they didn't get the toy they wanted from the store.

I think the thing that made him unique was that he could be such a serious work dog, but he was just as happy being a party dog, hanging around with the guys watching the Super Bowl. He was almost bipolar. Lex and a lot of the other high-level working dogs I had just wanted to work. That's what made them happy. Lex was a horrible house dog, not because he tore things up, but because he never could relax. He'd pal around with you for a little bit, but then it was, "Come on, let's go *do something!*" He'd stand there and just pace back and forth. Ivan was unusual in that he had an off switch. When it was work time, there was no more intense dog than him—ever. But when it was over it was over, and he instantly switched to couch potato. There was a real clown in him and people quickly fell in love with that. I had other dogs at the time, but everybody just loved Ivan.

He had a great, kind of frat boy sense of humor, too. He reminded me of the kind of guy who comes up behind you and hits you in the knees to make you fall down when you are standing in church—just to make you laugh. I remember one day I hadn't played with him much, and he was lying on the other side of the room just watching me while I studied. I had started studying for my real estate license then and I was working two jobs, and sometimes Ivan didn't get all the attention he felt he deserved. I could feel him staring at me, and I looked up at him and said, "What are you looking at?" He just went "Rrrr." I went back to my studying, and when I looked up again, he was lying in exactly the same position but about three steps closer. The next time I looked up, he launched into a full pounce and dove on me. My papers went flying and he knocked me out of the chair and started nuzzling my neck and face and kind of tickling me. It's like he was saying, "You are not going to ignore me!"

When Ivan was not working he was a big lounge lizard. He was a lot of fun just as a buddy to take out to the park or go to the river or just hang out and watch TV. I'd lie on the floor and he'd lie on top of me and start nuzzling and wanting me to pet him. Some of my working dogs weren't any fun that way, but he had no trouble relaxing and just being a silly dog.

And that's what was so strange about him. If he had been a more serious dog, his behavior quirks would not have been such a contradiction. What made them stand out is that otherwise he was such a playful, goofy dog. Sometimes I'd be sitting on the couch and he'd pounce on me and start licking my face, and I'd push him down on the ground and get him down in a headlock and roll around with him. He loved all that stuff. But trying to push him into the backseat of a car, or pull him out of one, could be dangerous. I have to admit, he was the strangest dog I've ever had. And I do always wonder about how he got that way.

There have been some new studies saying dogs don't remember anything past about two weeks. I absolutely believe dogs remember things beyond two weeks, but I also think it's easier than people imagine to replace habits born out of bad memories with new habits. It's not that dogs don't remember, but they have an amazing ability to get over it and move on to the next chapter of their lives. Everyone has either had a dog or knows a dog whom they interacted with at one time and who remembers them months or even years later. I've seen many of the dogs I've trained at Schutzhund trials, and years later I can go up to them and handle them the same way I always did. Of course those dogs remember me. Dogs just don't carry emotional baggage around with them all their lives.

For example, many people are getting dogs now from rescue organizations, and some of them have had an abusive or difficult past. I'm not saying that has no effect on the dog, but I do think people put too much stock in what a dog's previous life was like. They end up nurturing all the dog's fears and unpleasant memories, because *we* would have a hard time letting go of them. It seems as if when we know those histories, we project what our human story would be like onto the dog. It's almost better if you don't know the dog's history. Then you just work on whatever problems he's having and you end up helping the dog get over it.

To live with a dog like that, you have to know him really well, and you have to outsmart him. And to outsmart him, you have to remember that a lot of behavior quirks are based on context. A good example is the dog who is typically very friendly with people, good with strangers when you meet them at the park or even when they come over to your house, but tries to bite everyone who handles him at the veterinarian's office. That's an example of contextual behavior that most people are familiar with. Almost everyone I know has had a dog or known a friend's dog who is the nicest dog in the world, but turns into a monster when you take him to the vet.

The thing is, when a dog is experiencing extreme stress or fear, he takes in all of his surroundings and you never know which part of it he will ultimately associate with that negative experience. In other words, some dogs might react to the smell of a vet's office, some to the metal table in the exam room, and some to the sight of a syringe.

I found this out with Lex. He was great at the vet. He would stand quietly and let people give him shots, and I wouldn't even have to muzzle him or hold his head—as long as we stood outside. Take him inside the clinic and put him on that metal table with those vet office smells and he would get stiff and growl and show his teeth. He was cranked up and ready to go off on whoever got closest to him.

They had a waiting room full of dogs and cats and I just didn't want to take him in there and run the risk of somebody trying to pet him, because I knew he was going to be wound up. So the next time he needed shots, I called my vet and said, "Just meet me out in the parking lot." The vet gave him two injections and he barely moved; this is the same vet who, if we stepped inside the door and he attempted to touch Lex, that dog would have tried to kill him.

Somehow, Lex formed some kind of negative association with the textures and the smells in that building. And in fact, we see that a lot in police dogs. Before they are sold, they all have to have their hips X-rayed to certify that they are sound. In the United States, when we take a dog in for that kind of hip X-ray, he is sedated. But a surprisingly high percentage of dogs are sensitive to anesthesia. In Eastern Europe, they didn't want to take the chance that the dog might have an allergic reaction—plus they didn't want to spend the money for the anesthesiologist. So they'd get two big guys in, and the dog was muzzled and held down on a steel table. They flipped him on his back and one guy held his rear legs while the other guy held his front legs so he was all stretched out, and then the big X-ray machine was lowered over him. Imagine how traumatizing that is for a dog. And they can't do it until after the dog is a year old (because before that the dog is still growing), so he is still young, but old enough to really remember it. For many of those dogs, that was their first and only trip to the veterinarian. So getting up on a steel table at the vet's office probably makes dogs like Lex remember one of the most helpless, traumatic experiences of their lives.

But with all four feet on the ground, out in the parking lot, in a place Lex was used to, a little needle was no big thing. So from then on, for the rest of Lex's life, if I had any simple procedures that needed to be done at the vet's office, we'd just do it outside and Lex would stand there calm as you please.

Circumstance is a very powerful thing to dogs, and you can see entirely different types of behavior with the same animal in a different setting. I once had a crazy Malinois named Rico who competed quite successfully in Schutzhund. He was really difficult to deal with, and aggressive if you got near his crate or his food. But I could walk him onto a Schutzhund field anywhere and watch his eyes flicker. He turned into a completely different dog—easy to work with, compliant, a working machine. I could put my hands all over him and get away with a lot of corrections that, had I done them off the field, he would have eaten me alive.

Of course, about 95 percent of the time it's the opposite: The field is where the dog gets cranked up and more aggressive, but the point is still the same. How many people have nice, easygoing dogs whom everybody loves at home, but who turn into monsters when you take them to the park or for a walk? They act one way on their home turf and another way when they're out and about. It's important to understand that when you see a dog act a certain way, you have to consider that the setting may be responsible for the change.

So many people have told me they adopted a dog and the shelter or rescue group or friend they got him from swore he was housetrained. But they get him home and he pees on everything. Let me tell you something: "Housetrained" is a relative term. It means the dog is housetrained to that piece of turf he's been going on, and that's it. Now the odds are that if a housetrained dog has been going on grass, when you take him to a new home he's going to naturally seek out grass. But don't count on it. In a dog's mind, every home is a clean slate. If he doesn't have the exact same place to pee on, he might as well pee anywhere.

That will also happen if you move to a new home. Because the truth is that housetraining is a matter of habit and territory. Habit is about the surface—grass or a concrete floor or whatever. At the same time, not soiling your home turf is a territorial thing. If you take a dog to a new territory, why should he care about that?

The take-home lesson here is twofold. First, don't assume that your dog will generalize what he knows. Walking on a leash in your neighborhood streets is not the same as walking on a leash in the park. You need to teach your dog the same skills in a variety of settings. Second, when you have a dog who has an extreme reaction in a particular situation, change as many variables as you can, switch it up a little bit, and see what happens. You may be surprised at the results you get.

Ivan stayed with me until he was twelve. I had a friend who lived on a 1,200-acre family farm full of cows and horses, and he was great with dogs. He had been begging me for Ivan for a year, and I eventually relented. Especially since I was about to get married, and I just didn't trust Ivan around other people. I was going to be moving to a small place where he was going to have a small yard and not much opportunity to do anything. And meanwhile, this guy was going to be there all the time and really loved Ivan. And Ivan liked him, too.

Ivan the Terrible lived out his days riding around in a truck, checking on the farm, ruling the house and everything in it. I still have never seen a tougher or more beautiful dog.

# 8

# Bart and Tico

Bart and Tico. They're forever connected in my mind. I can't think of one dog without thinking of the other. In fact, they turned out to be inseparable—but not in a good way. I'll explain in a little bit, but first, let me introduce them individually.

Tico was the poster dog for the virtues of early socialization. He'd been raised in Hilversum, Holland, and by the time I met him he was working with Gerard, a dog training veteran and the father-in-law of Remco Whitkamp, one of the most famous protection dog decoys in Holland and a good friend of mine. Remco had been selected several times to be a decoy in the KNPV (Royal Dutch Police Dog Association) national championships, which is sort of like being chosen to referee the Super Bowl. Only the best get to do it, and I learned a lot of my decoy skills from Remco.

Gerard had seven grandkids, and he used to go over to his

son's house with Tico and let those grandkids play with him in whatever way they negotiated among themselves. I remember the first time I saw the dog, Gerard walked into his son's house, no leash on Tico, and the dog stood out in the middle of the room while the kids climbed up on the couch and jumped on top of him. Tico was clearly enjoying himself, and I thought it was pretty amazing.

He was great with other dogs, too, because Gerard was semi-retired and spent a good part of his day visiting around and cadging cups of coffee. He'd walk into people's houses—guys who also trained KNPV dogs—with Tico off leash, and they'd have their two or three big Malinois or German shepherds and all of them would just get along. Maybe the dogs would growl a little bit, so the guys would say, "Hey, shut up!" and it was over.

Gerard and Tico also worked four nights a week patrolling a busy shopping mall in Amsterdam. They took the commuter train to work, an hour and a half each way, and then spent their shift going up and down escalators and in elevators, which is great socialization for a dog.

Gerard was definitely old school when it came to dog training and had been very harsh with Tico early on. He wasn't that big of a guy, but he was notorious for being tough. If he got into an argument, it wasn't long before he started throwing punches. Everybody knew he had a red hot temper, and people did not talk back to him. Remco had a bit of a temper, too, but he was a lot more controlled. Suffice it to say, things were not always rosy between father and son-in-law.

Even in Holland, where hard handling was the norm, people thought Gerard was kind of abusive. In fact, his nickname was "the kicker." So when I first saw Tico, he spent his time around Gerard in a little bit of a crouch with his tail half tucked. When I finally bought him at age three and a half, I spent a lot of time building him up. He was such a great dog and so full of himself as a pet, but when I'd start working him I would see the pressure of those memories and he would be waiting for the boot to hit. It took me about two years of really working with him, not putting heavy corrections on him and freeing him up with a lot of fun work and a lot of praise, before he completely came around. The change was pretty amazing, too. When I got him from Holland he weighed about eighty-five pounds, and by the time I had him two years, not only had he put on some weight, but I swear he was taller, too. His whole working demeanor had changed; he was happier and he enjoyed the work.

I think it was a testament to his personality that he could survive a handler like Gerard. With some dogs, that style of training breaks down their confidence. But Tico had been blessed with a great genetic makeup, and that, combined with his life-long socialization, made him a dog with a deep sense of confidence about anything that might come up. He was a super working dog and a wonderful companion.

Tico was the sort of dog who could be a precision instrument in a police seminar and a wrecking machine in a field trial, but then I could bring him to a talk I was giving at my wife's school and take him off the leash with 300 little kids around and know he was 100 percent reliable. I'd see him with kids riding on his back, hanging on to his head in a headlock, and he'd actually grin and nuzzle them for more. If they did anything that really hurt, he'd just step out of the way.

But I don't want you to think Tico was a marshmallow. He just knew when to be tough and when not to be. He proved that the day the wrong guy came to our house. Jill, my wife, never had (and still doesn't have) any interest in working the dogs. There have been times I just needed her to hold a dog's leash for a moment while I was working him, but she doesn't want to have any part of it. She likes the dogs, but the protection aspect is just not her thing.

At the time I had Bart and Tico, we lived on a busy country road. One day Jill was home alone and she heard a banging on the door. She looked outside and in the driveway was this old, beat-up, windowless van. The driver had been banging on the side door and now he was walking around to the front of the house. He had no shirt on, was covered in tattoos, and looked really creepy. Frankly, the guy scared her—and Tico picked up on that immediately. In the front of our house we had a regular wooden door and then a full-length glass door, and when Jill got to the front, this guy was standing at the glass door, banging on it.

Tico came unglued. He started bouncing off the door, trying to take the glass out. Jill had never seen him explode like that before. He was not really barking; it was more like he was growling a deep, scary rumble and foaming at the mouth. (When I got home, there was spit all over the glass at face height.) Jill grabbed his collar just to keep him from breaking the door, and Tico was pulling so hard he was off his front feet. He wanted to get that guy and was going to do whatever it took.

The guy turned white, held up his hands, and quickly ran back to his car and drove away. As soon as he did, Tico settled down, although he was still on alert. Jill was amazed, because she never gave Tico a command. He just sensed her fear and went to work. Before that happened, whenever I was out of town she would put Tico in the kennel and bring Bart into the house, because Bart didn't really like anybody. But now she knew either dog would protect her.

Tico was an explosive worker, but he was also a big, goofy dog—kind of like the Marmaduke comic strip. This was back in the 1990s, when the Malinois as a breed was just starting to be really accepted in the United States as a superior working dog in law enforcement. Now, a typical Malinois looks a bit like a svelte version of a German shepherd with a shorter coat. Tico had the Malinois coloring—cream with a black muzzle—but he was not a pure Malinois. He had a Great Dane two generations back, which made him really tall and a bit gangly. And there was a bullmastiff somewhere in his pedigree, too, so he was very substantial with a broad chest. A good-size male Malinois is seventy pounds, but Tico always weighed right around hundred pounds.

He was a clown like Marmaduke, too. As he got more confident, he developed this walk where he'd prance like a Tennessee walking horse, picking his front feet up high and nodding his head in the same rhythm as his step. He was just so full of himself. If I had ten dogs out from my kennel, Tico was the one everybody wanted to be with. He was funny, he had a lot of energy, he loved people, and he craved attention.

Bart, on the other hand, was a dog without a sense of humor. I got Bart from Holland when he was about ten months old, and he had not really had any training. Bart was a Dutch shepherd, but he had some other things mixed in. Certainly, he had some pit bull in him—if you cut his head off and stuck it on a pit bull, it would match up perfectly. His ears stood up, though, like a Dutch shepherd, and he was tall and lean, so there was definitely something else in the mix. Dutch shepherds are black with a brown brindle pattern, but the brindle was so faint in Bart that from fifteen feet away you couldn't even see it.

In some ways, Bart was a cat in a dog's body. He was a stalker and a pouncer, a great hunter. He never did police work, even though he had the mechanics of it down perfectly and was not afraid of anything. His personality was just no good for the street. He was too quiet. Most police dogs are really loud— because barking is part of the intimidation factor. But if Bart got into a fight, he was going to hurt somebody; he wasn't going to do a hold and bark, because he realized early on that if they could hear him coming, they would either get ready or get away. So, just like a cat, he learned that silent stalking was the best way to get what he wanted.

Unlike Tico, who was big and intimidating and loud and so scary looking that he sent chills up your spine, Bart never exploded. Everything with him was stealthy, and I think it actually made him scarier. He would sit there and look at you with his cold eyes and pull his lips back and show you all his teeth. He'd barely even growl. It was plenty intimidating, but not in the explosive way police departments were looking for.

On the other hand, Bart would have been a great SWAT dog. I remember I saw a video of a police SWAT team with a dog who would crawl on his belly and sneak up on the bad guys. So I started training Bart for SWAT duty. He loved it.

Still, Bart was not shy about expressing himself. He just did it silently. If he was standing near someone he didn't really like, he would get right in front of them and shove his muzzle up between their legs and look right up at them with a look that said, "If I open my mouth, you're castrated." I can remember at least a dozen times when I had to tell him to cut that out.

I remember when Remco was doing some seminars in the United States and came to visit me. I'd told him about Bart, and he wanted to do some decoy work with him. The dog did fine, but when we were done and Remco took his bite suit off, he said to me, "There's something not right about him. I think there's a little evil in that dog."

In fact, a lot of times Bart was a big punk. I remember he did not take to my dad at all. My father is not a dog person, but he is a very intimidating man. When you meet him for the first time, you can tell right away that he's very forceful. It's hard to describe, because Dad's not a mean guy. His personality is just very commanding, and dogs pick up on that.

I remember one time I was out on Dad's farm with him and Bart and a female dog. Dad and I were walking side by side down the trail, and the dogs would come from behind and run past us going really fast, chase each other, and then come around and run back the other way. Bart started coming up from behind us and targeting Dad—he'd launch himself into the air and just brush Dad, shoulder to shoulder. One time he did it and I guess he misjudged, because he clipped Dad pretty good in the shoulder and knocked him forward. Dad yelled, "Hey!" in an aggressive way. As soon as Bart hit the ground, he spun around and was all up in Dad's face like, "Are you talking to me?!" Two tough guys squaring off. I told Bart to cool it.

Bart was also impatient, and that was always a problem in training. He would do great for about ten or fifteen minutes, and then he'd just had enough. In fact, he was like that with everything. Even me. Bart was one of those dogs who took a long time to warm up to anyone. He bonded very deeply, but affection made him just as impatient as everything else. His loving came in half-minute bursts. I might be sitting in a chair watching TV or reading and he would come up and nuzzle my hand with his head, and I'd pet him for thirty seconds. Then he'd walk off. As he got older, if I was lying on the floor watching TV he would come lie down against me and roll on his back for me to scratch his belly. But the truth was that Bart was very uncomfortable being in a submissive position like that, and he growled a little bit the whole time. If I sat up, that was too much looming over him and he'd snarl and get up. It seemed to me Bart was just a tortured little soul—although I never did figure out why.

In a way, I guess you could say Bart was the anti-Tico and Tico was the anti-Bart. Of course, they also had a lot in common. Both were imported from Holland, where they were raised in a sort of rough and ready way. Both were mixed breeds, designed to be the best possible working dogs rather than to have pristine pedigrees. Both lived in my house and were trustworthy with my family. And, because of their excellent early socialization in Holland, both were fine with other dogs, even unneutered males. That was especially true of Tico, who did bite work together with Arras (whom you'll meet later on). But Bart was also fine in the house with other males, even dominant ones.

The other thing they had in common was that they hated each other with a passion I had never seen before—right from the day they met. Nothing happened to set it off: no incident with food or a toy or anything. I just brought Tico home and the two of them instantly went at it. I don't mean they got in a bad fight, I mean it got to the point where both of them were on life support at the vet. They were a snarly, scary ball of tearing teeth. Twice, they almost killed each other.

It was one of those things you have to chalk up to bad chemistry. They just did not like each other from the get-go. And it was always that way. Bart brought out a side of Tico I never saw when he was with any other dog. Tico would sometimes get another dog riled up just for a goof, but he always walked away before things got too hot. Not with Bart, though. Those two hated each other, and neither ever backed down. They had a "let's fight to the death" thing their entire lives.

When you have several dogs, you can't assume they're all going to love each other just because they all love you. You have to figure out which combinations work. I had a Dutch shepherd puppy I was raising at the time and, surprisingly, Tico, who was usually such a friendly dog, was a real bully with that puppy. Meanwhile, Bart was super gentle with him and would lie on his back and let the puppy jump all over him, even when the pup got to be very big. It just goes to show that different personality combinations will bring out sides of your dog you didn't expect. If I was making predictions, I would have pegged Tico for the nurturing one. But it turned out to be Bart.

What makes a dog acceptable—or unacceptable—to another dog is something we can never really understand. We have a tendency to think that if a particular dog has ever been in a fight, he is dog-aggressive and can never be trusted near another dog. The reality is far more complex, because he may be trustworthy around some dogs but not others. And you'll never know how he decides which is which.

As a trainer, accepting this has been hard for me, because I'm the kind of person who likes to fix things. But you just have to be willing to let some things go. When you're dealing with animals, there's a certain level at which we cannot know them.

Another thing to consider about dogs who are aggressive with other dogs is that sometimes the handler is the one who triggers the aggression. Maybe you see another male dog approaching and you tense up a little bit, expecting a problem. Remember, tension travels right down the leash, and your dog picks up on your bad vibes and goes on alert. Then your dog's change in posture sends a signal to the other dog that he's ready to fight, and it all snowballs out of control.

Or it might be that your dog snaps at another dog and you think, "Cool! I have the toughest dog in town and the other dogs are afraid of him." You might be thinking this on a deep subconscious level, but your body language still reflects that. It's not that dogs can read our minds, but remember, they *evolved* to read our body language. They're very, very good at it. The next time you approach a dog, your dog knows his aggressive reaction will get some satisfying body language out of you. So he lunges.

Dogs also mistranslate things across the board. All kinds of nervous energy, from anticipation to excitement to dread, translates into a red flag for dogs, because the nervous energy is all they pick up on. The different kinds of nervousness we display can almost always be interpreted by the dog as, "Watch out! Something's getting ready to happen."

Never forget that dogs always look to us for cues. They only get it wrong when we inadvertently give them the wrong cue, or when they are trying to figure things out on their own. When that happens, sometimes they make the wrong choice. But when they look to us for cues, they are not going to make the wrong choice because we are going to tell them what the right choice is. That means we give clear commands and convey clear expectations of what we want—not a mixed bag of nervousness and tension.

With Bart and Tico, people would ask me, "Which dog will you get rid of?" But it's like divorced parents: If you love both of your parents and they can't be together, that doesn't mean your relationship with each one of them individually has to be over. So Bart and Tico became a management issue. Dealing with an issue like that begins with accepting who your dogs are and understanding that you've got a problem, and then finding a safe way to manage it.

Looking back on it now, the constant management was stressful for both me and Jill. But at the time, we just incorporated it into our routine. We had a long porch that went into a covered carport, and one day Bart and Tico had a little blowup out there when Jill was home alone. Very quickly they got tied up in a ball of dogfight, so Jill threw a blanket over them both and then opened the front door. They let go for a moment and Tico came out from under the blanket. Jill just put her foot on Tico, shoved him through the door, and slammed it shut.

To avoid these kinds of incidents, we figured out a rotation system where I would have one in the house and one in the kennel, then the next day the outside dog came in and the inside dog went out. All this time I had several other dogs, and Bart and Tico could mix with all of them. Sometimes there were four dogs sleeping in our bedroom at night; the only variation in the pack was whether Bart or Tico was joining us.

I did a lot of training with Bart and Tico to get them to relax around each other. I finally got them to the point where I could walk them together with one dog on one side of me and one on the other, and they didn't even look at each other. I could have them both on leash in the same room, too, and no fights broke out. After that had been going on for about a month, I was feeling pretty good about myself. Johnny super trainer.

What was really happening, though, was that they were tolerating each other as long as I was standing there, because they had to. The animosity between them hadn't changed at all, but it's like each was saying to me, "I'm not going to look at him just because you are standing over me." It's important to understand that management is for the life of the dog. There are some things you are never going to change. I learned that one the hard way.

One Sunday afternoon, Jill and I drove Bart and Tico over to this piece of property my dad owns for a long walk. I had them on long lines and things were going really well. They were tolerating each other, just running around with each doing his own thing. So I let them off the lines. They ran around for a second and then Tico went over and picked up a stick. Bart ran to grab the same stick, and it was like a bomb going off.

The two of them got tangled up in a big ball of snapping

teeth. Bart bit Tico on the chest and locked down like a pit bull and Tico had Bart's whole head in his mouth. I ran over there and tried to separate them (Caution! Do not try this at home!). I spent about thirty minutes trying all the ways I know to break up a dogfight, including going back to the car for blankets and other equipment to use to pry them apart—none of which worked. I finally ended up having to choke Bart unconscious with his collar. By then Tico was almost unconscious anyway because he had lost so much blood. Bart had more than hundred puncture wounds on his head and face and Tico had a hole in his chest that was so big I could put my thumb in it. It had cut one of his arteries and I had my thumb and forefinger inside Tico's chest pinching that artery shut.

It was the worst dogfight I have ever seen in my life. I remember I went back the next day to that property and there was blood spread everywhere over about a twenty-square-foot area. During all my work with the police I've seen my share of crime scenes, but I've never seen anything like that. I was horrified.

It was touch and go for a while at the vet's office. Both dogs eventually recovered, but Bart was never really the same after that. His head swelled up so bad that he had swelling in his brain, and it did change him a little bit. He wasn't more fearful or aggressive, it just seemed to age him. He lost his stamina and his drive to work.

It was a very painful reminder for me that I can never assume I've fixed something. By then, I'd had both dogs for years. It wasn't like some stray ran up and picked a fight with my dog—they were both my dogs and I loved them.

Maybe you've been thinking, from the way I described them,

that Tico was the better, more lovable dog. But that wasn't the case. They had totally different personalities, and they brought out different handlers in me. But the truth is, I loved them both equally.

Tico was Mr. Versatile. He could do anything with anyone. He was just one of those dogs who was along for the ride. He was a lot of fun and everybody loved him, he commanded attention and could be a total clown. But there was no denying him the other way; he could be a great working dog. He was big and powerful and had a lot of drive. There were decoys who refused to work him in a bite suit because he was a leg biter and leg bites can be really painful. When he was in working mode, he was tough as nails.

I loved the fact that he had the ability to wear different hats, and I loved his phenomenal energy and his inner will to be able to overcome his abusive past and not be scarred by it.

I once took him to a competition in the United States that we had organized using the same rules as the Dutch KNPV trials. We flew over one of their top judges and two decoys from Holland, and four or five top Dutch trainers came to see what was going on and to sell a few dogs over here. The judge was from the same city where Tico was raised, Hilversum. When the trial was over and they were handing out the awards, that judge asked me to bring Tico up on the podium. He was standing at the microphone and said, "I want everybody to know that I've known this dog since he was a puppy. I trained with him in his club, I know his owner who raised him, and today before me I see a different dog. Always in Holland the dog's tail was under his legs and he was a little bit afraid of the handler. But here I see a dog who is full of himself and he's a much better dog than he was in Holland. The dog was a good biting dog over there, but I see a force of power in him today that I never saw over there."

It was an amazing statement. The Dutch generally believe they sell great dogs to the Americans and we ruin them. They work their dogs in well-established clubs four times a week and we just don't have that opportunity here in the States, so it's true that imported dogs usually don't work as crisply two years later. But what that judge said confirmed for me—and for all the Dutch trainers and decoys who were there—that the way I was training was absolutely effective. It opened a lot of doors for me in Holland and was the reason I was able to get Arras (more about him Chapter 10). And I owe that to Tico and his amazing resiliency.

It's not as easy to explain what I loved about Bart. His personality was just an anomaly. It's rare to find a dog with absolutely no sense of humor, but everything seemed to make Bart kind of mad and grumpy. Not mean, but a lot like a grouchy old man. Sometimes when he got that way, Jill would say, "Oh, Bart, come here," and she'd make him stand still for a hug. He'd be grumbling the whole time, too.

I felt sorry for Bart a lot of times, like he was the wrong dog in the wrong body. It made me feel very protective toward him. But it wasn't just that. What I loved about Bart was that he had such a quiet strength and confidence. There was just no backing up with him. He was always so sure of himself, and so strong and silent, almost like a rock. If he was there, he didn't have to jump up and down in front of you and make a big show. But there was no mistaking when he was in the house; when he walked in, he was *there*.

He was loyal, too. I knew that he actually loved me to his core, even though it didn't manifest itself in that hug-me-pet-me kind of thing. He didn't need that. But there was such an unspoken bond with the two of us, and I appreciated that aspect of him. There is certainly something to be said for a dog who's a pet whore—one who lets everybody pet him and wants everybody to love him up. That was one of Tico's great attributes. But (and maybe this is a guy thing) there is something ego-boosting about having a dog who likes only you and nobody else. It makes you feel special. And that's how it was with Bart and me.

I'm going to tell you two stories about Bart. Both of them will tell you a lot about his heart, but in very different ways.

I'd been doing my radio show in Jackson, Tennessee, for several years when this first story took place. It was about 1997 or '98, and I was at the peak of my police dog work. I hosted a lot of regional seminars back then, sometimes with as many as hundred canine teams, and there had been some newspaper stories about that. So I was pretty well known.

One day this guy called me and said, "I saw something about your police dogs and I've got a German shepherd. I have to get rid of him; he's just too tough. So I'm thinking that if you could tame him down, he'd make a good police dog." The guy was probably in his early to mid-thirties, and was calling from a little town called Prezzant—it's hardly even a town really, just a stop sign in the road—and he was real country. I got those kinds of calls all the time, but most American-bred German shepherds just can't cut the mustard in police work, so I was only half listening.

Then he said something that got my attention: "I need to get rid of him because he's bitten and attacked a bunch of different people, and the last time he attacked somebody it was my cousin and he had to get more than two hundred stitches." I thought, "Okay, that's not a little run-over-and-bite-you-on-the-ankle type bite. A dog who can give somebody two hundred stitches got into a genuine brawl." I was interested.

We talked a bit and I told him I would come and take a look at the dog and do a standard courage test. He asked, "Now what exactly do you want to do?" I told him, "I'm going to put on a bite suit and pull up to the front of your driveway, then I'm going to call you on my cell phone and tell you to come out with the dog. I want you to come out on the front porch and just sit there, but don't tell the dog to come after me. Don't encourage it, but don't discourage it, either. You try and be passive and just let the dog go."

Then he said, "Tell me about this bite suit thing." I described it, and he asked, "What kind of a helmet do you have?" I said, "Well, I'm not going to have a helmet at all." The guy said, "No, no, no, you don't understand. This dog, he's a flying alligator. He'll bite your face off."

It turned out that he and his father owned the local tough-guy pool hall bar—the only one in Prezzant. The only way he'd agree to me doing the test was if I met him in town at the bar first, where he was going to have this big liability waiver in which I was signing my life away so I didn't sue him when the dog disfigured me. That should have clued me in to what was really going on, but I didn't get it quite yet.

I called one of my old training partners, Dave Taylor. At the time, Dave was living in Nashville. I told him the whole story, ending with, "This guy actually called the dog a flying alligator." Dave couldn't stop laughing. Finally he said, "Oh my God, you've got to take me with you because I have to see this."

When we drove over there, I brought Bart along in a crate in the back of the truck, because I figured I might need to show them the kind of things I look for in a police dog. Dave and I met this guy in town at his bar. It was filled with the usual assortment of pool hall tough guys, their hair lank and greasy and their shirtsleeves rolled up to reveal an assortment of biker tattoos. The owner was drawing up his liability waiver. He said, "Maybe tonight, if you all are still around town, you can come by because they are going to want to hear the story of this. Everybody knows about this dog in three counties."

Then he wanted me to show him the bite suit. When I did, he just shook his head and said, "Man, you are crazy. I just don't feel good about this. This dog, he's a flying alligator. I mean, he's going to tear your face off and you're crazy to do this." It played well to the crowd. I just said, "Let me worry about that."

The guy's house was up on a hill and there was a long tree-lined drive to get up there. I stopped partway up the drive, pulled on the bite suit, and took out a clatter stick. That's a piece of bamboo about three feet long that's split most of the way down into about ten pieces. When you shake it, all the pieces clatter together and it makes a lot of noise. You don't hit the dog with it—it's just a noisemaker. We use it because it's very distracting and really tests a dog's nerves.

Dave and I pulled up to the driveway, which was about 200 yards down a wooded hill from the house—which meant the dog was going to be coming downhill at me and picking up steam while I was running uphill. I called the guy and told him, "You are going to hear me yelling when your dog comes after me, but that's just me trying to intimidate him to see how he reacts." At this point, the guy said he was going to call an ambulance for me.

I got out of the car and could hear the dog barking. I started walking up the hill and the dog looked at me awhile. Suddenly, he realized I was coming up to the porch and he took off with a "Grrrrrrr!" I just kept walking like he wasn't even there. He was coming on pretty fast, and when he got about fifty or sixty yards from me, I started running straight at him, clattering the stick and yelling at him. Suddenly his voice went up the scale—an indication of the stress on him. Finally, when he got to the point where we were going to have to engage, he put the brakes on and his whole body posture changed. His ears were forward, his tail was up, and his hair was standing on end. He was showing all his teeth. Sheer terror. And he was squealing like a piglet.

I'm pretty sure I know what was going through his mind right then. "Why is this guy not running away? I made everyone else turn and run, what's the matter with him?" I stopped, but I didn't back up. He kept trying to go around behind me, and I kept turning and keeping him in front of me. He'd never seen anyone act that way before, and he was reaching his breaking point.

Dave had gotten out of the car and was standing down the hill, laughing. For anyone who knew dogs, the point had been made. But the dog was still running around me in circles, barking, and I knew those guys wouldn't realize how defeated the dog was. Dave gave me the thumbs-out sign, like, "Go ahead and drive the point home." So I went after the dog.

He started backpedaling. I ended up chasing that dog all the way up to the house. The whole family had gathered on the porch to watch the carnage, and he ran right around them to the back of the house and hid in the garage.

The guy and his father were absolutely speechless. They couldn't believe what had just happened. And that's when I realized they had never wanted to sell the dog to me. They just wanted to be able to go to the bar that night and say, "That big shot from Jackson, the police dog guy, came out here and my dog cleaned his clock." They were pretty mad.

Then they started making excuses. "Well, it was that you had that big suit on. If you didn't have that stick, he wouldn't have done that. No dog would go after a guy with that big suit on and that stick." I told them, "That dog never had anybody stand up to him before, and he didn't know what to do. He's really a very fearful dog and he's biting out of fear." Man, they didn't want to hear that!

They were pissing me off now, so I got Bart out of the back of the truck. Dave put on the suit and took the clatter stick, and he started yelling and running at Bart from about sixty yards out. Well of course, Bart started running toward Dave, not even barking. Dave was going good with the stick and yelling at the top of his lungs, and Bart was running full speed. When they got about fifteen feet apart, Bart left the ground and just about broke Dave's ribs. I mean, Dave's a very experienced decoy and never gets knocked down, but Bart hit him so hard that he knocked him right back.

We did it three or four more times. Then I asked Dave to take the suit off and Bart walked around Dave all cool and calm, and

Dave patted him on the head. I wanted these guys to see what a stable temperament a real police dog has. He can make decisions and follow directions without showing aggression. I knew they didn't think such a thing was possible, and I wanted them to see otherwise. As I walked off to put Bart in the car, I asked them, "What time do y'all open up the bar tonight so I can come by and tell everyone the story?"

My other story about Bart is not as easy to understand. In fact, I have to admit it mystifies me. After all the dogs I've worked with, I still can't explain it.

When this took place, we were living on the farm in Jackson. We had several hundred acres and my neighbor had about 600 acres, so a lot of the time I had the dogs off leash and running around. Sometimes one of the dogs would take off for five minutes or so, but he'd always come back. If he didn't, I'd send some of the other dogs out looking for him and they'd always bring him back. But one day Tico, who never, ever roamed, took off and didn't return.

Because of my radio show, everyone in Jackson knew me, and I asked all my listeners to be on the lookout for Tico. Some of the other shows on that station also made announcements. I put up posters and a piece appeared in the local newspaper. I knew all the cops in the area, too, so they were all on the lookout for him. I even offered a $5,000 reward, so I was pretty sure if somebody found him they would give him back.

At the time, I had Tico and Bart on a rotation schedule—each spent every other day in the house. Bart was very much of a homebody, so when he was outside and Tico was inside, he would stay right near the house anyway. But with Tico on the loose I couldn't leave Bart outside at all, because I kept thinking any minute Tico was going to come busting through the bushes and then we'd have another fight on our hands. I even boarded Bart at a kennel for the first week.

Jill and I were heartbroken, as was everyone who knew Tico. We kept up hope for about two weeks, especially with all the media attention and the police looking. I offered to pay the reward even if Tico was dead, because I just wanted to know. Then three weeks went by and I had just about given up. I figured by now he was either dead or someone had taken him.

Bart was back home and was staying in the house, since his war with Tico was no longer an issue. Bart had this routine where he would get the newspaper for me every morning. The delivery guy would throw the paper down by the road. Bart would get up right before dawn and come over and nudge me, and I'd open the door in the bedroom that went out to the deck. He'd go out, do his little morning rounds, pick up the newspaper, and put it at the front door. One time years ago I had sent him to fetch the paper for me, and then he'd developed the routine all on his own—one of those great connections where a dog just knows what you want him to do.

One Saturday morning while Tico was still missing, I got up like always and let Bart out at dawn. I got up myself at about 7 a.m., walked to the front door, and there was no newspaper. In two years, that had never happened. So I opened the door and stepped out. Bart was curled up asleep on the porch. About fifteen feet down from him was Tico, also curled up asleep.

At first I was in shock. Then, in about two seconds, I felt this rush of every kind of emotion you could think of: joy, elation, relief, excitement, confusion, terror. I wanted to scream and jump up and down, but as soon as I had that thought, another one just as powerful hit me: "If you scream, you'll wake them up. And if you wake them, they are going to blow up." So I eased the door shut and ran inside and jerked the big comforter quilt off the bed. The bed where Jill was still sleeping. When dogs are getting into it, one way to separate them is to throw something over one of them before they lock up. So I went back outside and threw that comforter over Bart like a casting net, then dove onto him and covered him up. He probably didn't know what hit him. Then I grabbed him, dragged him into the house, and put him in a crate in the utility room.

Tico woke up and started coming over my way, and I had to leave him outside for a second. When I ran back out, Tico was just standing there wagging his tail. He had been gone a month and a day, and he looked like he had not eaten that entire time. I mean, he was a huge dog, but now he was skin and bones.

When I opened the door for him, I yelled to Jill, who was still in bed wondering what the heck was going on. She sat up and saw Tico and he saw her, and he ran down the long hall and dove on the bed with her. She was crying and crying, because of all the dogs we've ever had, Tico was her favorite. It was like a lost child had come back.

He wasn't injured at all and he didn't have a mark on him, but he was worn out like he had been running the whole time. And he was just a bag of bones. There was no telling where he had been and what he had done. I looked at him and thought, "Buddy, if only you could talk. Where were you? What have you been up to?"

Tico and Bart went right back to hating each other's guts. But for some karmic reason, Bart gave him a pass that day. It was like he said, "You've been gone, you're half dead, I'm going to let you go." I guess I'll never be able to explain it. Nobody really knows the mind of a dog except God and the dog.

# 9

# Akbar

Akbar's story is a tale of redemption. He was literally minutes away from death when I agreed to take him, because nobody thought redemption was possible. But all things are possible when you open your heart and listen to a dog.

By the time I met Akbar, I had gained a reputation among police dog insiders in Europe and over here for being able to handle really difficult dogs. One day my phone rang and a friend of mine, a Dutch dog broker named Mishel, said, "I need a big favor."

I knew Mishel from back when I spent a lot of time in Holland, and I'd introduced him to some people in the United States. "I've got a three-year-old Czech German shepherd I sold to a SWAT team in California because they wanted a super-tough dog," Mishel told me. "But they have been doing really stupid things with the dog and he's chewed up a bunch of handlers. Now they're going to put him down—today."

They'd called Mishel to get a replacement dog and to ask if he wanted the shepherd back before they took him in to the police department vet. "He's a good dog and I think you can do something with him," Mishel said. "Can I send him to you? See if you can rehab him; there's got to be a chance. I'll pay to ship him to you if you'll just spend a couple of weeks with him."

I said no. I already had a lot of dogs in my kennel and a lot of work on my plate. I didn't need to take in someone else's mistakes. "I'll pay you for your time," he said. "Please try it. I just hate for them to put him down." I heard something desperate in his voice. I said okay.

Toward the end of that conversation, he just happened to mention that this was the same dog he'd called me about a few months earlier, when the dog had put his partner, Giard, in the hospital. I knew Giard, and he was a real tough guy. He used to be a professional boxer and a kickboxer, and he was as hard on dogs as he was on people. Giard had grabbed the dog to pull him out of a crate and kind of muscled him a little bit, and the dog blew up and hurt him bad. I remember at the time I was amazed, because Giard was very, very experienced and dogs did not get the better of him. At the time, Mishel had just said, "Yes, this is one badass dog."

All of a sudden I knew I was dealing with something different. It was pretty common in police departments for some of the tougher dogs to get paired with less experienced handlers and end up reacting aggressively. Usually those dogs might be a little bit hard in temperament, but an experienced handler could get them under control. But when Mishel told me it was the same dog who got the better of Giard, I knew we were talking about a very tough dog, because Giard had never been chewed up like that in twenty years. This was going to be interesting.

In the couple of days it took for Mishel to arrange the shipping, I tried to learn as much as I could about this man-eater. And the more I learned, the madder I got. The dog had been placed in a city with a big police canine unit, and they put him with a new handler who was going through the training program. Like a lot of old-style police dog training, those handlers were taught that dog training is all about dominating and controlling your dog. It's the "show him who's boss" mentality.

Well, the dog chewed up the first guy pretty good. But then they put him with another green handler. Big mistake. By the time he came to me, he had been with the department just six weeks and had already put three handlers in the hospital. And the last one he had knocked to the ground and stood on top of, mauling him. They had to hit the dog over the head with a nightstick and knock him out. When he woke up, they had already pronounced his death sentence—until Mishel stepped in.

I couldn't believe the K-9 trainers had been so stupid, especially because the severity of the attacks was escalating. When a dog feels like he's fighting for his life and he reacts aggressively and that stops the pressure, he learns that an aggressive reaction works. And when a dog gets you on the ground and dominates you the way Akbar did, it builds his confidence up to a dangerous level where he is really not afraid. He starts to feel as if he can take on anyone. In that last attack, especially, he was learning to give it all he had. Such a powerful dog could do some serious damage, and the escalating attacks were making him more dangerous by the day.

I picked Akbar up at the airport in Memphis. He was growling as I loaded his crate into my car, but not like so many dogs I had seen who were just putting on a big show. Lex used to rock the crate and snap his teeth. Akbar's growl was low and guttural and actually scary. In hindsight, it makes a lot of sense to me; he wasn't putting on a huge display because there wasn't a real threat in front of him. He really didn't want to initiate a fight, he just wanted everyone to leave him alone.

When we got back to my place, it was already dark. I put his crate out in a pen near the house, opened the crate door, and walked out, shutting the gate behind me. I had left a little food in the pen, but not much. And then I just went into the house. I never even looked back to see him come out of the crate. I would wait until morning for the unveiling.

The next day I went out and fed and watered all the other dogs, and got my first good look at Akbar. When I did, my jaw hit the ground. He was a bi-color German shepherd, which means he was almost all black except for his socks and his face, which were a rich brown. The black was shiny and deep. He wasn't that tall, but he was built like a rottweiler. He had a big, wide muzzle and a square, thickset body, and was a good twenty to twenty-five pounds heavier than most shepherds at that height. He didn't have any of that typical German shepherd slope to his hips, and his rear end looked like a pit bull with hair on it. He had thick thighs and very muscular legs—I mean, he was a powerhouse. For what I like, which is a compact, powerful dog, he was as good as a German shepherd gets.

His pen was right between two mild-mannered females, because I was hoping to minimize any distractions with him so he could just relax. With males, there might have been some fence fighting or posturing, and I didn't want anything to amp him up. I gave the other dogs food and water, and totally ignored him. When I got close to Akbar's pen, he flared up and snapped a bit, but I acted like he wasn't even there. He toned it down pretty quickly. Then I went inside and got my folding chair, set it out with my back to the fence surrounding his pen, picked up the newspaper, and sat down to read. As soon as I sat down he was hitting the fence and growling, but I kept ignoring him. I sat there and read the paper for an hour or so, then turned around, threw a little food into his pen, and went back into the house. I did that for about two days.

Now, I don't want you to think I didn't feed Akbar for two days. He got fed, but it was always from me. I didn't pressure him to take the food directly from my hand, because he clearly wasn't ready for that. But every piece of food he got, he saw in my hand first, and I made sure he watched me toss it into his pen. He knew it was coming from me.

On the third day, I filled my pockets full of treats. I fed the other dogs their regular meals, and by the time I was done Akbar was standing there watching me. As I walked by his pen I casually popped the latch, opened the gate and just started walking away. I didn't even turn around to see if he was coming out of the pen. I mean, I had him in my peripheral vision, but I was just taking a walk down the little country path on my property.

I could see him step out tentatively and he was kind of like, "Okay, nobody's telling me to do anything." He didn't really trust me yet, but I knew in my gut that he was going to follow me. Have you ever seen one of those silly movies where a dog's spirit somehow gets transferred into a man's body? There's always a moment when somebody throws a ball and the man can't help but run after it. There's a certain element of truth in that. Dogs can't help doing what they were born to do.

Dogs with a lot of working drive—and in fact, most dogs—have a need to follow a strong leader. But with the really tough dogs I was working with, I couldn't just clip on a leash and take control because that would initiate a fight. So a little trick I learned was to let them out where they didn't feel confined or threatened in any way, and then just walk away and expect them to follow—exactly the way a top dog would do it. I used this trick with Lex in the beginning, too.

Out of the corner of my eye, I could see Akbar start to follow me a little bit. He'd stop to smell things and pee on bushes, but he was pretty much keeping up. When he'd get ahead of me, I'd just turn and go in a different direction. His natural inquisitiveness kept getting the better of him, and he'd catch up. Without putting him on the defensive, I was subtly planting the seed of an idea: "You are following me. I'm leading." Dogs can't help but register that as part of the pecking order, and it's all been accomplished without having a confrontation.

As for the treats, every time he got close to me I handed one off to him. I never looked at him or even stopped moving when I gave him one, so there was no engagement. I was very careful in how I let him approach, too. If I had stopped and turned to face him, it would have been a confrontation. So instead, I'd walk along and as he got up next to my side in the heeling position, I'd reach into my pocket and pull out a treat and not even look at him while he took it from my hand and ran off. That's how we started to build the trust we needed for a real relationship.

We went for walks that way twice a day for about three days. The fourth day, I let one of my females out and the three of us went together. Eventually I called her to me and gave her some treats. Akbar saw that and also started coming when I called her, because he wanted treats, too. Watching the other dog do it and be successful and not get hurt gave him the confidence to come to me when I called.

The next day we went for a walk again. The guy who had the farm next to mine kept cows, but he usually had them on a different part of the farm. Every once in a while, though, they'd bust out or somebody would leave a gate open and they'd end up in a nearby pasture. This day, I noticed there were about a hundred head of cattle in the field adjoining mine, separated just by a little fence. Akbar noticed, too. His body language completely changed and he took off and scooted under the fence. I thought, "Uh oh, this is going to be a problem." I wasn't worried about the cows—they were big and mature and he couldn't hurt them. I was worried about how I was going to get Akbar back to me.

But as he started running, I could see that he wasn't just chasing the cows. He was herding them. One cow got away from the herd and he drove it back in like a pro. Most shepherd breeds have a little bit of innate instinct for herding, but when I saw him cut that cow, I knew it was more than that. This was a trained behavior.

I went to the edge of the fence and whistled, and he instantly stopped and looked at me. I made a hand signal to the left and he moved those cows to the left. I made a signal to the right and he moved them right. And at that moment, I saw him change. Akbar had been trapped in a world where nobody recognized him for who he really was. By accident, I had stumbled upon the key to his past and I knew how to address his future. His relief at finally being understood was almost physical—I could just see his anxiety drain away. At last, someone spoke his language!

That night I got on the phone with Mishel and said, "Look, I've done you a favor with this dog. Now I want you to do something for me. Find out as much as you can about his background."

It turns out Akbar had been raised by an old man who lived on a farm in what was then Czechoslovakia. The man used to be a trainer in a ZVV club (which is the Czech equivalent of Schutzhund), which told me Akbar probably already had a good foundation of obedience training. But by then the guy had retired and was living alone, so Akbar had not had the benefit of going to club training sessions and getting all the socialization that comes with being in a dog club. He'd had just one handler all his life, and that handler kept cows and taught him how to herd them. He worked at one job for one man—a man he probably spent every moment of his day with.

The way dogs are sold in Europe, it's fast and furious. The little brokers are buying for the big brokers, who are buying for the American brokers. These guys are running around with pockets full of cash, they look at a dog, they test him real quick and if he looks okay, they give the owner some money, grab the dog, put him in a crate and throw him in a car. If he's earned some kind of title, they get the records on that. But if not, there may be no paperwork at all. The guy who bought Akbar probably picked up hundred dogs that week. Akbar's history was lost in the shuffle.

I can't blame the old man who sold him, because the money he got for Akbar probably meant the difference between eating and not eating that winter. And I can't blame Akbar, who went from the farm where he was born and raised to a holding facility that had 400 dogs in it. He totally freaked out.

He eventually ended up in a kennel in Holland with Giard. As I said, Giard is a very tough guy and I know he manhandled his dogs. At a typical holding kennel, the dogs are tested for their courage and toughness by cracking a whip next to them or coming at them with a stick. The dogs who have had protection training know exactly what is going on and respond the way they have been taught to; it's a familiar training exercise for them. But for Akbar, who had been taught nothing but herding, it was all real. A stranger was coming at him and *threatening* him.

He probably responded explosively, because he thought he was fighting for his life—which just earned him a trip to the United States. That meant spending twenty-five hours in a crate on a plane, then time in a kennel with a bunch of other dogs. Akbar had never been in a kennel and probably hadn't even spent much time around other dogs. So while all the other dogs knew the drill, he must have been terrified.

When the SWAT unit he was sold to started doing bite work

with him, he thought he was being attacked for real again, and defended himself the only way he knew how. As they upped the pressure, he escalated his response.

Thinking about all this made me sad and angry at the same time. I decided then and there that I wasn't ever going to sell him. If he spent the rest of his life on the farm with me, that would be fine.

Two days after I figured out how to communicate with Akbar, we were doing on-leash obedience. I never had a growl out of him. He did phenomenal obedience work, and I just brushed it up a little by offering him treats for good work and not many corrections. He heeled like an AKC obedience champion—perfect posture, head up looking at me, body curled around my hip. It was a turning point for us.

A little more than a week after I brought him home, I thought he was ready to come into the house with me. I knew enough about how to read his body language and felt confident I wasn't going to make a mistake that might make Akbar feel cornered or pressured. Jill wasn't home, either, so everything was under my control. We had been making such great strides and he'd probably spent the nights inside with his old man back in Czechoslovakia, so I thought he might actually enjoy it. But it turned out to be a very sad night.

That day I took him for a run beside me on my four-wheeler, so I knew he was exhausted. When I brought him in, I sat down on the couch and figured I'd just leave him alone to settle down and relax. But Akbar started pacing. It wasn't the kind of pacing Lex did, like he was looking for something to do. Akbar's pacing was uneasy and haunted. I could tell he was tired and wanted to lie down, but he just kept pacing and pacing. I could see the anxiety grinding away at him.

Finally, he got under a table in the corner of the room and pressed his back into the spot where the two walls met. I heard a big sigh and then he dozed off. But if I moved an inch he would look up like, "What, what, what?" And that's when I realized he was just too nervous to sleep in the house. The boogeyman was still haunting his dreams and he couldn't lie out in the middle of the floor without feeling threatened. Even though he trusted me, the scars were deep.

I got a big crate, popped the door off it and stuck it in the corner of the room, so he wouldn't feel exposed. Akbar dove in and was snoring like a moose within ten minutes.

At first, I didn't try to do too much with him. We spent a lot of time together just walking and running around the farm. He was the one I would let out if I had to go work on a deer stand or take a drive on the four-wheeler or just go for an afternoon walk. As he relaxed, he became more and more lovable. He was very comfortable and affectionate with me and licked me all over my face.

I discovered that, at his core, he was exactly the kind of dog I liked. He turned out to be phenomenal in obedience work. He was tough, fair-minded, and clearheaded. By that I mean he was a very clear thinker and a good problem solver. A herding dog needs those qualities, and they also made him a great tracking dog because he could make decisions independently and act on them without instructions. When you are following a scent trail with a dog, you can't smell the trail, so you have to trust the dog to figure things out on his own. And Akbar was really good at that.

He was a medium-drive dog, which means that, unlike Lex, he had an off button. When he would finally relax around me, he liked to just lie around and be a little bit lazy, which made him a great companion. But when it was time to go to work, he was serious and hardworking.

Akbar was my kind of dog, but that, too, was bittersweet. I wished I could have had him right from the farm without all that trauma. "If I could have got you straight from the old man's place," I thought, "you'd be my dog."

But Akbar was never free of his demons, and sometimes they would ratchet up the anxiety in him until you could see the expression of his tortured soul on his face. It was hard not to get emotional when I could see some innocent little exercise or movement flash him back to those terrifying times.

I was running a protection dog business at the time, and if my regular guys were testing dogs, I could see Akbar getting really cranked up. He'd see them testing the other dogs and think, "These guys are getting ready to come and attack me next." So I started either putting him in a crate in the house or moving him to the other kennel, so he wouldn't see or hear what we were doing.

I tried to do some really easy bite work with him—the kind you do with a puppy—and he was certainly tough. But it was too realistic for him. He wasn't fearful and he wouldn't back down, but to him it was always a real fight.

Akbar was the sleeping giant: "If I think you are trying to hurt me or we're going to have a fight, it's going to be awful. But if we can avoid it, I'd rather not fight." I'm sure if I'd worked with him a couple of years, I could have eventually taught him that protection work was a sport, not an attack. But what was the point? At the end of the day, he would rather be out running on the farm, chasing the four-wheeler and herding a couple of cows. The bite work was so stressful for him, and I had nothing to prove with this dog. Akbar had enough bad experiences to last him the rest of his life, and I wasn't going to add to them.

In the police dog world, Akbar still had a reputation as a man-eater—the dog who chewed up three cops in six weeks. As a result, a lot of people tried to buy him from me. But I never considered it. I knew they were interested in him because they thought he'd make a tough, explosive protection dog, and I knew that was exactly what he didn't need. What Akbar needed was to stay with me.

Then I got a call from a guy named Tim. He was a bounty hunter in New Orleans and had heard about Akbar from a police officer in Lafayette who bought some dogs from me. I told him Akbar wasn't for sale. Tim knew a little bit about the dog's history from his friend and he said, "I'm not interested in using this dog for work. I live by myself. I had another companion dog for a long time and he just rode around with me eight, ten hours a day. We lived together and slept in the same bed and were together all the time. He died a couple of years ago and I'm ready to get a new dog now. Akbar sounds like what I need."

I said no. But at the same time, I was beginning to suspect I was not what Akbar needed and that this guy might be it. Akbar was a one-man dog. I think that stemmed from his lack of socialization as a puppy. There's a crucial period in a dog's life, from about five weeks to twenty weeks, when it's vital for a dog to experience a wide variety of people and places. When the dog misses that, it becomes tough for him to accept the unfamiliar. You add to that Akbar's untrusting nature and the fact that he had never really been around that many people, and it was easy to see that his pack was very, very small. He loved the one he was with, but he couldn't love anyone else.

I had gone away to Europe for a month and the woman who ran my kennel for me made it her mission to befriend Akbar. She had admired him from afar, and while I was gone she got him to the point where he would walk with her on a leash and accept her commands. When I got back, she wanted to show me how they were buddies now, so she got him out of his pen and handed me the leash. As she did, Akbar whipped around 180 degrees and hit the end of that leash, all teeth, and got right up in her face. It broke her heart. As soon as I was back, that was it for him. We were a pack of two and she was an outsider. It's a part of the canine mind that's hard for us to understand, but he just could not serve two masters.

Jill was pregnant at the time, and she sure couldn't be around Akbar. As much as I wanted to give him a life like the one he'd lost, where he was one dog spending all his time with one man, I knew I couldn't.

Meanwhile, it turned out that Tim and I knew a lot of the same people. So he had his trainer friends call me up and swear he was legit and that he would love the dog and spend every waking minute with him and never pressure him to do the work he could not do. Tim kept calling, too. For months.

Finally I said, "Look, if you come up here and spend some time with the dog, I'm not promising you anything, but that's the only way I'll even consider it." He agreed. The fact that he was willing to take time off from work and spend some money staying in a hotel for a week showed me his level of commitment. Before he even got here, I decided, "If this guy looks okay, I'm going to let him have Akbar."

It was a very, very tough decision for me. In the year I'd had Akbar, I'd grown to really love that dog. And I had made him a promise. But a lifestyle match is probably the most important part of owning a dog. People sometimes hold on to dogs who are ill-suited for them out of guilt or because they think it's a bad thing to give the dog away. The dog ends up alone in the backyard, having a mediocre life at best, because his owner feels guilty about giving him away but not about keeping him in the wrong situation.

I have given away a number of dogs, but it was always for just one reason: The person I gave him to could provide a better life for the dog than I could. Even then, even when I knew I had to do it, it was never easy. But if I knew somebody who had the perfect setup and was going to work really well with that dog's temperament, and that the dog was going to be in a better situation than he was with me, I had to take my personal feelings out of it and do what's best for the dog. That was for sure the thing with Akbar, because I swore I would never let him go.

So Tim came to my farm to spend five days with Akbar. Tim was in his early thirties and looked like you'd imagine a bounty hunter looks. He was six-foot-two, tough, and gritty. I could tell right away he knew about dogs. And when we got to talking, I realized that he wasn't exaggerating when he said Akbar would spend every minute of every day with him. I knew that was the lifestyle Akbar craved. The dog needed a buddy like the old man who had raised him. Tim was going to make him his constant companion. He didn't have any kids, he didn't have a wife—it was just going to be the two of them.

It was hard for me, because knowing that Akbar was not able to serve two masters, I had to distance myself from him that whole week Tim was there. I loved the dog so much that it was almost painful to ignore him. But for me to be able to give Tim an honest shot, I had to do it. At the end of the week, I let him have Akbar.

Tim called me for months after that to give me updates—that was part of the deal. I wanted to know everything about how it was going between them. And I made him swear that if he ever had even a hint of regret or it wasn't working out, I'd immediately get the dog back. But it turned out to be the perfect match.

The thing I hope you remember about Akbar is not the sadness in his life, but the redemption. I've been talking about this a lot lately with respect to fighting pit bulls—the dogs who are rescued from illegal dogfight operations. There was a time when people believed they were just killers and all those dogs were immediately put down. But it doesn't have to be that way. Probably 60 to 80 percent of them can be great pets, although they have to be placed with a lot of thought and care. You have to remember that dogs coming out of fighting operations have been encouraged all their lives to be aggressive around other dogs. So a very, very low percentage of those dogs will ever be able to be around other animals. But as long as their owners understand that, the dogs can be adopted out.

I think one of the pieces of the puzzle that often gets left out when people are trying to decide if a dog can be rehabilitated—maybe a dog who has had a damaging history—is temperament. You've got to figure out whether you are dealing with damage that has been done to a dog who is naturally a pretty stable, strong animal or whether you are dealing with a dog who has a genetic problem with nerves. Because the first one is fixable and the second one is not. I see a lot of dogs out there in shelters who are easily spooked, and everybody assumes it's because they were abused somewhere. That may be true, but more often than not I find out these are dogs who have a genetic nerve deficiency and they're just squirrelly.

Akbar's magic was that despite the fact that he had almost been beaten to death, at his core he was a genetic masterpiece. His pedigree was a who's who of all the great East German and Czech dogs, so genetically all the right stuff was there and the damage to him could be undone with proper training.

Now, even when you have a nervy dog, training can address a lot of his issues. But you need to have reasonable expectations. With a nervy dog, unless he bites out of fear, most of the problems are more annoying than anything else—fear of storms, wariness around strangers, and so on. These are a hassle, for sure, but you can set up a reasonable training program and understand that it's for the life of the dog. And yes, you can have a wonderful life with a dog like that, but you have to be realistic in what you expect them to be able to do, so you don't get frustrated.

Pit bull owners, especially, have to take responsibility for what they have. These are dogs who are genetically hardwired to go after other dogs. It's irresponsible and just not smart to show up at a dog park and cut a pit bull loose to play with the other dogs. He may be fine 99 percent of the time, but that 1 percent when his genes kick in, there will be a fight. If I had a super defensive protection dog, I would never take him out to a public park and cut him loose around people. And if you have a gamey breed of dog, you can't let him loose around other dogs.

With all that said, pit bulls from fighting kennels, while they are very dog-aggressive, tend not to be nervy at all and can be great around people. We saw that with the dogs seized from the facility owned by Michael Vick, the football player who ended up going to jail for dogfighting. The ASPCA evaluated the forty-nine pit bulls there and recommended that only one should be euthanized. They felt the other forty-eight could be rehabilitated and placed. Fortunately, the judge overseeing the case took their recommendations. I met Dr. Pamela Reid, vice president of the ASPCA Animal Behavior Center, after she worked on that case, and she told me she had to fight long and hard to make that happen.

I think about those pit bulls sometimes, and I hope they ended up like Akbar. People were calling me for years about Akbar and Tim. They became known as the dynamic duo. Akbar liked to ride in the car, so he spent most of his day in the front passenger seat of Tim's pickup truck. The dog was attached to Tim's hip 24/7. Finally, he got to live out his dream life.

# 10

# Arras

The dog ate my wedding ring. Honest! My wife, who works as a teacher, had sure heard this excuse before. But it was true.

It was the day I brought Arras and a couple of other dogs home from the Atlanta airport, where they'd been shipped to me from Holland. I stopped at a rest station to let the dogs have a bathroom break, because they had been in their crates for more than twenty hours on the plane. I was a bit wary with the dogs I didn't know, but Arras and I were old friends. So I let myself get a little distracted while I was putting him back in his crate—a place he did not want to be after that long trip. We ended up getting into a serious scuffle. My shirt was torn where I got bit in the chest. My hands and arms were bloody, too.

That kind of encounter with a dog is no big deal for me, and I decided to drive over to the bathroom to wash up, take inventory, and see if I needed to go to a doctor. But when my hands hit the steering wheel, I realized my wedding ring was gone.

I spent the better part of an hour searching that rest stop on my hands and knees, looking for my ring. It wasn't just that I was scared of what Jill would say. That was my father's wedding ring. My mother gave it to him, and it was engraved inside with their names and the date they got married. I took out some of the dogs who are specially trained to recover lost articles and searched the area, but the ring never did turn up. I assumed Arras swallowed it and, reluctantly, I headed for home. I had him X-rayed the next day, and it wasn't inside him. But it was still his fault, because for sure he ripped that ring off my hand.

I guess the story just added to Arras's legend—which was already formidable on both sides of the Atlantic. Arras's father was a Malinois named Pecco, who was owned by a man in Holland named Hans Pegge. Hans had developed a bloodline of dogs who were phenomenal. Hans also had his own little bloodline going—four children—and they all lived in a typical Dutch house, which is very small by American standards. He kept three or four of those dogs at home with his kids, so they were super socialized. But when it came time to work, they were incredibly tough and athletic. They were all what we call hard-hitting flyers, too; they really launched themselves at the decoys and their bite work was explosive.

Everybody knew about Pecco because he was a great breeder and had been invited to the Dutch championships. Only the top ten dogs in the country receive invitations each year, so just competing is a lifelong pursuit that many trainers never attain. Hans had bred Pecco to a Dutch shepherd who was very famous herself and came from a bloodline of really big dogs. Arras was black brindled, because those color and pattern genes from the Dutch shepherd are so dominant. As an adult, he weighed more than ninety-five pounds, which is freakishly big for a KNPV dog. He had those launching attacks, just like Pecco, but he threw an extra thirty or forty pounds behind them.

By the time Arras was eight or nine months old, he had already built a name for himself in Holland and decoys started coming from other clubs to work him. Dutch decoys are some of the best in the world, and there's a lot of pride that goes along with the job. Those guys take some unbelievable shots from the dogs, because for most of the bite work, the dog has about a hundred yards of running room to build up steam before he hits the decoy. So the decoys are taking hits from dogs running at full speed. When you've got a dog who launches himself from twenty feet out, the way Pecco and Arras did, it's like getting hit in the back with an eighty-pound dumbbell thrown at thirty-five miles an hour.

Those guys were like boxers in the sense that if they got knocked off their feet, it was considered a disgrace. But by the time Arras was three years old, decoys were coming from all over the country to work with him and if they got knocked down by Arras there was no shame, because everybody did.

Arras got his KNPV-1 title when he was three, then a year later he got a KNPV-2 title and qualified for the national championships. I was in Holland that year, partly because Arras's reputation had reached all the way to Tennessee and I wanted to see him. A friend had introduced me to Hans on a previous trip, so I decided to say hi and get a look at the dog before the trial.

KNPV trials last all day and are a grueling affair, so the handlers all rest their dogs before and between events. But that morning I found Hans out on an adjacent soccer field with a tennis racket, hitting balls as far as he could for Arras to chase. He was making the dog sprint fifty or sixty yards at a time, thirty or forty times in a row, because he knew that by the time the trial started, if Arras was too loaded up with drive, he wouldn't make it through the competition without getting out of control. I thought, "Wow, this is a very different animal we are dealing with here; a different level of drive."

Arras ended up finishing in fourth place. He also knocked down two decoys. Now, being in the championship is the same for the decoys as it is for the handlers: They are professionals, and only the best are selected. They are the kind of guys dogs *cannot* knock down. But Arras knocked one off a bike in an exercise where the decoy wears a bite suit and flees on a bicycle, and got another during the flee and attack exercise. That was in 1996, and people still talk about it today.

Of course I wanted him. You couldn't see a dog work like that and not want him. And what I'd achieved with Tico, the reputation that dog helped me build in Holland, enabled me to convince Hans to sell Arras. He took a lot of heat for it, though, because Arras was a great dog and a proven breeder, and they didn't want those dogs leaving the country. People were calling up and cussing him out. He told his kids and they started to cry, because Arras lived in the house with them and they all loved him. In fact, I started worrying that Hans might change his mind. So when he called me up and said, "Get this dog out of here before my family disowns me," I asked my friend Appie

Kamps (who is one of the most famous KNPV trainers ever) to go get the dog right away.

The night before I was flying back to the States, I worked Arras at Appie's KNPV club. By then everyone knew Arras was going to be leaving soon, and decoys drove in from all over just to work with him. One guy drove down from Friesland, which is the northernmost part of Holland, two and a half hours in his little Fiat with his bite suit in the backseat, to work that dog one time before he left. We did a flee and attack. This is the longest, most dangerous exercise for the decoy, because you are walking away from the dog and you don't look over your shoulder, so the dog is hitting you with a hundred yards of steam and you just have to be ready for it.

This guy was about six-foot-four and weighed about 260 pounds, and when Arras hit him I saw feet in the air and then a cloud of dust. Arras cartwheeled the guy.

These KNPV training clubs have little clubhouses and it's all very social. The wives are in there making coffee and getting beer and pastries ready, and people do a lot of sitting around and chit-chatting, European style. So I thought this decoy would stay for a beer afterward. But he just came over and thanked me for letting him work the dog, got in his car and left. He never even shook my hand.

Two days after I got home to Tennessee, Appie called to tell me the decoy had driven himself straight from the club to the hospital. Arras had hit him so hard that it tore his shoulder out of the socket.

Nobody who worked around that dog, here or in Europe, would ever say they had seen a dog with more drive. He was also huge—maybe twenty-eight inches at the top of the shoulders. He was big like a German shepherd, with a big head and a very broad chest. Usually, the bigger a dog is, the less athletic he is. But not Arras. He was known as a flyer; he'd take off and travel almost fifteen feet through the air before he hit a decoy.

Arras was a freak working dog. I ended up using him for demonstrations at seminars and working dog trials, because everybody wanted to see that dog work. After a while it got hard to find a decoy who would work him because he'd knock them down all the time. He was just a master at breaking somebody down. A lot of times I'd have to work him myself, which is the reason I've got lower back problems now. I was fast becoming known as one of the best decoys in the country, and I had people calling me to do decoy seminars and classes. I needed to be able to stay on my feet with the best dogs in the country, and I had the best sitting right in my house to practice with.

Because I didn't always have a decoy, other than me, I had to be able to work Arras at a distance, without a handler standing next to him. He learned it easily. I could put him in a down-stay while I had a bite suit on, or he would heel next to me and I could walk down the field and send him at myself and learn to take the shots. It was very valuable for me, because believe me, when I walked onto a training field, I felt strong. Not that I never got knocked down, because it's always going to happen from time to time, but once you've been beaten up by Arras or one of his offspring, nothing fazes you.

Arras always bit at the top right shoulder or the back of your arm. Then, as you were standing up, he'd swivel around and place his front paws at the top of your hip and pull back all his weight while he was pushing on your hip, even sometimes to the point of picking his back feet up off the ground. All that weight would be pulling you backward while you were trying to stay on your feet. He wouldn't let go, either. He understood the idea of leverage and used it against you. A lot of my guys, when they worked him, would leave the buckles on the jacket of their bite suit undone. Once Arras made the initial hit and bit down, they would shed the jacket because they didn't want to have to stand there with him; that's when you got brutalized. They'd just throw the jacket off and Arras would stand there, still clamped down on the jacket. (As scary as that sounds, he was very bite safe that way. With a lot of police dogs, you shed a jacket and they'll just spit it out and come after you.)

So Arras had the size, the athleticism, and the drive everyone wanted. He had a very stable, even temperament, and wasn't handler-aggressive. He also had the look. Back in the 1990s, when Malinois were just coming into use by police departments in the United States, there was a problem because they are thinner and smaller than German shepherds and most of them are kind of light colored. So even though they are great working dogs and very tough, they are not very intimidating looking. But Dutch shepherds, even though they're about the same size as Malinois, are all black with brown brindle, and that combo is kind of scary.

Arras also had something else everyone was looking for: He wasn't aggressive with other dogs. There were times when Tico would bowl him over, yet they got along fine. If another dog turned around and snapped at him over a piece of food or something like that, Arras would just shrug it off and walk away. I mean, he would totally turn the other cheek. That's a highly prized quality for a police dog, especially if you work for a department that's got a lot of dogs. If you've got a police dog who's aggressive with other animals, when you are out on the street there's always a stray dog running around, a cat, or something, and you can get into a lot of trouble if your dog is distracted. It happens more than you might think. I've been to more than one police dog competition where two guys were working their dogs off leash and they got too close to each other and a fight broke out. Many times, the men ended up fighting each other, as well.

That set of traits all in one dog, on top of that flying gene—it was like the perfect storm. It's incredible to have all that in one dog to begin with. But Arras's legend did not stop there. His ability to pass on all his super traits . . . well . . . I've never seen anything like it, ever, in any breed. It was the most incredible example of a dog being able to reproduce himself. He was like a Xerox machine. He was bred to German shepherds, Malinois, Dutch shepherds, and every single dog came out almost a carbon copy. In fact, from a working standpoint they were better because he was so over the top in terms of drive that to water him down a little bit was a good thing.

Arras had been bred well over a hundred times before I brought him from Holland. When Hans announced that he was going to let me take the dog, his phone was ringing off the wall. People were inducing heat in their bitches just so they could breed to Arras. He will go down in history as probably one of the greatest producing dogs in Holland ever. He was five years old when I brought him to the States, and in the first year I had him, I bought and imported six of his sons, all from different mothers. They were so similar to him that it was a little scary. I was at a police dog competition in Las Vegas recently, and four guys came up to me and told me they had Arras sons or grandsons.

Arras's legend as a great sire extends beyond his ability to produce spectacular offspring. He also had a sex drive to match his work drive. In Holland, they bred him two or three times a week. I mean, he was like a porn star—always ready to go. He was just too big and heavy for most of the girls to breed naturally, so I used to take him to the veterinarian to collect semen for artificial insemination. Most of the time when you do that, the vet has to have a bitch in heat in the office to get the dog going. But Arras would walk into the vet's office and wink at him, because that dog knew it was breeding time. (I'm going to leave it to you to imagine how a veterinarian collects semen from a dog, but yes, it's just the way you imagine it.)

Arras was a lover in another way, too. He used to make me crazy with what we called his Arras hug. He would come and sit next to you and lean on you, because he wanted to be petted all the time. If you were done petting him and started to walk away, he'd jump up and kind of hug you around the waist. He'd grip really tight, too, and push his head into your stomach so you could pet him there. You could keep walking, but he would walk around on his hind legs behind you, as if you were both dancing. It wasn't a dominance thing and it wasn't a breeding thing—he just didn't want you to leave.

That big bear hug was another unusual thing about Arras, because it was totally about affection. Some dogs who are prolific breeders like to grab a leg every once in a while, but he never did that. He knew the difference between man and beast.

He just loved to be loved. If Jill and I were watching TV, Arras would sit in the middle of the room and look back and forth at us, thinking, "Who is going to be more likely to pet me the most?" Then he'd start inching over, still in a sitting position. He'd scoot two inches at a time so you never saw him move, but every time you looked up he'd be a little closer. Then all of a sudden he was practically in your lap.

He was always so charged up, too. It's as if he vibrated with energy all the time. It was good energy, though—it wasn't like he was about to blow up. He was a very happy dog, so it was more that he was always wishing somebody would say, "Okay, let's go." I don't think in all the years I had him that I ever caught him sleeping more than once or twice. Even though he had very good manners, it was always like he was barely able to keep a lid on it.

Still, every other high-drive dog in a kennel run spins and paces and barks and jumps because he just can't stand the inactivity. But Arras would just sit there at the front of the gate, showing you nothing at all. Of course, the first time I snapped a leash on him and brought him out, he started shaking he was so geared up. There were waves of energy coming off him. Despite that, though, he was very easy to handle and I could take him straight out of the run and start doing work with him.

Because he had so many offspring and because they were so visible in the police dog world, I learned a lot about the powerful influence of genetics from Arras. For example, there obviously is a flyer gene in dogs, because his father, Pecco, did it and a huge percentage of his offspring do it. Usually, launching into the air to hit a target is something that has to be trained, but all of Arras's offspring just do it naturally.

He always produced size, as well, even when he was bred to smaller bitches. And there is some kind of genetic thing he throws so that none of his puppies show dominant-aggressive behavior with other animals.

It's hard for me to overemphasize how valuable that predictability is when you're buying a working dog. I imported several of Arras's sons and grandsons, and they all went to different police departments, but I had them all long enough to see the unbelievable similarities they had to Arras. When I bought a dog who was a son of Arras, I knew I was going to pay more, but I also knew when that dog came off the airplane I could walk right up to him, snap on a leash, and get to work. I knew what kinds of things that dog was going to be able to do well and where he might need a little bit of extra work. Remember, all of these dogs were being imported from different people, bred to different mothers, and raised in different families. When you throw in all those variables and consider the fact that these dogs kept coming off the conveyor belt like little clones when the only thing they had in common was the genetics of their father, it's totally amazing. It's proof of the power of genetics in dogs and how it determines much more than the size, shape, and color of the dog. So much of the behavior is hardwired from birth, and we waste a lot of time thinking we can change things that we can't.

I imported Jacco, Arras's son, about six months after I got Arras, and living with the two of them really drove that point home for me. Jacco was Arras's son from a Dutch breeding, and they had never met one another. But, true to form, they got along great right from the start. They looked like father and son, too, so I started a flashy little dog routine with them working as a brace (that's what we call it when two dogs work side by side). They would heel together, shoulder to shoulder, actually touching—it was beautiful. I taught them to heel with me on a bicycle, the way they do it in Holland. Then I would flip them from one side to the other with a voice command; they'd come around smartly and both end up in a brace again, almost as if they were attached at the shoulder.

I also did brace bite work with them, and there are very, very few dogs you can do that with. In fact, it's kind of dangerous, because when dogs get that worked up it's difficult to handle them and usually the males are going to get into a fight. That's why doing multiple attacks with two males is almost unheard of. But I could do all kinds of dual bite scenarios with Arras and Jacco or Arras and Tico. I never could work Jacco and Tico together, though. They got along fine and could live together, but in a bite training session there was too much testosterone between them. But Arras worked beautifully with either one of them.

To get off the subject for a second here, bite work with two dogs is an awesome thing to see. You've got to have a very adventurous decoy, though. Paul was the only guy in my whole region who would do it, and he was one of these kamikaze skydiving types. Tico was a leg biter, so he would run and hit you in the back of the legs or at the top of the hip. Then you had Arras, who would fly over Tico's back and lock down on your shoulder.

It was a high-low combination. Paul was never the same after those workouts. He had to go to the chiropractor for years.

Having Jacco really helped me understand how much of himself Arras passed on to his offspring. In a kind of replay of Arras's last workout in Holland, I had Jacco with me at a Schutzhund trial and one of the top-rated decoys in the United States, a guy named Alan, told me he wanted to work the dog because he had heard so much about him. Alan did a Schutzhund courage test, where you're running at the dog and he's running full speed at you. Jacco knocked him right down. When Alan finally picked himself up, he said to me, "I'll never do that again. That absolutely scared me to death. I've never been hit that hard by a dog. He almost knocked my shoulder out of the socket."

Jacco had the flying gene, too. In fact, because he wasn't as heavy-bodied as Arras, he could launch himself farther. One time we actually measured and found he was traveling eighteen to twenty feet through the air, totally off the ground. In other words, he was running that fast and could jump that far. That meant if you were working Jacco on a runaway, where the decoy fled and didn't turn and look back, he would hear the thump, thump, thump, and then just silence. And then the sledgehammer would hit him.

Arras's amazing genetic legacy is still very much alive, too. At that police dog trial in Las Vegas, I met a guy who had a son of Jacco—a grandson of Arras. He raised that dog from a puppy, police certified him, narcotics certified him, and qualified for the nationals in Schutzhund. He liked him so much that he found a bitch who was an Arras daughter and bought her, too.

This guy is a police officer in California, and when I met him he told me, "I never met you before, but I've heard your name a lot and I want to tell you about the dogs I've got." As we started talking, I told him more and more about Arras and Jacco and all their little idiosyncrasies, and the guy was just nodding his head. He said, "You know, until I got this female and saw the similarities, I just thought I had a phenomenal dog and it kind of made me feel like I was the greatest trainer in the world. But when I got the female she was already an adult and I couldn't believe how similar she was. It spoils you, doesn't it?"

"Are you going to breed that female?" I asked him.

"Yes, probably. I might even breed her back to Jacco's son."

I told him I've got to have a puppy out of that bloodline again. And I mean it. But I have to admit, those puppies are a pain in the behind to raise. If you walk through a yard of six-week-old Arras puppies, when you walk out again you are peeling them off your pants legs. They are attached to every part of your body they can reach, like ticks. It's an indication of that redline working drive, and they all have it. Anything that moves, they'll grab it. And once one puppy grabs on, the others see and they all want it.

That kind of drive is so extreme that it can be dangerous. It's not that there's some monster lurking under the surface. It's just that when you activate something—that is, you make it move—a dog with that much drive *has to* have it. Arras was 100 percent free of any malice in his makeup, but if you kept something from him, or if he thought you had a tug toy or something like that, he would lose all control.

Some of that behavior I can trace back to Hans. And in fact, he did say to me once that if he had Arras all over again he would do some things differently. But the traditional thing you do with those dogs when you are trying to get them ready for KNPV is to build that possessive drive in them when they are young. It's a way to take what they've been given genetically and juice it up a little bit. But Arras was already so high-drive, and the training really put him over the top. I mean, you would literally see it in his face: He would be overwhelmed with the desire to have something and he absolutely couldn't control himself.

I don't think it made him dangerous. After all, Arras lived in Hans's house with his kids. And he lived in my house with my son Parker, too. In fact, he was great around kids. I used to take him and Tico when I gave talks at the local schools. He'd let the kids climb all over him the same way Tico did, although I could see that Arras didn't love it. He would stand there and let them do whatever they wanted, but his eyes were looking right at me, waiting for me to ask him to do something. He would have shrugged those kids off him in a second if I had shown him a decoy and said, "Go get him."

Arras had very good house manners, too. He never jumped up, and as high-drive as he was, when I walked into the house with him and people were sitting around, if he wanted to be petted he would go straight over to you and just sit and lean against you. Hans had trained him to be good that way. But he was always just kind of quaking—a bundle of energy all the time.

Then came the teddy bear incident. Jill's friend Kendra, her roommate and basketball teammate in college, had twin boys who were about three at the time. They came over to our house for a visit. One of the kids got out of the car carrying a teddy bear. They were walking from the driveway into the garage, where Jill was standing, holding Parker in her arms. Kendra looked at her boy and said, "Don't bring that bear in here, just throw it back in the car." The kid was five feet from the car and he tossed the teddy bear into the backseat.

Arras was standing in the yard, saw him toss the teddy bear and, like a rocket, dove full speed. I wasn't home at the time, but Jill told me he launched into the backseat of that car from about ten feet out and grabbed the teddy bear. Jill yelled at him to let it go and went over to the car, but he was totally freaked out over it and she had Parker, so she went in and put Parker down first. When she came back outside, Arras had his feet on the bear and was ripping it to shreds. She went over to him and said, "Let go of that," and kind of popped him upside the head. He just locked down on the bear even harder. Arras would do this thing where he would shut out the rest of the world, and you could have beaten him with a sledgehammer at that point, but he would not let go. Once he had that bear, he had to neutralize it.

Jill decided, "I'm not going to get in the middle of this," and she left him alone. When she came out about twenty minutes later, it looked as if it had snowed in the driveway. An hour later, when I got home, there was still stuffing floating all over the place. And there was not a piece bigger than a quarter left of that teddy bear.

Now, dogs tear stuff up all the time. But there is a dark cloud over that kind of situation. You can't predict what kids are going to do, and if that boy had made a motion to throw the teddy bear but then didn't let go of it, or if he had seen Arras grab it and decided he wanted to get it back, there could have been a problem. Arras was 100 percent focused on the teddy bear because the boy had activated it—made it move. But with that much focus, the boy's arm could easily have ended up in the dog's mouth and Arras would not have let go, because the arm then becomes an extension of the bear. Arras would have had no sense that he was biting the boy—just that he was going after a moving object.

There's a process that happens here, and it happens most often between two or more dogs. I think the vast majority of really serious dog mauling cases I read about are the result of this possessive/competitive process. Perhaps the most famous was the Diane Whipple case in San Francisco. In January 2001, Whipple was killed by her neighbor's two Presa Canarios—guard dogs originally from the Canary Islands. It was a horrible, savage attack in which one dog started and then the other joined in. Yes, those dogs were aggressive to begin with, but you had two dogs who lived together in a small apartment and there was a lot of pent-up tension there because the people who owned them didn't really understand the breed.

I believe what really happened was that a competition was going on between those dogs under the surface that the owners were unaware of. Then the male dog had an aggressive confrontation with Whipple over a close quarters thing in the hallway, and the female dog thought, "Well, what is that? If there's something over there that you want, I want it first." As the female went forward, the male was like, "I don't think so." In milliseconds, it turned into a tug-of-war where, in the minds of those dogs, Diane Whipple ceased to be a human being and just became an object that each one of them was driven to possess. While the trigger may have been aggression, in a split second it turned into a competition between those two dogs. I don't think it ever would have happened if those dogs had confronted Whipple individually. The male may have bitten her, but it would never have turned into what it did.

I saw behavior like that all the time when I was doing brace bite work—which is why that kind of work is so dangerous. I would stand there, getting ready to send the dogs while both were in full drive, barking. Both dogs would hold a line (which means you heel up off leash to a spot and then the decoy runs in yelling and the dogs have to sit there and wait for you to tell them to go) and were 100 percent solid when I worked them separately. But when I worked them together, if one of them moved an inch too quickly, the other one was gone. I always had to have them on a leash. It was as if they were saying, "I'm going to work and be a good boy until I see that he's cheating. Then I'm gone, because he's not getting there before me." Even with dogs who are well-trained (and I don't believe the dogs in the Diane Whipple case were), that competitive thing can throw good training out the window.

It's a low percentage possibility, but there is a very scary chain of events that can happen with dogs who live with each other and have a competition going. Something that happens in a lot of these horrific dog bites is that a kid is running down the street and two dogs are walking along who know each other—maybe they're living together or are fence mates—and there's some of that natural pack competitiveness going on. One of the dogs reacts and zeroes in on the kid, and the other dog reads that and says, "I don't think so, that's going to be mine." The other dog probably didn't even care until the first dog showed interest, but now it escalates out of control faster than the dog owners can react. And the kid isn't even a kid anymore—he's just an object that both dogs want. You find yourself asking, "Why would that dog want to bite that kid?" But the truth is the dog didn't want to bite that kid. He just wanted to get something before the other dog got it.

So how can you protect yourself in a situation like that? First and most important, you've got to stop being a moving object. You've got to be very still, and, if you can, turn and confront the dogs and shout "No!" so you snap them out of their prey drive. I know this is not easy for a little kid or an older person to do, but at the very least they have to understand that movement and running is what stimulates the dogs and keeps the attack going. As soon as you stop and stand still, the game's over. In fact, a lot of times they'll run right by you—I've seen that happen firsthand.

I saw a more benign example of this competitive drive one day when Jill and I were out walking on the farm with Arras and Jacco. We had 260 acres, and we were back on almost the farthest point, about a mile and a half from the house. There was a heavy plastic gas can that somebody had left in the woods. It was empty, and Jill said, "You need to get that gas can and take it back to the house." I said, "I wonder if it's got any gas in it?" and I nudged it with my toe. Well, both of those dogs were about equal distance from the gas can when I did that. Me just tapping that thing activated it for them, and Jacco whipped around and locked in on it. Just as Jacco's head was whipping around, Arras noticed him looking at that gas can and, of course, he heard me nudge it and saw that it moved. Instantly, it was about who was going to get it first.

They hit the gas can like a bomb. Both of them locked down on it. I yelled at them to let go, but they were in another world. They were having a tug-of-war over that gas can, and they had bitten it so hard that they punctured the heavy plastic. At first I was mad and decided to make them let go. But then I thought, "You know what, you idiots? Have your tug-of-war, I don't care. We're out of here." Jill and I kept walking, and I figured after a few minutes they'd tire themselves out.

Ten minutes later I turned around and they were following us, but they both still had a death grip on that gas can. If we stopped walking, they would commence to tugging it away from each other. We walked all the way home, more than a mile and a half, and we took our time, too, and these two dogs kept it up all the way. It was almost two hours that they were locked down like that. The amount of energy it takes to bite down and compress on something that hard and to hold on to it while another dog is trying to rip it out of your mouth is unbelievable.

When we got back to the house, they were both falling to the ground but still not letting go. The gas can was starting to tear apart at that point. I thought, "I'm going to see how long these idiots will go." And they just lay there on the ground, neither one letting go. About ten minutes later, they both got a little energy and they started tugging again and the gas can ripped into two pieces. Once each one of them had a piece, they just spit it out and didn't give it a second look.

This kind of thing can happen with just one dog, as well, if he has a strong prey drive. And that brings me back to Arras.

That dog had no people aggression, but the drive part of him was so high that he could create a competitive thing without there being other dogs around. If I was walking along with him and I acted like I was hiding something behind my back, just that little bit of body language would send him into orbit. He would literally scream like a child. And then he'd try to get around me and would start bulldozing me. Whatever it was, he had to have it. Within about two or three seconds he was totally out of control. I'd show him my empty hands and it would take him a second, but then I could see his eyes clear up and he'd be like, "Okay, sorry." It was definitely something he couldn't control.

We had a little baby in the house, and the teddy bear incident was enough to convince me that Arras's days were numbered as our house dog. I knew a guy who had a kennel in Texas. He was a cop, and his wife was Dutch and had been a secretary at a KNPV club there. Of course they knew Arras. They were breeding Dutch shepherds and had imported a couple of really nice females. They had no kids and it was a good place for him. So Arras went to live with them.

It's never easy for me to let a dog go. And it was especially tough with Arras, who was so spectacular in so many ways. But I always, always send a dog to a situation that I know is going to be better for him. Arras was such a lover, and I knew he wasn't going to be happy living in my kennel. By then he was almost eight years old, which is pretty old for a dog that size. But he kept breeding, stamping out those replicas of himself. To the end, he was always ready to go.

# 11

# Lex's Last Days

At the core of everything between Lex and me was mutual respect. Lex was not the fastest, the biggest, or the strongest dog I've ever had. Certainly, I had other dogs who were much more impressive and flashy. But with Lex, I could always see his inner warrior.

As Lex got older, his body started to fail him. But his fierce spirit never did. It was that spirit I loved best in him, and it only seemed to grow stronger over time. Even as he got more and more infirm, he would still do things that left me in awe. Nothing could extinguish his fire.

Lex had a bad accident when he was six years old. I had a brand-new dog trailer I had recently had custom built, and I was taking Lex to a Schutzhund trial and a rottweiler I'd imported from Czechoslovakia to his new owner in Nashville. My brother, David, was visiting me, and the road out from my farm was tricky, so he was going to follow me part of the way. I loaded the dogs in the trailer and we headed out.

We got on a long stretch of country road when David started blinking his lights and pulled up alongside me. "Hey, man," he yelled, "you lost your dogs back there. Both of them stepped off the trailer. I almost ran them over."

I thought he was kidding, because when I looked at the trailer, all the doors were shut. "Look inside," David said. I went to unlock the door to the dog box and realized it was already undone. The box that held the dogs had a faulty latch, and when I started driving, the vibrations had popped the latch open. So the door was unlatched and had been flapping open and shut. Lex just walked out on the back of the trailer, looked around, and stepped off. I was going almost sixty miles an hour, and he tumbled across the pavement. Then the rottweiler jumped off and hit the grass on the shoulder. David wasn't sure either dog was still alive.

I was on my way to Nashville, which was 120 miles away. If David hadn't been behind me, I would have driven all the way there and arrived in Nashville with no dogs and no idea where they were. Who knows where they would have wandered off to by the time I got back. I felt a little sick just thinking about it.

We started slowly driving back the way we came, and soon we saw the rottweiler standing on the side of the road looking confused. The poor dog had been on a plane from Europe just three days ago and had no idea what hit him. I looked him over and he was skinned up a little bit, but no broken bones or other injuries. About half a mile farther back, we found Lex standing on the side of the road with a look on his face like, "Is somebody coming to get me or what?" Old cartwheeling Lex; he was smart, but not smart enough to figure out that you don't step off of a trailer going sixty miles an hour.

His knees and muzzle were skinned up, and there was a raw patch on one ear. He was limping, too. I drove straight to the vet and had both dogs X-rayed. Unbelievably, they were fine.

I went ahead and delivered the rottweiler, but I decided not to put Lex in the Schutzhund trial because I figured he'd be so sore that he wouldn't be able to move. I wanted to go anyway, though, to see the other dogs who were competing.

When we got there, I took him out just to check on how he was feeling. He was kind of stiff for a second but he quickly shook it off. He saw all the activity and action going on around him, and he started bouncing and barking and getting wound up. He wanted to be in it. So I decided we'd just do the obedience part of the trial because it's not very physical. Lex blew through it with his usual style and precision. So I thought, "Okay, we'll do the tracking part the next morning. If he starts showing any signs of discomfort, though, I'm going to pull him from the trial."

You already know the end of the story, don't you? We finished the competition and won High in Trial. Because that's the kind of dog Lex was. But he also ended up with a certain stiffness in his rear end that got progressively worse as he got older.

His mind, though, never stiffened up. I showed Lex when he was nine in Los Angeles in a big professional protection dog trial. Nine is pretty old for a German shepherd, but he was as sharp as ever. In Schutzhund, you know what's going to happen in the competition and can train for it. But at these professional trials, there are certain exercises that they don't tell you about until the actual day of the trial. So the dog always needs to think on his feet, just like in a real patrol situation.

It's not all that hard to train a dog to follow a sequence of behaviors when the sequence is always the same. For example, it's easy to teach a dog to sit and then lie down and then stand up. But then if you ask him to sit when he's lying down or stand when he's sitting, a lot of them won't understand what you're asking. They'll be thinking, "Wait! The sit comes first and the stand comes *after* the down."

At the trial, they told us the obedience exercise was that you had to tell the dog to lie down, then walk thirty paces away, turn around, and tell him to sit up from a down and then stand from the sit. Lex had never done that particular sequence on command in his life, and it's something most dogs would probably need about a week to learn. They give you the lunch break to work on the exercise before you're tested, so I took Lex in the parking lot. We trained for fifteen minutes, then he went out there and did it flawlessly.

I know that doesn't sound as exciting as the explosive bite work Lex was so famous for, but it was, in some ways, more difficult. Dogs get used to doing certain things in a certain way. And as they get older, they become more and more inflexible. They're like crotchety old folks: "This is the way we've always done it, by God, and we're going to keep doing it this way." But Lex was always thinking and processing new information. He never stopped learning, all the way to the end.

The best analogy I can think of is a guy who has been an athletics coach for thirty years. I think of myself as more of a coach than a trainer anyway, because I am taking dogs who have varying levels of athleticism and natural ability and I'm coaching them to focus those abilities on a specific task. That might be working for a police department, finding drugs, finding people, or competing in sports. I am always taking some natural ability and molding it. I have coached so many tremendously gifted athletes who accomplished a lot, but many times there were mental barriers that caused them to hit a ceiling with their training.

In fact, I run into that a lot more than I do a dog hitting his physical limitations. Bart is a good example. He was a tremendously athletic, powerful dog, but his mind allowed him to go down only one path. He didn't like change, he liked routine. He was set in his ways, and once he learned something, it was hard to go off in another direction with him. With dogs, that's a lot more the norm than the exception. If you spend years training a dog in one capacity, that becomes his world. But Lex was such a sponge for new information and new types of training. You match that up with an internal drive that was in high gear all the time, and you understand why he could work through any problem, physical or mental.

Lex's mind never, ever failed him. But eventually, his body did. The time I felt the sorriest for him was at a trial in Los Angeles. This was the national championship for professional protection dogs. Lex and Arras had qualified at the regionals in Dallas, so I took them both to L.A. Lex was ten by then and was starting to have problems with his back. He would get out on the field and be running, and the lower part of his back down through his back legs would either cramp up or just go dead on him and he would fall right over.

When Lex was hurt, there was no picking him up because he'd eat you alive. So when this sort of thing happened, I'd just sit there with him for a few minutes and he'd whimper a little bit—which for Lex must have meant he was in horrible pain. Then he'd kind of bust through it and loosen up and he'd be fine and ready to go a hundred miles an hour. And it usually wouldn't happen again at the same trial.

Anyway, we were at this trial and we were in first place going into the finals. We were doing a call-off—the decoy is at the other end of a field and you send your dog to bite him, but at the last minute you call the dog off and he must stop. Most dogs really sprint down the field, because they know they're going to get a bite, and Lex did, too. But he was also 100 percent reliable in that exercise and I never had any trouble calling him off. This time, he started running and his legs just went out from under him as if somebody had shot him. I had to go out on the field and get him, and I knew it was going to be a problem. I knelt down beside him and it was obvious he was really hurting bad. I tried to pick him up, but he popped me pretty good on the arm and drew a little blood. The last thing I needed was a big fight out there with a lot of people watching. So I told him to quit biting me. Then I started picking him up, and he was growling and snapping, but he was hurting, too.

After I got him up on his feet, I held up my hand to the judge and told her, "I need a minute." Lex just stood there for a few minutes and then we walked off together. He would not be carried.

When Lex was thirteen and could barely move in the rear, he was in my car with me and we passed a patrol car that had pulled somebody over. He saw those blue lights flashing and went into a barking, snarling fit in the back of the car, jumping up and down, just wound up and ready to go. When he was like that, I'd be left standing there open-mouthed, thinking, "This dog will *never* quit."

A few months after that, I took in a Malinois named Max for a cop friend of mine who wanted to tune up the dog's training a little bit. By then we had stopped working Lex because his hips were very arthritic and he had some problems with his lower spine. Sometimes his rear end would go numb and lock up on him.

I was working Max with a decoy named Chris, and Lex was about sixty yards away in a pen, watching. As soon as he saw Max nail Chris, Lex started barking at the fence, as if to say, "Let me out! Let me out! I want to do this!" He had gotten his legs up under himself pretty well, and was braced up against the fence. There was no way I was taking him out to do bite work, though, so I just ignored him.

Then I heard Chris yell, "Lex is out!" Lex was in a little temporary pen I had near the house, and he'd pulled up the corner of the chain link and peeled it back. He could not run anymore, and he was just kind of hobbling across the yard, almost dragging his legs. But he was coming. I put Max in a down-stay because I didn't want there to be a dogfight. And then Lex was on Chris.

Lex didn't have any rear leg strength at that point, but he managed to jump up and was hanging on to the bite sleeve. He wanted to be out there so bad and show everybody he still had the stuff. I told Chris, "Just sit down on the ground and let him wear himself out. At least he's having a good go." Chris got on his hands and knees and Lex had him on the shoulder and was really kind of wrestling with him, giving it everything he had. It was heartbreaking to watch, but I was also happy for him. As broken as his body was, he was furiously doing his dominant high tail wag. Lex was in his favorite element and he was having a great time.

I remember thinking at the time, "If the lights could go out right now, it would be the best way for him to go." But the truth is, Lex was happy about it for days, kind of like, "I showed you I still have it. Don't count me out yet."

Lex was living in my house by then, although he still didn't settle down much. We had a routine at night where I'd sit out in the backyard and he would run around as best he could and maybe go a little ways into the field behind the house. Because of his arthritis, he couldn't go far. And I'd always be out there with him. Well, about three weeks after the incident with Chris and Max, we were out for our usual night run when my cell phone rang. I often made my end-of-day calls then, and while I was on the phone Lex would check in with me every ten minutes or so, then vanish into the darkness for a little while.

That night, after the second or third check-in, he came up and got in my lap and really leaned on me. I was in the middle of a conversation and I wasn't paying much attention, but even so, I realized there was something different. After a few minutes he wandered off and I finished my phone call. About thirty minutes went by and I started to wonder where he was. Then I started calling. Then I started hollering. He could not have gone far, so I thought maybe he just couldn't get back to me. I ended up searching all night.

The next day, I got every police officer in the county looking for him. There were only a few houses near us, and I knocked on the doors of all of them. I started driving up and down the county roads, stopping everyone I saw. I made announcements on my radio show. I offered a reward. Everyone was looking for Lex.

I still went out in the backyard every night at our regular time, because I missed him so much and I was hoping he might come home. Four days after he'd gone missing, I was sitting out there and I swore I heard him barking. I know all my dogs' barks very well, and I was absolutely sure it was Lex. He sounded fine, too: It was his regular "I'm in the pen barking at the world" bark. A sense of relief flooded me as I realized one of my neighbors must have found him wandering and taken him in. I visited them all, checked everyone's yard and barn, and nobody had seen Lex. It wasn't like I found another dog barking, either. There were no other dogs.

A few days later, I thought he must be dead. Maybe he got hit by a car, or, because he looked so much like a coyote, a farmer shot him. I put the word out that I'd still pay the reward, because I figured at least someone would know where his body was. I *had to* know what had happened to him.

But no one ever saw him and no one ever called. Lex, the dog of my heart, the old samurai warrior, had vanished into the night.

# Epilogue

Abigail Elizabeth sleeps on the bed with Jill and me. That's a new development, because until recently she was peeing all over the house and there was no way I was having her in my bedroom. But she's a year old now and she's become reliable, so here she is on the bed. And I will say this for her: A ten-pound shih tzu takes up a lot less space on the bed than a ninety-pound German shepherd. And if I wake up in the middle of the night and she's on my legs, I just reach over and pick her up and dump her on Jill.

Back in the Introduction, I said I would take the same basic approach to training a shih tzu as I would to training a rottweiler. If I had trained Abby, I would have. But I left her training to my family. And mistakes were made.

It all comes down to personnel. If I was with her by myself for any length of time, I could snap her into place and get her to where she wasn't peeing in the house at all. But as soon as the others would return and start not following the program, it all went to hell in a handbasket.

Abigail's training, or lack of it, is all the proof you need that consistency is key. And not just consistency over time, but consistency within the family. With dogs, too many times we say, "Well, we've sent this dog to obedience school so she's learned the commands and knows what they mean." That's great, but that's where it ends. We think dogs either know something or they don't. So they are housetrained or they're not, they know how to sit or they don't. But it's not really like that. They can know something, but they also know who to do it for. Dogs have individual relationships with each person in the family, and what kind of success rate a person has with the dog depends on what kind of relationship they have with her. Her following those commands for the mother, the father, child one, child two, child three, all depends on them. This has never been more evident than it is with Abby, because I've been constantly undoing bad training or backtracking in her training.

A perfect example of this is that if I've been gone for a day or two, when I drive up in the driveway I'll usually see Jill, all three of my kids, and one or two of the neighbors running around trying to catch this little black and white flash of a dog who's running in circles and making everybody fall all over themselves staying just out of reach. That little circus act means only one thing: Abby has gotten out again and they can't catch her. This has happened so many times that I can't even count.

Usually, I get out of the car and tell everybody to go inside. I might whistle for Abby once, but I don't tell her to come, because you never give a dog a command that you can't enforce.

(That just teaches them that the command is worthless.) Then I'll look at her to see how crazed she is, and if she looks like she's all into the chase-and-catch-me game, I just go inside the house.

After a few minutes I might come back out with some food and set it down. She'll see me do that and come on over, which is when I give it to her and clip on the leash. I don't punish her or anything, because she'd interpret that as being punished for coming over to me.

Another trick I use is to walk out the door and go do other things. I act like she's not even there. And pretty soon, as I am moving away from her, she can't help it—the pack dog in her has to see what I'm doing and follow me. This trick sounds familiar to you, I know, because it's the same one I used with Akbar. You really do train the little ones the same way you do the big, tough dogs. Anyway, when Abby gets in close enough, I kneel down on the ground, act like I'm getting something out of the grass, and she gets even closer to me. Then I reach down and pick her up. I don't make a big fuss about it. I just pick her up, give her a little treat, "good girl," and we go in the house.

The point is, me chasing her is not part of our relationship. So she doesn't run from me the way she does from the others. With them, as soon as she gets out she starts with that look of, "Come get me, come get me." It's a game to her, and she knows the rest of my family will play along. But she and I *never* play that game.

The housetraining issue dragged on much longer than it needed to, though. And that was because of her feeding schedule, which wasn't very regular. Plus, they were giving her too much freedom in the house and almost no crate training.

You may be wondering how that happened with a dog who lives in my house. But it turned out to be a mistake of convenience. You need to put up puppy gates to keep the dog in the kitchen, but when you've got a two-year-old who can't get over the gate, every time he wants to come in and out of the kitchen you've got to either lift him over or undo it. It just became a nuisance and Jill stopped putting up the gates. It's easier to pick up an occasional pile of poop from a little dog than to have to go through all that.

We finally fixed the problem by putting Abby on a schedule and limiting her access around the house. It's all about opportunity. I just didn't give her an opportunity to pee in the house. If I was sitting in the living room watching TV, then the only room she was allowed in was the one I was in, so I could watch her. Then we got her on a consistent feeding schedule—because what goes in on schedule comes out on schedule. And then all the bathroom problems magically evaporated. We could anticipate when she'd need to go and take her outside. After a while she got so used to going outside that she would ask to go out.

As for her sleeping in the bedroom, that transitioned over time. We got to where we were letting her sleep in the sunroom at night, which has a couch but also has a tile floor that's easy to clean. There was a period of time when she would occasionally have an accident in there. With little bitty dogs like Abby, though, I'm inclined to give them a bit more leeway overnight because they have small bladders and sometimes they just physically can't hold it as long. But one week I went away on a business trip and Jill started letting Abby sleep on the bed, and the dog proved she could handle it.

One of the biggest problems we had was with her and Chandler. This goes back to me ignoring my own advice about not getting a puppy if you have kids under the age of four. Chandler turned three a few months after Abby was one. The first eight months of those two nutcases going at it, of him constantly teasing her and pulling on her and rolling on top of her and picking her up by the tail right when I told him not to and her using him as a teething toy . . . I had to break up something between them all the time. He's picking and poking and then she's nipping and mouthing and sometimes it hurts and he gets upset and he hits her. Somebody's always hurt and it requires constant supervision.

If you have a young dog, especially a teether, you cannot leave her alone with small children. You just can't do it. It can turn negative in a millisecond. So after all of this, I steadfastly stand by my original advice: *Do not* get a puppy if you have kids under the age of four.

Abigail also had a tendency to be very mouthy. I think some of that has to do with the fact that she has bad teeth, so her teething phase just went on forever. And the kids always perpetuated it by teasing her with their hands and letting her mouth and nip and gnaw them. Constantly playing with her that way made the mouthy phase drag on way longer than it should have. When you're teasing a dog, the only way she can fight back is with her mouth. Then the kids end up whining and saying, "Oh, it hurts!" But five minutes later they are sitting there tugging on her and teasing her again. So really, that about covers all the bases of all the things you can do wrong.

Now, if your dog nips your kid because the kid is teasing the

dog, it's the kid's fault, yes, but you still don't want the dog nipping. I mean, you can say to the kid, "If you don't play with the
dog that way, she won't nip you." But just telling them to stop
and not play would never work. Because what's the point of having a dog if you can't play with her? I understand that. So it's
about figuring out ways they can play safely and then teaching
them those ways, rather than saying, "Leave the dog alone."

The thing that really helped me was teaching the kids how to
do something different. That is, when Abby started chewing on
them, to just say "no" and then stick a toy in her mouth. Or
start playing with her using the toy in the first place, instead of
their hands. Because as children, what they wanted to do was
play with her; they just didn't know how. By getting them some
easy-to-hold toys that Abby could grab on to, they found out
they could play with her and it didn't hurt.

Another thing you have to be aware of if you have pesky
small kids and any age dog is that the dog needs a break from
the kids, just like the parents do. With Abby, there were times
when you could see the kids were making her crazy and she
wanted to escape. She was tired. She needed a peaceful place
during the day to take dog naps. For us, it meant recognizing
when she was tired and putting her in a crate in a room the
kids couldn't get into. Consequently, she's not defensive and she
sleeps very soundly, because she doesn't feel like somebody's getting ready to grab her while she sleeps.

With a little dog like Abby, I wasn't too worried about the
mouthiness. Now, if I had a rottweiler, or any big dog, I would
take a more serious approach and only allow the kids to play
and interact while I was there to supervise. And that's another

thing about Abby: I'm used to having a more serious role in raising dogs, because the dogs I've had around have been more serious. But Abby is like a pesky little fly. After all, she's not going
to do any real work. So after a while, even I end up just letting
some of her antics go.

And yes, that's yet another example of me being a hypocrite,
because I do get on people who have little dogs and let them get
away with murder. Now that I have one, I understand why they
do it, though, especially if there are only adults living in the
house. But that's not the right way to raise a dog, because then
the dog starts habituating some pretty undesirable behaviors,
and after a while bad behavior just isn't cute in any dog. We've
actually been able to correct the serious stuff. Abigail doesn't
nip the kids anymore, she's sleeping in the bedroom all night,
and for the most part she's doing better about coming when we
call.

Mind you, as I'm writing this she's just walked into the other
room and got herself a nice flip-flop and is commencing to chew
it up. (Does she not have any dog toys?) I chalk that up to the
fact that she's got horrible teeth and they don't fit her mouth.
She'll eventually need to have a bunch of her teeth pulled. In
fact, Abby is a genetic mess. She's still got the lazy eye I saw way
back in the pet shop. I've also realized that these housedogs are
bred to just be companions—little balls of fluff who run around
the house and are kind of cute. But boy, their level of trainability and overall intelligence is not what it is for working dogs!

Jill and I got into an argument about this the other night. She
was saying, "Oh, Abby is so great." I asked, "What's great about
her?" She said, "What do you mean?" And I said, "What does

she do that's unusual or neat or spectacular? Name one thing."
And Jill couldn't come up with anything.

But when I think about it, the best thing about her is the way
my kids light up around her. She's funny and silly the way they
are—not serious like my working dogs. She does this thing with
Chandler where she'll steal his pacifier and hide with it under a
big chair where he can't quite reach her. Sometimes he'll lie on
the floor with the pacifier in his mouth and kind of taunt her,
and she's lightning quick and will jerk it out of his mouth without ever touching his face. Then she'll run around with the
pacifier in her mouth, looking like a little baby doll.

She's also brought back a lot of the puppy playfulness in
Nord, my six-year-old German shepherd. He plays goofy little
games with her that just make me laugh. And he comes in the
house more often now because he likes to be with her.

Nord eventually fixed Abby's oral fixation by letting her chew
on him. It's actually pretty funny. When they are in the house
together, Nord walks over to her and stands with his head up
and his tail wagging. Abby will stand at the tail end of him,
jumping up trying to catch his tail in the air as it's wagging. I
mean, she jumps and almost does backward somersaults, just
barking and snapping. It's hysterical. In the other game they
play, Nord stands next to the couch and Abigail gets on it so
they are nose-to-nose. Then she nips him on the chin. As she
growls and snaps and paws at his muzzle, he just sits there kind
of growling and wagging his tail and showing his teeth while
she's pawing and batting his face. It's like two fighters in the
ring, but one is standing on a chair. Usually, Nord has an expression on his face that says, "What's this clown doing?" He's

snapped at her two or three times, but mostly he's very tolerant. Nord weighs about ninety pounds and Abby is just a little tiny dog, so it doesn't hurt him. And, like me, I don't think he takes her seriously.

In a lot of ways, Nord has really mellowed her out. This goes back to what I have said before about the necessity of dogs being with other dogs. Yes, Abby turned one year old a few months ago and that has certainly settled her down. But so has being able to run with Nord. Nord and Abby spend most of their alone daytime hours together, and both of them have benefited enormously from that. The two of them chase each other around the yard and play and tumble, even though he's huge and she's tiny. Getting all that adolescent energy out of her system has made her a much better dog for us. It's good for her sociability, because she's quit chewing on us. And Nord has toned down a lot, because he's tired and gets all that playing out with her. There's an old adage that a tired dog is a good dog, and there's a lot of truth in that. And both of them are just happier dogs all the way around.

Their relationship has changed the advice I give out on my radio show. Now, more and more, I find myself recommending two dogs. In the past, it's not that I was against it, but I just didn't think of it as often when listeners called in with behavior problems that stem from the frustration a single dog experiences when he has nothing to do. It could be chewing, digging, or a host of different manifestations, but the core of those kinds of problems is that the dog is really bored and alone a lot of the time. I used to say things like, "Teach the dog a game, something you can do when you get home." I still say that. But now

I find myself also suggesting that they find another dog as a companion. That's especially true for families where both adults work and the dog is sitting home alone for ten hours a day with no stimulation at all.

As much as we want to pat ourselves on the back about being great dog owners, dogs are pack animals and there are some needs other dogs can fulfill for them that we can't—no matter how much we wish we could. I'm not saying that a dog who never lives with another dog has an unfulfilled life. But I promise you, even at eight or ten years old, if you give your dog some time to get used to another dog, you'll see a different part of him come out and overall he will be a happier, more fulfilled animal. That rolling and playing and all that smelling—all those things that we don't do as people and that dogs do naturally—is so fulfilling for them. It's a part of their world (or at least it should be), and they can't get it anywhere else.

I have to admit, begrudgingly, that I am sort of liking Abigail these days. Just a little bit, mind you. I like the companionship. I mean, it's nice to have a dog in the house all the time. Of course, part of the bond I've always had with a dog is loving the way they work and respecting the limits we set for each other, and it's never going to be that way with me and Abby. But I love the way my family loves her and the way she makes us all laugh and the fact that she doesn't take up too much space on the bed.

If I did everything wrong in the way we picked Abigail, I did everything right in the way I selected Ruger, my new pit bull. I do a lot of speaking these days about pit bulls and breed-specific legislation. But when I started, I didn't actually have a pit bull, and that seemed to take away some of my credibility. Plus, I wanted one. Because I grew up with PJ, I just like the personality of an old bulldog.

It's kind of a funny thing, but while a lot of the top police dog trainers I talk about in this book have $20,000 K-9s who do all that high-performance work, when it comes down to just having a pal dog, they have pit bulls. I was talking to my friend Ken the other day and he said to me, "When you come in the house, you gotta see my buddy dog. I got this great pit bull and he's the greatest house dog in the world. I do a little bit of training with him, but he's my big football watching couch potato buddy."

I started looking for my own pit bull the right way: by checking out breeders. I was looking through some ads in *Dog Fancy* magazine and there was one that caught my attention because the dogs in the pictures were massively muscled and really big and strong looking. Then I noticed the phone number had an area code and prefix from west Tennessee, not far from where I live. I did a little more research, and I found out the guy is one of the top breeders in the country. He works for the sheriff's department in the same county where I worked Lex as a police dog. Talk about full circle!

I called him and told him what I was looking for, and asked about what type of dogs he was breeding and why. These days, pit bulls are almost three or four different breeds. You have short, heavy ones; bigger, more agile dogs; smaller dogs; lines bred for gaminess; lines bred for no gaminess; lines bred for hunting; and everything in between.

This guy is breeding really heavy-bodied dogs. They are not

working-line dogs, so they are pretty low-key, and he's trying to breed a lot of the gaminess out of them. His males are all intact (which means they're not neutered), and he socializes them a lot with other males. The first time I went to his house to look at his dogs, he had four adult, intact males running around in the same pen together. Pretty impressive.

I like the type of dog he's producing, and he's doing the right things to make good general pets for people. However, like a lot of breeders, he has a full-time job and limited time to work with his dogs. So he's got a lot of dogs who spend a whole lot of time together in a pen. They've been very well socialized to other dogs, but not so much to different kinds of people. They've got good nerves, everything is there genetically, and they act solid. But I know they haven't had that foundation socialization during the critical five-week to twenty-week period. So I knew from the get-go that any dog I got from him, I'd have to work with and watch carefully at first.

Having had enough of puppy antics (and female dogs) with Abby, I got a six-year-old male named Ruger who had been one of his top stud dogs for a long time and was slated to be retired. I actually looked at three or four other males, but I felt they had too much drive for what I needed. So I ended up with Ruger, who is a more mellow sort.

When I first met Ruger at the breeder's place, it was immediately clear that he didn't have much training. He didn't even know how to sit and barely knew how to walk on a leash. I wanted to take him away from his home to see how he'd react, so we took him over to a tennis court at the local park. I brought along a tennis ball, and he was really into it. He wanted to chase it down and carry it around in his mouth, so I just started right then with temperament testing him. I reached in and pulled the ball out of his mouth. And he let me take it. Then I held the ball down, kind of in my fist, and he didn't try to jump and chomp at it; he gently took it out of my hand. So that part of him I liked right away. He was a big teddy bear, too. He'd come up and lean on my leg, and as I started petting him, he would slowly start tucking and rolling until he was on his back and presenting his belly for scratching. He also snorted like a pig. What a character!

Ruger is a little tank. His shoulders come just about as high as my knees, but at 101 pounds of solid muscle, he is not a small dog. He's what we call red (really a reddish brown), with the same color nose, a white splash on his chest, cropped, upright ears, and yellow eyes. Very intimidating looking. In fact, that was one of the things I wanted, and here's why.

I got to thinking about what I wanted to do with the dog, besides having a good house dog who was real durable with the kids. I wanted a dog I could use in my public presentations to change people's minds. If I had a long-eared, friendly looking pit bull, it's not going to have the same impact as walking out there with a dog who looks scary. Then, after everyone listens to my twenty-minute talk and are all petting the dog and the kids are sitting on his back, I know I've made a real change in people's minds.

I ended up taking him home, and I am telling you, within forty-eight hours my family was totally in love with him. He was sleeping in the bedroom and on the couch. One day we had all the neighborhood kids over in our backyard playing and running and he was the perfect balance of engaging the kids but not bulldozing them over or demanding all their attention. They could hand him a snack and he wasn't taking any fingers off. If he got their ball, they could walk over and pull it out of his mouth. It was just phenomenal—a perfect fit.

When I saw how accepting he was of strangers, my fears about his lack of socialization melted. I still planned to work with him before I took him out on the road, but I knew there would be no ugly surprises. I mean, there is not a malicious bone in his body. I started thinking about him as the breed ambassador. He's got a huge barrel chest, so I had a kind of Miss America banner made for him to wear across his shoulders. He's the Pit Bull Ambassador.

Just a few weeks after I got him, the craziest thing happened. Jill and I were in the car, with Ruger in the backseat. We were driving through Jackson, Tennessee, which is where I did my original pet dog radio show on 101.5 FM. They have a hugely popular morning show from 8 a.m. to 11 a.m., and the guy who does it, Bill Way, is the same guy who gave me my first break in radio fifteen years ago with *Pet Talk*. He's a big animal lover, too.

Anyway, I decided to tune in, and what was Bill talking about? Pit bulls. Somebody had called in and said that a pit bull had attacked and killed her border collie, who had gotten out and was running loose in the neighborhood. It ignited a firestorm of anti-pit bull opinions. And, as sometimes happens in talk radio, things started spinning out of control. Even Bill was getting into it, saying things like, "I never trusted pit bulls. Those dogs will turn on you."

I was ten minutes' drive from the studio, so I called the station manager and told him, "I'm listening to Bill's show and I just happen to be going through town. I've got this big pit bull in the backseat of my car and I'm coming over. Don't tell anyone."

So live, on the air, I walked into the studio with Ruger on a leash. Bill's eyes got as big as saucers and the guy who was running the board behind him just about jumped up on the table. Bill recovered quickly and said, "Harrison Forbes just walked in with the biggest pit bull I've ever seen. I'm afraid to move." I sat down and ended up doing a twenty-minute segment, talking about the dog, berating Bill for all the misinformation he was repeating, and chiding him for getting caught up in the moment when he knows better.

The thing I started talking about right away was all these people calling and saying the pit bull who killed the border collie should be put down. I said to Bill, "Let's change the scenario for a second. If a mother is sitting inside her house and she gets on the phone or just gets caught up in an episode of *One Life to Live,* and her three-year-old eases out the back door and walks out in the street and gets hit by a car, what's the fallout of that publicly?" And he said, "They hang the mother out to dry."

"Right. They will go after her as an irresponsible parent, in some cases even to the point of prosecuting her for neglect. Why is it that we do that, but when it comes to dogs, it's a totally different set of rules? What's wrong with putting some responsibility on the border collie's owner for letting that dog get out and run loose?"

And he said, "Yeah, but dogs are going to get out."

"Well, yes and no," I said. "But still, I haven't heard a single caller ask why that dog was running loose. If the border collie got hit by a car, would people be calling up suggesting that they ban cars? It's really unfortunate that her dog came out on the losing end of a fight, but there is responsibility on her shoulders, too. When it comes to our kids, we are expected to be responsible. If we have a gun in the house, we take the ammunition out of it, we hide the gun, we lock it up in a safe. We are well practiced as parents in keeping things away from kids and keeping them safe and in the house. Why is it so different for our pets?"

It was an intense conversation. And while it was going on, Ruger went up to Bill. Bill has various exotic pets, including llamas and pigs, so he smelled very interesting to a dog and Ruger started sniffing him all over. And Bill started petting him. At first he was really afraid, but Ruger crept up and put the front part of his body in Bill's lap. Suddenly, Bill was petting him on the top of the head and telling his radio audience, "This is the nicest dog." It was a huge change right there.

But then Bill said, "Let me ask you another question. If I walked in here with my little Brittany spaniel male right now, what would happen?" And I said, "Bill, I'd love to say that everything would be roses, but there are a lot of intangibles. If your dog came in here and jumped on top of this dog aggressively, I'm not sure that Ruger would just stand there and take it. I don't know. But that's part of being respectful of what you've got.

"Honestly, I would not put Ruger in that position. If I needed those guys to get along, I would set up their first meeting where

I could work with the dogs. It would be done in a way where I could make sure nobody got hurt. That's just part of being a responsible dog owner."

The other thing I talked about on Bill's radio show that day is a plan I have for owning big breeds like pit bulls and rottweilers and making sure people do it responsibly. Back about fifteen years ago in Tennessee, they implemented a requirement for young hunters that you can't legally hunt if you are under eighteen and haven't completed the state's two-day hunter-safety course. When they started enforcing that, within several years the hunting accidents involving minors went down 90 percent.

Meanwhile, the insurance industry has been putting all large dogs—German shepherds, pit bulls, rottweilers, Doberman pinschers—under the same "aggressive" umbrella and denying their owners' home owner's insurance. It's a way to legislate against these breeds without actually having to pass a law. And of course, it hits the responsible dog owners. A thug running down the street with a pit bull who's up to no good doesn't care about home owner's insurance. A responsible dog owner does.

Since the insurance companies are forcing the issue, I'd love to see a requirement for owning a big dog with the potential to do some harm that's similar to the one we have in Tennessee for hunting. I'd be happy to put together a responsible dog ownership class for potentially aggressive breeds. Heck, I'd do it for free. People could pay a fee to the city or state and sit through a one-day seminar, then take a little test and get a certificate that allows them to own the dog and get regular home owner's insurance. We already do that with so many other things. I mean, you don't drive a car without going through a course and taking a driver's test, because a car can turn into a deadly weapon if it's not used correctly. Well, what's the difference?

Now, once a person has taken the course and is certified, if they screw up and their dog gets out and attacks a person or a dog through the owner's lack of responsibility, I say nail them to the wall. The thing with pit bulls is that you punish the deed, not the breed.

I also told Bill, "I'm against the idea of homogenizing all the breeds, the idea that every breed of dog ought to have the same personality—love strangers, love everybody, great for kids, and just a big teddy bear. People have different needs and they want different dogs. If I want a guard dog and I get myself a dog who is a little bit aggressive with strangers, well fine. I think people should be able to own dogs like that. But then the responsibility is heaped on their shoulders. And if they screw up, there should be consequences."

I had to leave right after that, but Bill was on the air for two hours more, and I tuned in while we were driving. There were people who had been on hold and wanted to go off on pit bulls, and Bill started combating them. He said, "If I hadn't seen this dog fifteen minutes ago, I'd still be with you, but Ruger just changed my mind and got me back to center." Then people started calling in saying, "I'm glad Harrison came up there. I've got a pit bull and he's a great dog." Those people had been afraid to call in before, but now everything changed. The few minutes I was there with Ruger changed thousands of people's perceptions. It was a big moment. And I knew right then, this is a calling. I've got the platform and this is something I need to do. And Ruger is the perfect dog to do it with.

His story is so phenomenal because of people's knee-jerk reaction to pit bulls. You just can't deny that he is a great dog and that his personality comes from his breeding and not from the way he was raised. When he was with the breeder, he was around a few kids but not many and not regularly. He came into the breeder's house for a few hours once a month and spent most of his time in a kennel with other dogs. But within two days I was able to have him in my house 90 percent of the time. He went right to the door when he wanted to go out to the bathroom. Immediate housetraining, immediately good around kids—this goes back to great genetics and a very solid temperament. People say it's all in how you raise them, but I pulled a six-year-old dog out of a kennel, and it wasn't that I did any magic with him. His temperament was right to begin with, and that made for a very easy and quick transition.

The first day I had him in the house, we ended up having a bunch of kids over and some of them were really loud. I mean, we're talking about six- and seven-year-olds and they were playing some game in the house. Ruger and I were walking through the kitchen and four kids came barreling around the corner at full run, screaming at the top of their lungs. That certainly would have spooked Nord, and a lot of other dogs, too. Ruger just kind of winced, because he thought he was going to get run over. Then he stepped out of the way and they brushed by him. He sort of shrugged, as if he was saying, "Whoa, that was intense."

Certainly, Ruger and Chandler is a lot easier than Ruger and Abigail. Chandler always wants to hug Abby and lie on top of her, even though she weighs just ten pounds. But he can get

Ruger in a headlock and roll all over him and nobody's going to get hurt, so I don't have to hold my breath all the time.

One night soon after I got Ruger, I was lying on the couch, snuggling with him, talking baby talk and doing kissey faces. Jill was astounded. She said, "In the fifteen years we've been together, I have never seen you act like this with a dog." I started thinking about it, and I guess it's true. The last time I acted like that with a dog was when I had PJ.

Certainly, Ruger reminds me of PJ. But there's something else, too. One of the things about being a handler of overbearing, tough, dominant dogs is that my role as the pack leader and trainer has to be more authoritative. I forgot how much I love to have a big old huggie dog.

It feels great to come back to this place with a dog—a place I haven't really enjoyed since I was a kid. I can just have fun with Ruger. Of course, I've been training him, but that's more just to make sure he has some basic skills and to keep things interesting for me and for him. Other than his role as Pit Bull Ambassador, Ruger doesn't have any particular job to do. My family got themselves a pet with Abby. Ruger is my pet. It's been such a long time since I was just a boy and his dog.

# Index